American Favorites

AMERICAN FAVORITES

All-American Cooking

for a New Generation

★

BETTY ROSBOTTOM

HOUGHTON MIFFLIN COMPANY

BOSTON   NEW YORK

For information about permission to reproduce selections from this book, write to
Permissions, Houghton Mifflin Company, 215 Park Avenue South,
New York, New York 10003.

Library of Congress Cataloging-in-Publication Data

Rosbottom, Betty.
    American favorites : all-american cooking for a new generation / by Betty
Rosbottom.
        p.   cm.
    Includes index.
    ISBN 0-395-97171-3
    1. Cookery, American. 2. Low-fat diet—Recipes.
    3. Quick and easy cookery   I. Title.
TX715.R829 1996
641.5973—dc20   96-26768

Printed and bound in the U.S.A. by World Color, Taunton, Massachusetts

Designed by Susan McClellan

10 9 8 7 6 5 4 3 2 1

For Emily Bell and Emmy Clausing,

my assistants, whose creativity, culinary skills

and dedication made this book a reality,

and

As always, for Ronny and Michael,

who provided the two most important ingredients:

love and laughter

Acknowledgments

THIS BOOK WOULD STILL BE JUST A FIGMENT OF MY IMAGINATION if it were not for the support and hard work of many people. Judith Weber, my literary agent of many years, believed in this project from the beginning and found a wonderful home for it at Chapters Publishing.

Cindy Leland did an extraordinary job of transforming my recipes from sheets laden with illegible notes into pristine computer pages. She also coordinated the recipe testers for this collection, spending many hours sending recipes to volunteer testers all over the country and carefully recording their comments. Her work was invaluable to me.

For the volunteers who tested day after day, week after week, for almost two years, there are simply not enough words of gratitude for their generous help. More than 25 cooks from the Midwest, the South, New England and across the land participated. I thank them all, especially Wendy Gabriel, Wendy Kersker, Marilyn Thompson, Alice Ford, Char Shiff, Elly Persing, Claire Farina, Jackie Murrill and Brenda McDowell.

To my longtime assistant at La Belle Pomme Cooking School, Sheri Lisak, I offer thanks for helping prepare the proposal for this book. To assistant Charles Worthington, who came on board during the final months of this work, thanks for tirelessly retesting so many dishes. I would also like to thank Barrie Kane at University Hospitals Synergy in Cleveland, Ohio, for nutritional advice. And to Emily Bell and Emmy Clausing, my culinary assistants, I am indebted to you both for your long hours of work and your constant striving to perfect the recipes.

Many of the recipes on the following pages have appeared in *Bon Appétit* magazine, in *The Columbus Dispatch* and in my column for The Los Angeles Times Syndicate. I would like to thank my editors at each of these publications for permitting those recipes to be used.

I am grateful to all the people at Chapters Publishing for their excitement and enthusiasm for this work. Thanks to the whole team: editor-in-chief Barry Estabrook, designer Susan McClellan, Cristen Brooks and Melissa Cochran. Most particularly, I feel lucky to have had Rux Martin as my editor. Wisely, she kept asking more of me with her questions, her requests for rewrites and her appeal for clearer descriptions. This book is better because of her guidance.

To photographer Louis B. Wallach, publicist Laura Baddish, copyeditor Janet McDonald, proofreader Susan Dickinson and indexer Rose Grant, I am appreciative of the invaluable roles you played in this project.

Finally, I would like to thank my husband, Ron, and son, Michael, for their love and patience in seeing me through this long and time-consuming work. You guys are the greatest!

—Betty Rosbottom
Amherst, Massachusetts

Contents

Introduction

SEVERAL YEARS AGO, after almost 20 years of teaching cooking classes that focused on French and European foods, I sat down at my desk and wrote the description for a new course called simply "American Favorites." For the menu, I had planned such familiar-sounding dishes as meat loaf, mashed potatoes, popovers and spice cake. Despite my own enthusiasm, I worried that the students would not share my excitement and that enrollment would fall short. Much to my relief, the phone began ringing immediately. Experienced as well as beginning cooks, young people as well as older ones, men and women alike were all eager to sign up. For the next year, I offered several more sessions of "favorites." Each time, the result was the same: The courses sold out, and there was always a waiting list.

The runaway popularity of what began as a whim planted the idea for this book in my mind. I knew there were plenty of cookbooks on American food, but I wanted to do something different. My goal was to update the classics: adding a new ingredient here or there to refresh a dish, streamlining times and cooking techniques and addressing nutritional concerns by lowering fat when flavor was not jeopardized.

In my meat loaf, I replaced the usual ground beef with ground chicken, which is lighter in taste and calories. I also added finely diced root vegetables and grated apples for moisture and seasoned the mixture with thyme. Instead of a heavy pan gravy, I created a quick, intensely flavored one with shiitake mushrooms. Rather than traditional mashed potatoes, I prepared mine with Yukon Golds, a glorious pale gold variety, which I combined with buttermilk and fresh herbs. I made innovative changes in other dishes too. I roasted chicken with an apple in its cavity and basted it with cider, and I enhanced corn bread and biscuits with simple additions of cheese and herbs. I studded ordinary chocolate brownies with chunks of white chocolate. As my students said, I was giving their favorites a facelift.

MY PURPOSE was to spruce up the traditional, immediately recognizable standbys—chowders, pot roasts, baked beans, potato salads and apple pies, for example—by giving them unexpected twists. I also planned to make room for some new favorites without a long past history, recipes inspired by ingredients that have recently appeared on grocery shelves. Grains like couscous; mushrooms such as portobellos; dried fruits, including cranberries and sour cherries; mild or hot peppers; fresh herbs and myriad varieties of fish are all a part of our changing marketplace and have substantially influenced American cooking.

Such ingredients have found their way into the recipes in this book. Chipotle peppers, a smoky dried chile pepper available in many supermarkets, lend an exciting flavor to Smoky Peppers Chicken Noodle Soup. Spicy Tomato and Cheese Macaroni retains the spirit of the traditional but is made with creamy Havarti cheese and enlivened with a tomato sauce seasoned with fresh basil. Fennel and prosciutto raise the taste of chicken potpies to new heights, while little bits of toffee make simple sugar cookies distinctive.

Such embellishments need not take more time. Throughout, I've kept in mind the convenience of the cook. I don't hesitate to rely on ready-made items when they are appropriate. Quick Rosemary Cheese Straws—thin, crisp pastry twists—take only minutes to assemble, because they are made with purchased puff pastry. The same is true for Glazed Winter Fruits over Pound Cake, because the cake is the store-bought variety.

IN ORGANIZING THIS BOOK, I have tried to make it simple to use and have filled it with helpful extras. Each recipe, for instance, includes an overview of the dish's important features and lists the following:

* Time required from start to finish to complete the dish (arrived at by averaging the results of the book's testers) as well as the actual working, or "hands-on," time;
* Whether it can be made in advance and/or frozen;
* The best season to make it.

I have also included notes on shopping for special ingredients, substitutions, explanations of cooking techniques, shortcuts, menu suggestions and variations for reducing fat—all in response to questions that my students frequently ask.

My family and friends have responded to these recipes with unparalleled enthusiasm and, in what is always the ultimate test, have accorded them a permanent place in their own collections. In this high-tech age, when many of us are still struggling to master our VCRs or learning to use our computers, we are often happy to return to the reassuringly familiar at mealtime—our favorite dishes, reinterpreted with fresh, imaginative touches.

Chapter 1

All-American Appetizers *and* Drinks

One-Bite Biscuits *with* Apple Butter *and* Country Ham

SMALL MUSTARD-AND-PEPPER-SCENTED BISCUITS spread with apple butter and topped with slices of ham and white Cheddar are so satisfying that I could make a meal of them. I like to serve these during cold weather, especially during the holidays. These biscuits are best baked, filled and served immediately, so have all ingredients assembled before you begin. Although they make a splendid appetizer, they would be equally tempting as part of a brunch menu with a plate of scrambled eggs and a bowl of fresh fruit. (*See photograph, page 33.*)

Mustard Biscuits (page 289)
½ cup store-bought apple butter
4 ounces thinly sliced baked country ham (*see Shopping Note*)
4-6 ounces medium-sharp white Cheddar cheese, thinly sliced

1. Prepare Mustard Biscuits as directed.

2. Split biscuits and spread bottom halves with apple butter. Add a slice of ham and a slice of cheese, cut to fit biscuit. Place tops on biscuits.

3. Serve warm, arranged on a serving tray or placed in a napkin-lined basket.

MAKES 18 TO 20 APPETIZERS

From Start to Finish:
45 minutes

Actual Working Time:
25 minutes

Make Ahead: No

Can Be Frozen: No

Best Seasons:
Fall and winter

Shopping Note:
Try to buy ham with a pronounced smoked flavor; Black Forest is a fine choice. If you are lucky enough to find one, a Virginia ham, such as a Smithfield, would be good in this recipe.

Silver-Dollar Crab Cakes *with* Roasted Red Pepper Sauce

MAKES 30 TO 32
CRAB CAKES

From Start to Finish:
1 hour 45 minutes
Actual Working Time:
45 minutes
Make Ahead: Partially
(see steps 1 and 2)
Can Be Frozen: No
Best Seasons: All year

Shopping Notes:
  Hellman's makes a good
reduced-fat mayonnaise.
  For a recipe like this one,
in which a small amount of
roasted peppers is called
for, I buy peppers already
roasted in the deli section
of the grocery, or I
purchase a jar of roasted
peppers found in the aisle
with canned vegetables or
condiments. Mancini
is a reliable brand of
commercially roasted
peppers.

I HAVE YET TO MEET A PERSON who does not love crab cakes. No matter how many I make, there are never leftovers. In this version, the crab cakes are bite-sized so that you can pop them into your mouth all at once. Sautéed until crisp and golden, they are packed with crabmeat and are enlivened with lemon and orange zests. The crab cakes could easily stand on their own, but they are even more tempting when dipped into a quick sauce of roasted red peppers. (*See photograph, page 41.*)

FOR CRAB CAKES

1   medium or large egg
3   tablespoons reduced-fat mayonnaise
      (*see Shopping Notes*)
4   teaspoons Dijon mustard
1   tablespoon fresh lemon juice
1   pound best-quality crabmeat, such as Maine
      crabmeat, picked over to remove cartilage,
      drained and patted dry with paper towels
¼   cup finely chopped green onion
2   tablespoons finely chopped fresh flat-leaf parsley
½   teaspoon *each* grated lemon zest and orange zest
      (yellow and orange portions of rind)
1   cup fresh bread crumbs
½   teaspoon salt
¼   teaspoon cayenne pepper

FOR ROASTED RED PEPPER SAUCE

1   medium-sized red bell pepper, roasted
      (*see Shopping Notes or Cooking Technique*), skin,
      seeds and membranes discarded
1   cup reduced-fat mayonnaise (*see Shopping Notes*)
2   large garlic cloves, coarsely chopped
½   teaspoon fresh lemon juice, plus more if needed
1   teaspoon Dijon mustard

2 tablespoons finely chopped fresh flat-leaf parsley

1 tablespoon *each* unsalted butter and vegetable oil,
plus more if needed

1. **To prepare crab cakes:** Place egg, mayonnaise, mustard and lemon juice in a bowl and stir to mix. Add crabmeat, green onions, parsley, lemon and orange zests, bread crumbs, salt and cayenne; stir well to mix. Shape into small, flat cakes the size of a silver dollar; you should have about 30 to 32 cakes. Place crab cakes on a baking sheet, cover loosely with plastic wrap and chill for 1 hour or overnight. (These crab cakes do not contain a lot of bread crumbs to bind them, so it is important to chill them well before they are sautéed.)

2. **To prepare sauce:** Coarsely chop roasted pepper and place in a food processor fitted with a metal blade along with mayonnaise, garlic, ½ teaspoon lemon juice and mustard. Process until pureed. Taste and add more lemon juice, if desired. Transfer to a serving bowl. (*Sauce can be made 1 day ahead. Cover and refrigerate.*) Stir in parsley before serving.

3. **To cook crab cakes:** Heat butter and oil in a large, heavy skillet over medium heat. When hot, add just enough cakes to fit comfortably in pan and sauté for about 2 minutes per side, until browned. (Lift them gently when turning.) Repeat until all cakes are cooked; use extra butter and oil if needed. If not serving immediately, you can place on a baking sheet, cover loosely with foil and keep warm for 30 to 40 minutes in a 250°F oven.

4. To serve, place a bowl of sauce on a serving tray and surround with crab cakes. Spoon a little sauce over each crab cake and serve out of hand, or if you prefer, arrange crab cakes on small plates and serve with a fork.

Variation: The roasted red pepper sauce also makes a delicious dip for fresh raw vegetables.

Menu Suggestion:
These little crab cakes are perfect to serve before Mahogany Spareribs (page 179) or Mustard and Pepper Flank Steaks (page 172).

Cooking Technique:
To roast peppers, place them directly on a gas burner or on a baking sheet about 7 to 8 inches from the broiler. Roast, turning occasionally, until peppers are blackened and charred on all sides. Wrap peppers in damp paper towels and place in a plastic bag; seal bag. Allow peppers to steam in bag for 10 to 15 minutes. Remove black charred outside skin from peppers with a sharp paring knife; you may need to run peppers under cold water to remove all skin. Using a paring knife, remove seeds and stems. Peppers can be placed in a jar or bowl, covered with olive oil and refrigerated, covered, for up to 3 days. Drain and pat dry before using.

"Melt-in-Your-Mouth" Summer Corn Cakes

MAKES ABOUT 20
CAKES

★

From Start to Finish:
40 minutes

Actual Working Time:
30 minutes

Make Ahead: No

Can Be Frozen: No

Best Season: Summer

THE RECIPE FOR THESE DELECTABLE CORN CAKES was given to me many years ago by a student who grew up in the South, as I did, and loved anything made with cornmeal. The cornmeal batter, to which fresh corn is added, takes only a few minutes to assemble and then is dropped by spoonfuls into a hot skillet. The corn cakes are quickly baked until crisp and golden and are best served hot from the oven.

1 cup yellow or white cornmeal

2 teaspoons baking powder

1 teaspoon salt

½ teaspoon baking soda

1 cup buttermilk

¼ cup vegetable oil, plus 1-2 tablespoons
   more for skillet

1 cup fresh corn kernels (scraped
   from 2-3 ears of corn), uncooked

2 tablespoons chopped fresh chives
   or flat-leaf parsley for garnish

1. Preheat oven to 425°F.

2. Combine cornmeal, baking powder, salt, baking soda, buttermilk, ¼ cup oil and corn in a large mixing bowl. Stir well.

3. Pour just enough oil (1 to 2 tablespoons) into a large, heavy oven-proof skillet (preferably cast-iron) to coat bottom. Place skillet in oven and heat until hot, about 10 minutes. Remove from oven and drop batter by tablespoonfuls into pan, leaving about ½ inch space around each cake to allow for spreading while cooking.

4. Return skillet to oven and bake for 4 minutes. Turn cakes and bake for 2 to 3 minutes more, until crisp and golden on both sides. Transfer to a serving plate, cover loosely with foil and keep warm while preparing remaining cakes. Continue baking corn cakes until all batter is used. (If you have 2 skillets, you can bake 2 pans at a time and speed up the process.)

5. To serve, arrange corn cakes on a serving plate and sprinkle with chives or parsley.

Menu Suggestion:

These go well with the same dishes as the crab cakes (see page 13).

Hot *and* Sassy Chicken Wings

**SERVES 8 TO 10
AS AN APPETIZER**

★

From Start to Finish:
Overnight marinating,
plus 1 hour 20 minutes
Actual Working Time:
30 minutes
Make Ahead: Partially
(see step 1)
Can Be Frozen: No
Best Seasons: All year

THESE SPICY WINGS REMIND ME of the Cajun food I loved during my college days in New Orleans. The wings are marinated overnight in a mixture of vinegar, honey, red pepper sauce and spices, then roasted to a rich mahogany brown. Crusty, yet tender, the chicken has both a hot and sweet taste.

1 cup white wine vinegar
2 tablespoons red pepper sauce, preferably Tabasco
½ cup light brown sugar
2 tablespoons dried thyme leaves
2 tablespoons cayenne pepper
4 tablespoons garlic powder
4 teaspoons salt
5 tablespoons honey (*divided*)
2 pounds chicken wings, split at joints into two
  pieces, wing tips removed (*see Cooking Technique*)
1 bunch green onions, cleaned, with roots and all
  but 2 inches of green tops cut off on diagonal

1. Combine vinegar, pepper sauce, brown sugar, thyme, cayenne, garlic powder, salt and 4 tablespoons honey in a large, resealable plastic bag. Add chicken wings and toss well to coat with marinade. (If you do not have a plastic bag, you can place chicken in a shallow glass, ceramic or other nonreactive pan and cover with plastic wrap.) Refrigerate overnight. Turn wings several times in marinade.

2. Preheat oven to 375°F. Line a baking pan with aluminum foil. Coat a cooking rack with nonstick cooking spray and place it in baking pan.

3. Drain chicken, pouring marinade into a medium, heavy saucepan. Arrange wings on rack. Place marinade in pan over high heat and cook until it has reduced by half, 5 to 7 minutes or more. Brush wings generously on all sides with reduced marinade.

4. Bake for 30 minutes. Turn wings and bake for 15 minutes more. Then brush wings lightly with remaining 1 tablespoon honey and bake for 5 minutes more.

5. Remove and arrange on a serving plate. Garnish with clusters of green onions.

Menu Suggestion:

These wings are ideal to serve before Smoked Turkey Gumbo (page 82).

Cooking Technique:

It is best to remove and discard the wing tips, since they burn easily when the chicken is baked for a long period in a hot oven. Once the tips are removed, the wings should be split at the joints into two pieces. You can have the butcher prepare the wings, if you prefer.

Grilled Ginger Shrimp

SERVES 10 TO 12 AS
AN APPETIZER

★

From Start to Finish:
1 hour 5 minutes
Actual Working Time:
30 minutes
Make Ahead:
Partially (see step 1)
Can Be Frozen: No
Best Seasons: All year

Shopping Notes:
Molasses can be either sulfured or unsulfured. Unsulfured is lighter and has a cleaner flavor. If you can't find it, buy light molasses.

The size of shrimp is determined by the count of unshelled shrimp per pound. This is a guideline:
Medium: 31-40 per pound
Large: 21-30 per pound
Extra Large: 16-20 per pound
Jumbo: 10-15 per pound

Menu Suggestion:
Serve with Michael's Grilled Rosemary Steaks (page 176) or Mustard and Pepper Flank Steaks (page 172).

FRESHLY CHOPPED GINGER, chopped garlic and soy sauce combined with molasses and balsamic vinegar make an excellent marinade for shrimp. After they have marinated for half an hour, the shrimp are skewered and grilled until pink and tender.

FOR SAUCE

⅓ cup reduced-sodium soy sauce
⅓ cup unsulfured molasses (*see Shopping Notes*)
3 tablespoons balsamic vinegar
3 tablespoons chopped garlic
1½ tablespoons chopped (not grated) peeled gingerroot

3 pounds uncooked large, unshelled shrimp
(21-30 per pound; *see Shopping Notes*)

Small bunch fresh watercress, cleaned and patted dry, for garnish

1. **To prepare sauce:** Combine soy sauce, molasses, vinegar, garlic and ginger in a nonreactive bowl and whisk well to blend. Set aside. (*Sauce can be made 1 day ahead; cover and refrigerate.*)

2. If using wooden skewers, prepare them by soaking in water for 30 minutes. Dry them before using.

3. Peel and devein shrimp. Marinate shrimp in ginger sauce for 30 minutes. Thread shrimp onto skewers.

4. Arrange a rack 5 to 6 inches from heat source and preheat grill. Grill skewered shrimp until pink and curled, 3 to 4 minutes per side. (Alternatively, preheat a broiler and arrange a rack 5 to 6 inches from heat source. Broil for 3 to 4 minutes per side.) Remove from heat and arrange on a large platter. Garnish with watercress. Serve, either skewered or unskewered, warm or at room temperature.

Peppered Almonds

THESE HOT, ZESTY ALMONDS make a fine opener for a Southwestern meal. They can be baked weeks in advance and stored to have on hand for last-minute entertaining. If you like to take a little gift when invited for dinner, these nuts can be packed in a small basket or container tied with ribbons.

- 3 tablespoons unsalted butter
- 2 teaspoons red pepper sauce, preferably Tabasco
- 2 teaspoons cider vinegar
- 1 pound (about 3 cups) whole blanched almonds
- 2 teaspoons crushed red pepper flakes
- 2 teaspoons ground cumin
- 1 teaspoon salt
- 1 teaspoon chili powder
- ½ teaspoon garlic powder
- ¼ teaspoon cayenne pepper

1. Preheat oven to 350°F. Line a 15-by-10-by-1-inch pan with aluminum foil.

2. In a large skillet over medium-high heat, melt butter. Stir in pepper sauce and vinegar. Remove from heat; add almonds, stirring to coat well. Spread almonds evenly in foil-lined pan. Bake, stirring occasionally, until nuts are a rich, deep golden color, about 20 minutes.

3. While nuts are in oven, combine remaining ingredients in a large bowl.

4. Remove nuts from oven; add to seasoning mixture, stirring to coat well. Return nuts to baking pan, spreading evenly. Bake for 5 minutes; remove from oven and stir. Cool completely. (*Nuts can be prepared 3 weeks ahead; store in an airtight container. You can freeze them for up to 2 months; defrost before serving.*)

MAKES ABOUT
3 CUPS

From Start to Finish:
40 minutes
Actual Working Time:
15 minutes
Make Ahead: Yes
(see step 4)
Can Be Frozen: Yes
(see step 4)
Best Seasons: All year

Menu Suggestion:
You might like to serve these nuts before a Southwestern dish such as Spicy Tortilla Soup with Vegetables (page 70), Santa Fe "Lasagna" (page 112) or Grilled Chicken with Pineapple Salsa (page 166).

Crispy Prosciutto Cheese Toasts

SERVES 8

★

From Start to Finish:
45 minutes

Actual Working Time:
35 minutes

Make Ahead: Partially
(see steps 2 and 5)

Can Be Frozen: No

Best Seasons: All year

Shopping Note:

Goat cheese has a slightly acidic taste that pairs well with many foods. Although France has long provided goat cheeses to the United States, local producers in Vermont, New York and California are now making fabulous varieties. For this recipe, a smooth, creamy cheese, either domestic or imported, works well. Goat cheese is relatively low in fat, averaging about 5 to 6 grams per ounce rather than the 9 grams or more per ounce in Cheddars, blues and other cheeses.

I AM CRAZY ABOUT THESE flavorful little toasts. The prosciutto is cut into paper-thin strips and quickly sautéed until crispy, then used to top toasted French bread slices that have been spread with a thin layer of goat cheese.

40 slices French bread, cut about ⅜ inch thick
    (a baguette 2½-3 inches in diameter works well)

8 ounces lean prosciutto, sliced paper-thin

4-5 ounces goat cheese, preferably a soft,
    smooth one (*see Shopping Note*)
    Several generous dashes dried thyme leaves
    Several fresh thyme sprigs for garnish (*optional*)

1. Preheat oven to 350°F.

2. Place bread slices in a single layer on 1 or 2 baking sheets. Bake, turning once, until crisp and just lightly browned, about 10 minutes. Remove and cool. (*Toasts can be prepared 3 to 4 hours ahead. Cover loosely with foil and leave at cool room temperature.*)

3. Stack 4 or 5 prosciutto slices on top of each other and cut off any fat around edges. Roll slices tightly into a cylinder shape and cut into ¼-inch slices to make strips. Repeat with remaining prosciutto.

4. Coat a large, heavy skillet (cast-iron works well) generously with nonstick cooking spray and place over medium-high heat. When pan is hot, add prosciutto and sauté, stirring and tossing constantly, until strips are crispy, about 5 minutes. Remove and drain on paper towels.

5. Spread toasts with a thin layer of goat cheese, top with prosciutto and sprinkle with dried thyme. Return toasts to baking sheet. (*If not baking immediately, cover loosely with foil and let sit at room temperature for up to 1 hour.*)

6. To warm toasts, bake for about 5 minutes. Place toasts on a large serving tray and garnish with fresh thyme sprigs, if desired.

Variation: For more color, arrange the toasts on a serving plate and garnish them with bundles of blanched young green beans and some black olives.

Menu Suggestion:

These toasts are delicious before Mustard and Pepper Flank Steaks (page 172) or you could offer them alongside Spinach Salad with Brown Mushrooms in Lemon-Garlic Dressing (page 250).

Mushrooms Stuffed *with* Roasted Garlic *and* Rosemary

MAKES 16
MUSHROOMS

⋆

From Start to Finish:
1 hour 55 minutes

Actual Working Time:
45 minutes

Make Ahead: Partially
(see step 4)

Can Be Frozen: No

Best Seasons:
Fall and winter

WHEN COMBINED WITH SOURDOUGH bread crumbs and rosemary, roasted garlic, with its sweet, mellow flavor, makes a sublime filling for mushroom caps. These mushrooms make a fine appetizer before grilled steaks or lamb chops.

1	whole medium-sized garlic head
3	tablespoons plus 1 teaspoon olive oil (*divided*)
16	mushrooms (½-¾ pound), about 1¾-2 inches in diameter, cleaned
1	teaspoon unsalted butter
¾	cup fresh finely ground sourdough bread crumbs
1	tablespoon chopped fresh flat-leaf parsley
1½	teaspoons chopped fresh rosemary or ½ teaspoon dried
¼	teaspoon salt, plus more if needed
¼	teaspoon freshly ground black pepper, plus more if needed
	Several flat-leaf parsley and/or rosemary sprigs for garnish

1. Preheat oven to 400°F. Remove loose paper from garlic head and cut and discard a thin slice off top (pointed end), exposing cloves. Place garlic head, cut side up, in a small ramekin and drizzle with 1½ tablespoons oil. Cover tightly with a double thickness of aluminum foil. Roast for 30 minutes, remove foil and roast for 15 to 20 minutes more. Garlic should be golden brown and tender when pierced with a knife. Remove and cool.

2. While garlic is roasting, prepare stuffing. Twist off stems and scoop out mushrooms with a small spoon. Finely chop stems. Heat butter with 1 teaspoon oil in a medium, heavy skillet over medium-high heat. When hot, add chopped mushroom stems and cook, stirring, for 3 minutes. Add bread crumbs and stir constantly, cooking until lightly toasted, 3 to 4 minutes. Remove from heat and stir in chopped parsley, chopped rosemary, ¼ teaspoon salt and ¼ teaspoon pepper. Set aside.

3. Separate roasted garlic into cloves and peel; reserve oil. Using a fork, finely mash enough garlic in a bowl to measure 1½ tablespoons. (Save any extra garlic for another use; it is delicious spread on toasted French bread slices.) Mix in reserved oil. Stir garlic mixture into chopped-mushroom mixture. Season with salt and pepper.

4. Line a large baking sheet with foil. Spray with nonstick spray. Brush mushroom caps with remaining 1½ tablespoons oil. Place caps, hollowed sides up, on sheet and lightly salt them. Spoon stuffing into mushrooms, mounding it in center. (*Mushrooms can be prepared up to this point 1 day ahead. Cover and refrigerate.*) Bring to room temperature 15 minutes before baking.

5. Preheat oven to 375°F. Bake mushrooms, uncovered, until tender, about 20 minutes. Arrange on a platter and garnish with parsley and/or rosemary sprigs.

Sun-Dried Tomato-Basil Toasts

MAKES 24 TOASTS

From Start to Finish:
45 minutes

Actual Working Time:
30 minutes

Make Ahead: Partially
(see steps 3 and 4)

Can Be Frozen: No

Best Seasons:
Spring and summer

Food Storage Note:
Unused sun-dried tomatoes can be kept, tightly covered in the jar and refrigerated, for several weeks.

THESE MOUTHWATERING TOASTS represent a fresh, new style of canapé. Sun-dried tomatoes are combined with shallots, garlic, basil and red pepper flakes and blended with cream cheese and Parmesan cheese to make a spread for crisp toasted French bread.

1   16-ounce jar sun-dried tomatoes packed in oil
¼   cup finely chopped shallots
2   teaspoons finely minced garlic
½   teaspoon salt, plus more if needed
¼   teaspoon crushed red pepper flakes
1   teaspoon dried basil leaves
¼   cup chopped fresh flat-leaf parsley
8   ounces reduced-fat cream cheese, softened
     (*see Variation*)
¼   cup freshly grated imported Parmesan cheese
24   slices French bread, ⅜ inch thick, preferably
     from a loaf 2½ inches in diameter
2   tablespoons fresh basil, cut into ¼-inch
     strips, for garnish

1. Drain 2 teaspoons oil from sun-dried tomatoes and place oil in a medium, heavy skillet. Chop enough sun-dried tomatoes to make ½ cup.

2. Heat oil in skillet over medium-high heat. When hot, add shallots and sauté, stirring, until softened, about 3 minutes. Add garlic and sauté, stirring, for 1 minute more. Add chopped sun-dried tomatoes, salt, red pepper flakes and dried basil and cook for 2 minutes more. Remove from heat and stir in parsley.

3. Blend cream cheese and Parmesan together in a bowl. Measure 2 teaspoons more oil from sun-dried tomatoes and add to cheeses, along with sautéed shallot mixture. Mix well and taste. Add more salt if needed. (*Cheese can be prepared 2 days ahead. Cover and refrigerate; bring to room temperature 30 minutes before using.*)

4. Arrange a rack at center position and preheat oven to 300°F. Place bread slices on a baking sheet and bake for 10 to 12 minutes, turning once, until golden and crisp. (*If not using immediately, store in an airtight container for up to 1 day. If necessary, reheat to crisp in a preheated 300°F oven for 5 minutes.*)

5. To finish, spread toasts generously with cheese mixture. Preheat broiler and broil toasts 5 to 6 inches from heat for about 1 minute, or until hot. Watch constantly so they do not burn.

6. Serve toasts on a serving plate. Garnish each toast with basil strips. Serve warm.

Variation: You can substitute a creamy goat cheese for the cream cheese.

Menu Suggestion:

These toasts can precede Roast Chicken and Potatoes with Rosemary, Thyme and Lemon (page 135), or they can be served with Mixed Greens in Orange Balsamic Dressing (page 247).

Quick Rosemary Cheese Straps

MAKES 44 STRAWS

★

From Start to Finish:
50 minutes

Actual Working Time:
30 minutes

Make Ahead: Yes
(see step 5)

Can Be Frozen: Yes
(see step 5)

Best Seasons: All year

Shopping Notes:
Cracker Barrel mild white
Cheddar cheese works well
in this recipe.

Pepperidge Farm makes
good puff pastry dough; it
is located in the freezer
section of the supermarket.

Parchment paper is
available in cookware shops
and in some supermarkets.

THESE THIN, CRISPY, HERB-SCENTED CHEESE STRAWS have two benefits for the busy cook: they are made with only four ingredients, and they can be prepared several days in advance.

¾ cup (3 ounces) grated mild white
    Cheddar cheese (*see Shopping Notes*)
¾ cup (3 ounces) freshly grated imported
    Parmesan cheese
1 tablespoon plus 1 teaspoon dried rosemary leaves,
    crushed
1 sheet frozen puff pastry
    (half of a 17¼-ounce package),
    defrosted (*see Shopping Notes*)
    Fresh rosemary sprigs for garnish (*optional*)

1. Line 3 large baking sheets with parchment paper (*see Shopping Notes*) and set aside. Arrange a rack at center position and preheat oven to 425°F.

2. Place Cheddar, Parmesan and rosemary in a food processor fitted with a metal blade and process for several seconds until mixture is finely ground to a coarse powder. Remove and set aside. (Alternatively, by hand, mince together cheeses and dried rosemary with a sharp knife.)

3. Place pastry sheet on a lightly floured work surface and roll into a rectangle 18 by 11 inches. Place pastry sheet so that a long end is in front of you. Starting at the short end on your right, cover half of pastry with ⅓ cup cheese mixture. Fold clean half of pastry sheet over cheese and press lightly with your hands. Repeat, rolling pastry to an 18-by-11-inch rectangle, sprinkling half of sheet with ⅓ cup cheese, then folding and pressing dough together, 2 more times for a total of 3 times. Let pastry rest for a few minutes if difficult to roll.

4. After all cheese has been incorporated, roll dough into an 18-by-11-inch rectangle a final time. Cut dough in half crosswise to make two 11-by-9-inch rectangles. Cut each rectangle into about 22 thin strips, or straws, ½ inch wide by 9 inches long. Twist each strip a few times and place on baking sheets, pressing ends onto parchment and spacing evenly. Bake straws, 1 sheet at a time, until golden brown, about 8 minutes. Watch carefully; check after 5 minutes.

5. When straws are done, remove from oven and cool for 5 minutes. Serve warm or at room temperature. (*Cheese straws can be made 2 to 3 days ahead and kept in an airtight container at room temperature. If desired, rewarm in a 350°F oven for 5 minutes. They can also be frozen; defrost before using and crisp in a 350° oven until hot, about 5 minutes.*)

6. To serve, arrange in a napkin-lined basket or in a wide-rimmed wine goblet. Garnish with a few fresh rosemary sprigs, if desired.

Menu Suggestion:

These cheese straws make a satisfying yet not too filling appetizer to serve with red or white wine. They can also be offered in place of bread with Orange and Basil Tomato Soup (page 58).

Warm Goat Cheese *and* Smoked Salmon Cakes

SERVES 6 AS AN
APPETIZER

★

From Start to Finish:
1 hour 30 minutes

Actual Working Time:
45 minutes

Make Ahead: Partially
(see step 2)

Can Be Frozen: No

Best Seasons: All year

Shopping Note:
Look for a smooth,
creamy goat cheese, either
domestic or imported.
Make certain it contains no
herbs or cracked pepper;
you want a simple, plain
goat cheese. Chavrie is a
brand often available in
supermarkets that works
well.

I LOVE THE FLAVOR OF SMOKED SALMON blended with creamy goat cheese in these seafood cakes. They are shaped into little patties and coated with bread crumbs, then sautéed just to warm—but not melt—the cheese.

4   ounces thinly sliced smoked salmon
2   ounces (about ¼ cup) smooth, creamy
      goat cheese, softened (*see Shopping Note*)
4   ounces reduced-fat cream cheese, softened
1   teaspoon grated lemon zest
      (yellow portion of rind)
1   teaspoon fresh lemon juice
¼   cup plain dry bread crumbs
½   teaspoon freshly ground black pepper
½   teaspoon dried thyme leaves
2   tablespoons olive oil, plus more for coating pan
2   tablespoons chopped fresh chives or
      flat-leaf parsley
      Fresh watercress sprigs, cleaned and dried,
      for garnish (*optional*)

1. Coarsely chop salmon and place in a mixing bowl. Add goat cheese, cream cheese, lemon zest and lemon juice and mix well to blend. Shape into 12 patties and flatten slightly so they are about 2 inches in diameter. Chill cakes to firm for 15 minutes.

2. Combine bread crumbs, pepper and thyme and place on a dinner plate. Gently press salmon patties into crumbs on both sides. Place patties on another plate and cover and refrigerate for at least 30 minutes or up to 3 hours.

3. When ready to serve, heat 2 tablespoons oil, or enough to lightly coat bottom of a large, heavy skillet, over medium heat. When hot, sauté enough patties to fit comfortably in skillet for 1 to 2 minutes per side, just to heat. Do not overcook or cheese will start to melt. Remove and loosely cover with aluminum foil. Repeat until all patties are cooked.

4. To serve, arrange 2 salmon patties each on 6 small plates. Sprinkle each serving with fresh chives or parsley; garnish each with a sprig of watercress, if desired.

Menu Suggestion:

These cakes could be followed by grilled lamb chops or chicken.

Fiesta Tortilla Triangles

MAKES 36
APPETIZERS

From Start to Finish:
50 minutes

Actual Working Time:
35 minutes

Make Ahead: Partially
(see step 1)

Can Be Frozen: No

Best Seasons:
Summer and early fall

Shopping Note:
I use Guiltless Gourmet
Mild Black Bean Dip, which
is available in the health-
food or snack sections of
many supermarkets. It has
no fat and is a delicious
topping for the tortillas.
Other black bean dips can
also be used.

THESE BRIGHTLY HUED TORTILLA WEDGES look as if they take far more skill and time to assemble than they actually do. Flour tortillas are spread with goat cheese—which is lower in fat than traditional Cheddar or Jack cheeses—and black bean dip, then topped with sautéed red and yellow peppers. Diced plum tomatoes and chopped parsley add final splashes of color.

2	tablespoons olive oil
1½	cups chopped red bell peppers (about 2 large, cut into ½-inch dice)
1½	cups chopped yellow bell peppers (about 2 large, cut into ½-inch dice)
1½	cups chopped green onions, including 2 inches of green tops
	Scant 1½ teaspoons crushed red pepper flakes
	Salt
6	8-inch flour tortillas
4	ounces soft, creamy goat cheese (*see Shopping Note, page 28*)
¾	cup black bean dip (*see Shopping Note*)
¾	cup diced plum tomatoes (5-6 tomatoes, unpeeled, seeded)
2	tablespoons chopped fresh flat-leaf parsley

1. Heat oil in a large, heavy skillet over medium-high heat. When hot, add bell peppers and cook, stirring constantly, until softened, about 5 minutes. Add green onions and red pepper flakes. Cook, stirring, for 2 to 3 minutes more. Season to taste with salt. (*Peppers and onions can be sautéed 1 day ahead. Cool, cover and refrigerate.*)

2. When ready to assemble, preheat oven to 350°F. Place tortillas on 2 aluminum-foil-lined baking sheets. Bake for about 5 minutes, just to crisp slightly. Remove from oven; leave oven on. Cool tortillas for a few minutes; spread each with 1 tablespoon goat cheese. Cover each with 2 tablespoons black bean dip. Divide pepper mixture evenly and distribute over tortillas. Sprinkle 2 tablespoons tomatoes over each.

3. Return tortillas to oven and bake until hot and crisp, 8 to 10 minutes. Remove from oven and sprinkle with parsley. Cut each tortilla into 6 wedges and serve warm.

Menu Suggestion:

These appetizers can precede Chilied Ribs (page 180) or Grilled Chicken with Pineapple Salsa (page 166).

Grilled Pepper Jack *and* Spinach Tortillas

SERVES 6 TO 8

★

From Start to Finish:
30 minutes

Actual Working Time:
30 minutes

Make Ahead: Partially
(see steps 1 and 2)

Can Be Frozen: No

Best Seasons: All year

QUESADILLAS ARE THE FAMOUS Mexican cheese-filled tortilla "sandwiches," which are fried and served warm. In this version, tortillas are spread with a pepper-Jack-cheese blend, then covered with shredded spinach and store-bought roasted peppers. For a lighter flavor, the tortillas are grilled rather than fried.

6 ounces soft goat cheese (*see Shopping Note,* page 28)
4 ounces (1 cup) grated pepper Jack cheese
4 tablespoons chopped fresh cilantro leaves
¼ teaspoon cayenne pepper
8 8-inch flour tortillas
⅔ cup store-bought roasted red bell peppers
   (*see Shopping Note,* page 12)
1⅓ cups cleaned spinach leaves,
   cut into ½-inch-wide strips

1. Place goat cheese, pepper Jack cheese, cilantro and cayenne in a mixing bowl; mix well to blend. (*Cheese mixture can be prepared 1 day ahead. Cover and refrigerate. Bring to room temperature before using.*)

2. To assemble tortillas, spray 4 tortillas on one side with nonstick cooking spray and place on a work surface, sprayed side down. Divide cheese mixture evenly and spread over tortillas. Cut roasted peppers into pieces approximately 1 inch square. Divide and arrange peppers over cheese layer. Divide and sprinkle spinach over peppers. Cover with remaining 4 tortillas and spray tops with nonstick spray. (*Tortillas can be made 1 hour ahead. Leave loosely covered with aluminum foil at room temperature.*)

(continued on page 49)

ONE-BITE BISCUITS *with* APPLE BUTTER *and* COUNTRY HAM, *page 11*

CORN *and* WILD RICE SOUP *with* SMOKED SAUSAGE, *page 80*

PECAN GRIDDLE CAKES *with* ORANGE BUTTER, *page 304*

BROILED TROUT *with* SESAME SEEDS *and* CHIVES, *page 125, and*
RED-SKIN POTATO *and* ASPARAGUS SALAD *with* WARM MUSTARD DRESSING, *page 260*

SCALLOP POPOVER *with* TOMATO-ORANGE SAUCE, *page 122*

CHILIED RIBS, *page 180, and* BLACK BEAN *and* CINNAMON RICE SALAD, *page 274*

GLAZED WINTER FRUITS *over* POUND CAKE, *page 348*

GRILLED CHICKEN *with* PINEAPPLE SALSA, *page 166*

SILVER-DOLLAR CRAB CAKES *with* ROASTED RED PEPPER SAUCE, *page 12*

CAJUN SHRIMP PO' BOY SANDWICHES, *page 338*

SALMON POTPIE *with* BUTTERMILK CRUST, *page 96*

Out-of-the-Ordinary SPICY TOMATO *and* CHEESE MACARONI, *page 110*

SMOTHERED PORK CHOPS *with* APRICOTS *and* PRUNES, *page 154, and*
SUGAR SNAP PEAS *with* PROSCIUTTO *and* MINT, *page 199*

THE OTHER BLT, *page 335*

BLACK *and* WHITE CHILI, *page* 76

VANILLA *and* CHOCOLATE LAYERED CHEESECAKE, *page 374*

3. Preheat a grill. Spray a rack with nonstick cooking spray and arrange 5 inches from heat source. When grill is ready, place tortillas on grill; watch constantly. Turn after 30 to 60 seconds, or when undersides start to brown and crisp. Cook on the other side in the same way. (Alternatively, you can broil tortillas: Arrange a rack 6 to 7 inches from heat source, and broil, watching constantly, until brown and crisp. Turn and cook on other side.)

4. Remove, and with a large, sharp knife or kitchen scissors, cut each tortilla into 6 wedges. Arrange tortillas in a napkin-lined basket and serve hot.

Menu Suggestion:
These tortillas taste delicious with the dishes mentioned on page 31.

Wild Mushroom Tart *in* Cheddar Crust

SERVES 6 TO 8

★

From Start to Finish:
3 hours 25 minutes
(includes 30 minutes for
chilling dough and 1 hour
for soaking mushrooms)

Actual Working Time:
55 minutes

Make Ahead: Yes
(see steps 3 and 7)

Can Be Frozen: No

Best Seasons:
Fall and winter

Shopping Note:
Dried mushroom
varieties, such as cèpes or
porcini or a combination
of these or others, are fine
for this dish.

THIS IS A TART OF ASSERTIVE FLAVORS. Grated Cheddar enhances the flavor of the crust, while dried mushrooms combined with fresh white ones and prosciutto add robust accents to the filling. The tart is best served warm from the oven, but it can be made ahead and reheated when needed. This savory pie could also be offered as a light main course along with a salad for lunch or supper.

FOR CRUST

1 cup all-purpose flour
½ cup (about 2 ounces) grated medium-sharp
    Cheddar cheese (*see Variation*, page 52)
¼ teaspoon salt
3 tablespoons well-chilled unsalted butter,
    cut into small chunks
2 tablespoons well-chilled vegetable shortening,
    cut into small chunks
3 tablespoons ice water

FOR FILLING

1 ounce dried wild mushrooms (*see Shopping Note*)
1 cup chicken broth, hot
2 tablespoons vegetable oil
2 ounces thinly sliced prosciutto, coarsely chopped
1½ cups chopped onions
1½ tablespoons minced garlic
1 pound fresh white mushrooms,
    cleaned and thinly sliced through stems
¼ teaspoon salt, plus more if needed
¼ teaspoon freshly ground black pepper,
    plus more if needed
1½ teaspoons dried tarragon leaves
2 tablespoons all-purpose flour
1 cup milk

1 large egg, plus 1 egg white, lightly beaten
1 tablespoon chopped fresh tarragon or flat-leaf
  parsley for garnish (*optional*)

1. Arrange a rack at center position and preheat oven to 375°F.

2. **To prepare crust:** Place flour, cheese and salt in a food processor fitted with a metal blade. Place butter and shortening on top. Process, pulsing, until mixture resembles coarse crumbs. Add water through chute and process until a ball of dough is formed. (Alternatively, you can prepare dough by hand: Combine flour, cheese and salt in a bowl. Cut in butter and shortening with a pastry blender or 2 table knives until mixture resembles oatmeal flakes. Gradually add water, mixing just until dough holds together. Transfer dough to a lightly floured surface. Using heel of your hand, smear ¼ cup dough at a time across surface to form a 6-inch strip; continue until you have smeared all dough. Smearing dough ensures that fats are blended evenly into flour.) Gather dough into a ball and flatten into a disk. Cover with plastic wrap and refrigerate for 30 minutes.

3. On a floured work surface, roll dough into an 11-inch circle and fit into a 9-inch tart pan. Fold overhanging dough in and push it against edge of shell to reinforce sides. Pierce bottom of crust with a fork. Line shell with aluminum foil and fill with pie weights or dried beans. Bake for 10 minutes, then remove foil and beans and bake until crust is light golden, 10 to 15 minutes more. Remove and cool shell. (*Shell can be made several hours in advance. Leave at room temperature, loosely covered with aluminum foil.*)

4. **To prepare filling:** Place dried mushrooms in a small mixing bowl and cover with broth. Let soak for 1 hour. Drain (straining and reserving soaking liquid); chop mushrooms. Set aside.

5. Heat oil in a medium, heavy skillet over medium heat. When oil is hot, add prosciutto and onions and sauté, stirring, for about 3 minutes. Add garlic and cook, stirring, for 1 minute more. Add chopped mushrooms, mushroom soaking liquid, fresh mushrooms, ¼ teaspoon salt, ¼ teaspoon pepper and tarragon and sauté, stirring often, until mushrooms soften and all liquid evaporates, about 10 minutes. Taste

Menu Suggestion:
This is a substantial dish and could be offered with Mixed Greens in Orange Balsamic Dressing (page 247) for a light lunch or supper.

Cooking Technique:

White sauce, or béchamel sauce, typically is made by melting butter, then adding flour to form what is known as a roux. After the roux has cooked for a couple of minutes, milk is added. For this new version, I have omitted the butter and cooked the flour alone for a few seconds before whisking in the milk. White sauce made this way works beautifully and has the added advantage of being lower in fat.

and season with more salt and pepper, if needed. Remove from heat and set aside.

6. Place flour in a medium saucepan over medium heat. Cook, whisking constantly, for 30 seconds; whisk in milk. Continue to cook and whisk until mixture has thickened, 3 to 4 minutes. Remove from heat and stir sauce into mushroom mixture. (Taste and add salt, if needed.) Stir in egg and egg white. Pour filling into prepared shell.

7. **To bake:** Preheat oven to 375°F. Bake tart until filling is firm and crust is a rich golden brown, 30 to 35 minutes. Remove and cool for 5 minutes. (*Tart can be baked 2 to 3 hours ahead; leave at room temperature and reheat at 350°F for 10 to 15 minutes.*) Garnish with chopped tarragon or parsley, if desired. Serve warm, cut into wedges.

Variation: For a stronger cheese flavor in the crust, you can use smoked Cheddar in place of regular Cheddar.

Warm Spiced Cranberry Cider

THIS DRINK IS SIMPLICITY ITSELF—cider and cranberry juice are simmered with orange and cinnamon seasonings.

1 medium navel orange, skin left on, cut into large chunks, plus 8 thin orange slices for garnish
4 cups cider
4 cups cranberry juice cocktail
2 cinnamon sticks, plus 8 more sticks for garnish
2 teaspoons light brown sugar

1. Put orange chunks in a food processor fitted with a metal blade or a blender, and pulse several times until coarsely chopped, or coarsely chop with a knife by hand.

2. Place chopped orange, cider, cranberry juice cocktail, 2 cinnamon sticks and brown sugar in a large, heavy saucepan over medium-high heat. Cook, stirring often, until hot, 8 to 10 minutes. Using a large sieve, strain mixture and return to saucepan. (*If not using immediately, cool, cover, and refrigerate for up to 1 day. Reheat before serving. Cider can also be frozen, defrosted and reheated.*)

3. To serve, pour into mugs or cups and garnish each serving with 1 cinnamon stick and 1 orange slice.

MAKES 8 SERVINGS
(1 CUP EACH)

From Start to Finish:
25 minutes
Actual Working Time:
15 minutes
Make Ahead: Yes
(see step 2)
Can Be Frozen: Yes
(see step 2)
Best Seasons:
Fall and winter

Menu Suggestion:
A plate of English Toffee Cookies (page 386) tastes good with sips of this cider.

Orange *and* Spicy Mulled Wine

SERVES 10

★

From Start to Finish:
30 minutes

Actual Working Time:
10 minutes

Make Ahead: Yes
(see step 1)

Can Be Frozen: No

Best Seasons:
Fall and winter

Menu Suggestion:
Serve with a plate of
robust cheeses and fresh
pears and apples.

T HIS IS ANOTHER PERFECT DRINK for sipping on a chilly evening. The aroma is enticing even before you taste the warm wine.

2   whole oranges, plus 10 orange slices for garnish
16 whole cloves
2   cups water
1   cup sugar
6   cinnamon sticks, plus 10 more sticks for garnish
2   750-ml bottles dry red wine

1. Cut whole oranges in half. Stud each half with 4 cloves. Bring 2 cups water to a boil in a large, heavy nonreactive saucepan. Add orange halves, sugar and 6 cinnamon sticks and stir over medium-high heat until sugar dissolves. Simmer for 5 minutes. Add wine, adjust heat so that mixture is almost simmering and cook for 20 minutes; do not boil. Remove orange halves and cinnamon sticks from wine. (*If not using immediately, cool, cover and refrigerate up to 1 day. Reheat before serving.*)

2. Ladle wine into mugs and slit each orange slice and attach to the rim of each mug. Garnish each with a cinnamon stick and serve.

Peach *of a* Tea

I OFTEN OFFER THIS SPECIAL ICED TEA before my summer cooking classes. Without fail, students always ask for the recipe. Peach-scented herb tea and English Breakfast tea are steeped together along with fresh mint leaves. Served chilled with a thin peach slice and a mint sprig, it is a tempting summer drink.

8 cups water

¼ cup sugar

3 regular (not family-sized) English Breakfast tea bags (*see Shopping Note*)

5 regular (not family-sized) herb peach tea bags (*see Shopping Note*)

3 fresh mint sprigs, plus 12 more sprigs for garnish

8 cups ice cubes, plus more for serving

1-2 large ripe peaches, peeled

1. In a 4-quart or larger nonreactive saucepan over high heat, bring water and sugar to a simmer. Reduce heat to low and simmer, stirring often, until sugar dissolves, 3 to 4 minutes. Remove from heat and add tea bags and 3 mint sprigs; let mixture steep for 25 minutes. Remove tea bags and squeeze them over pan. Discard mint sprigs. Add 8 cups ice to dilute. Cover and refrigerate for at least 1 hour to chill. (*Tea can be made 1 day ahead; keep covered and refrigerated.*)

2. To serve, fill 12 tall glasses with ice and pour tea over ice. Cut 12 half-inch wedges from peaches and garnish each serving with a peach slice and a mint sprig.

SERVES 12

From Start to Finish:
35 minutes, plus 1 to 2 hours to chill tea

Actual Working Time:
10 minutes

Make Ahead: Yes
(see step 1)

Can Be Frozen: No

Best Season:
Summer

Shopping Note:
I have used Perfectly Peach Tea and English Teatime Tea (either decaffeinated or caffeinated), both by Bigelow, for this recipe.

Chapter 2

Soups

Old Favorites *with* New Twists

Curried Carrot *and* Parsnip Soup

TWO UNDERRATED VEGETABLES—carrots and parsnips—are paired in this soup with leeks and a generous seasoning of curry powder. The result is a rich and satisfying potage that can either begin a cold-weather dinner or anchor it as a main course.

2 tablespoons unsalted butter

1½ cups cleaned, chopped leeks, white part only (about 2 large; *see Cooking Technique*)

1 pound carrots, peeled and coarsely chopped

¾ pound parsnips, peeled and coarsely chopped

8 cups chicken broth

1¾ teaspoons curry powder

½ cup whipping cream (*see Healthful Variation*)

2 tablespoons chopped fresh flat-leaf parsley for garnish

1. Melt butter in a large, heavy pot over medium-high heat. Add leeks and sauté until just softened, about 4 minutes. Add carrots and parsnips and sauté for 3 minutes. Add broth and curry powder and bring to a boil. Reduce heat to low and simmer until vegetables are very tender, stirring occasionally, about 30 minutes. Cool slightly. Puree soup in small batches using a food processor fitted with a metal blade, a blender or a food mill. (*Soup can be prepared 1 day ahead. Cool, cover and refrigerate. It can also be frozen; defrost before continuing.*)

2. Return soup to pot and bring to a simmer. Just before serving, stir in cream, and cook for 1 minute more.

3. To serve, ladle soup into bowls and sprinkle with parsley.

Healthful Variation: To lower the fat, you can use ½ cup evaporated skim milk instead of whipping cream.

SERVES 8

From Start to Finish:
1 hour

Actual Working Time:
30 minutes

Make Ahead: Partially
(see step 1)

Can Be Frozen:
Yes (see step 1)

Best Seasons:
Fall and winter

Cooking Technique:
To clean and prepare a leek for cooking, cut off and discard root ends and dark green portion of leaves (unless the recipe calls for including the dark green parts). What remains—a section that is white near the root end and pale green at the other—is considered the "white part" of the leek. Make a lengthwise slit down the leek and hold under cold running water to wash out any sand or grit that may be trapped in between the layers. Pat dry and use as directed.

Orange *and* Basil Tomato Soup

SERVES 8

From Start to Finish:
65 minutes

Actual Working Time:
25 minutes

Make Ahead: Yes
(see step 2)

Can Be Frozen: Yes
(see step 2)

Best Seasons:
Spring, summer and fall

TOMATO AND ORANGE HAVE A NATURAL AFFINITY. I love the way their flavors work together in this soup, which is also seasoned with red pepper flakes and basil. Light yet assertive in taste, this makes a good first course. Although I always serve it warm, my students have liked it chilled equally well.

¼ cup olive oil

1½ cups chopped onions

⅔ cup chopped carrots

2 teaspoons chopped garlic

2 teaspoons dried basil

Scant ½ teaspoon crushed red pepper flakes

2 28-ounce cans Italian-style plum tomatoes, drained well and coarsely chopped

3½ teaspoons grated orange zest (orange portion of rind), *divided*

Generous pinch sugar

½ teaspoon salt, plus more if needed

6 cups chicken broth

6 tablespoons freshly squeezed orange juice

2 tablespoons fresh basil leaves, cut into fine strips

1. Heat oil in a large, heavy pot over medium-high heat. When oil is hot, add onions and carrots and sauté, stirring, until vegetables are softened, 3 to 4 minutes. Add garlic, dried basil and red pepper flakes and sauté, stirring, for 2 minutes more. Add tomatoes, 2 teaspoons orange zest, pinch of sugar, ½ teaspoon salt and broth. Bring to a simmer and cook, uncovered, until vegetables are quite tender, 25 to 35 minutes.

2. Puree soup in batches in a food processor fitted with a metal blade, a blender or a food mill. Return soup to pot in which it was cooked and stir in orange juice. Taste; if it is too acidic, add a little more sugar. Add more salt, if necessary. (*Soup can be made 2 days ahead to this point. Cool, cover and refrigerate. It can also be frozen; defrost before continuing.*)

3. When ready to serve, reheat, stirring frequently, until hot. Ladle into 8 bowls. Sprinkle each serving with a generous pinch of remaining grated orange zest (⅛ teaspoon or more) and garnish with basil strips.

Menu Suggestion:

This is such a light, refreshing soup it can easily be followed by substantial fare like roast chicken, broiled lamb chops or grilled steaks.

Summer-Garden Corn, Tomato *and* Zucchini Chowder

SERVES 8

From Start to Finish:
1 hour 5 minutes

Actual Working Time:
35 minutes

Make Ahead: Yes
(see steps 3 and 5)

Can Be Frozen: Yes
(see step 3)

Best Season: Summer

BY LATE SUMMER, the local farmers' market where I shop is brimming with baskets of deep red tomatoes, crates of just-picked corn and boxes of small, tender zucchini. I am always enticed to buy several bagfuls, for I know they can be put to good use in this soup. The vegetables are simmered in broth and, when tender, finished with an addition of milk and grated pepper Jack cheese.

2 tablespoons olive oil
1½ cups chopped onions
4½ cups fresh corn kernels (scraped from about 9 ears)
7 cups chicken broth
¾ teaspoon salt, plus more if needed
⅛ teaspoon freshly ground black pepper,
   plus more if needed
   About 5 small zucchini, ends removed,
   cut into ½-inch cubes (about 3 cups)
   About 8 medium plum tomatoes, stemmed,
   halved lengthwise, seeds and membranes removed,
   cut into ¼-inch dice (about 2 cups)
1¼ cups 1% milk
1½ cups (6 ounces) shredded pepper Jack cheese

1. In a large, heavy, deep-sided pot over medium-high heat, heat oil until hot. Add onions and cook, stirring, just until softened, about 3 minutes.

2. Add corn and cook, stirring, for 3 minutes more. Add broth, ¾ teaspoon salt and ⅛ teaspoon pepper. Bring to a simmer and cook, uncovered, until corn is tender, 15 to 18 minutes.

3. Add zucchini and cook until tender, about 6 minutes. Add tomatoes and cook for 3 to 4 minutes more. Remove from heat; set aside for a few minutes. (*If you plan to freeze the soup, do so at this point. Cool, cover and freeze; defrost before continuing.*)

4. In a medium, heavy saucepan over medium-high heat, heat milk until hot but not boiling. Gradually whisk in cheese, a handful at a time, making certain each addition has melted before adding more. When all has been incorporated and mixture is smooth, remove from heat.

5. Place soup over medium heat and gradually pour cheese mixture into it, stirring constantly. Taste and add more salt and pepper, if desired. (*If not serving immediately, cool, cover and refrigerate. Soup can be made up to 1 day ahead. Reheat, stirring, when ready to serve.*)

6. To serve, ladle soup into 8 individual bowls. Serve hot.

Menu Suggestion:

In the summer, I serve this soup as a main course with warm sourdough bread and a salad of mixed greens in a light dressing.

Cucumber *and* Tomato Soup *with* Cayenne Croutons

SERVES 6

★

From Start to Finish:
  1 hour 20 minutes

Actual Working Time:
  45 minutes

Make Ahead: Partially
  (see step 2)

Can Be Frozen: Yes
  (see step 2)

Best Seasons:
  Spring and summer

CUCUMBERS ADD AN UNEXPECTED TOUCH of freshness to this warm tomato soup, but by far the best feature is the topping of cayenne pepper croutons. To make them, I spread slices of French bread with a highly seasoned butter flavored with garlic and cayenne pepper. I bake the croutons until crisp and golden and then serve one floating on top of each bowl of soup.

  2 tablespoons unsalted butter
  2 medium onions, coarsely chopped
  4 small garlic cloves, minced
  2¼ pounds ripe tomatoes, cored and quartered
  3 large cucumbers, peeled, halved lengthwise, seeded and coarsely chopped
  1 teaspoon salt
     Freshly ground black pepper
  1½ tablespoons tomato paste
  4½ cups chicken broth
     Dash red pepper sauce, preferably Tabasco

FOR CROUTONS

  3 tablespoons unsalted butter, softened
  1½ teaspoons minced garlic
  ½ tablespoon minced fresh flat-leaf parsley
  ¼ teaspoon cayenne pepper
  ⅛ teaspoon salt
     Dash red pepper sauce, preferably Tabasco
  18 ¼-inch-thick slices French bread

  6 green onions (white part and all but 2 inches of green tops), cut into very fine slices, for garnish
  2 tablespoons minced fresh tarragon leaves or flat-leaf parsley for garnish (*optional*)

1. Melt butter in a large, heavy saucepan over medium heat. Add onions and garlic and sauté for 1 minute. Add tomatoes and cucumbers and sauté for 1 minute. Add salt; season with pepper. Stir in tomato paste, then broth and red pepper sauce. Bring to a boil, reduce heat and simmer until vegetables are very soft, stirring occasionally, about 30 minutes.

2. Puree soup in batches in a food processor fitted with a metal blade, a blender or a food mill. Strain, if desired. Taste and adjust seasonings, adding salt, pepper and red pepper sauce, if desired. (*Soup can be prepared 1 day ahead. Cool, cover and refrigerate. It can also be frozen: defrost before continuing.*) Return soup to pan and reheat, stirring frequently.

3. **To prepare croutons:** Preheat oven to 300°F. Mix butter, garlic, parsley, cayenne, salt and red pepper sauce in a small bowl. Spread mixture on both sides of bread. Arrange on a baking sheet. Bake until golden brown, about 5 minutes per side.

4. To serve, ladle soup into 6 bowls. Garnish with green onions and tarragon or parsley, if desired. Float 1 crouton in each bowl. Pass remaining croutons separately.

Menu Suggestion:
This soup works well as a first course before Grilled Salmon with Roasted Garlic (page 168), or serve it as a light main course with a salad of mixed greens.

"No-Cream" Cream of Cauliflower Soup

SERVES 6

★

From Start to Finish:
1 hour 20 minutes

Actual Working Time:
35 minutes

Make Ahead: Yes
(see steps 2 and 3)

Can Be Frozen: Yes
(see step 2)

Best Seasons:
Fall and winter

ALTHOUGH CAULIFLOWER has never taken center stage at America's table as a simple vegetable, it's a star in this rich, creamy soup. It is simmered in broth along with aromatic vegetables. Then the mixture is pureed and enriched with low-fat milk, rather than cream. The result is absolutely delightful. A sprinkling of golden toasted bread crumbs and chopped parsley adds color to the finished soup.

2	tablespoons vegetable oil
¾	cup chopped carrots
¾	cup chopped celery
¾	cup chopped onions
8	cups cauliflower florets (about 2 medium heads)
7½	cups chicken broth
1½	cups 1% milk
⅛	teaspoon cayenne pepper
	Salt
1½	teaspoons unsalted butter, melted
½	cup fresh bread crumbs
1½	tablespoons chopped fresh flat-leaf parsley for garnish

1. Heat oil in a heavy, deep-sided pot over medium-high heat. When hot, add carrots, celery and onions and sauté, stirring constantly, until just slightly softened, about 5 minutes. Add cauliflower and broth and bring to a simmer. Lower heat and cook, uncovered, until vegetables are very tender, about 40 minutes.

2. Puree in a food processor fitted with a metal blade, a blender or a food mill. Return mixture to pot and reheat, stirring in milk and cayenne. Season to taste with salt. (*Soup can be made up to 2 days ahead. Cool, cover and refrigerate. It may also be frozen; defrost before continuing. Reheat over medium heat, stirring, until hot.*)

3. Heat butter in a small, heavy skillet over medium-high heat. Add bread crumbs and cook, tossing continuously, until crumbs are deep golden brown, 3 to 4 minutes. Transfer to a bowl. (*Bread crumbs can be prepared 1 to 2 days ahead. Cover loosely and leave at room temperature.*)

4. To serve, ladle soup into 6 individual bowls. Sprinkle each serving with bread crumbs and parsley. Serve hot.

Variation: One New Year's Eve, I added 2 tablespoons (about 1½ ounces) of lobster meat to each bowl of this soup. My guests raved about the resulting dish. Two or three shrimp per serving also make a special garnish.

Menu Suggestion:

This hearty soup tastes good before roast chicken or lamb. It can also stand on its own as a light main course offered with a mixed green salad.

Butternut Squash *and* Sausage Soup

SERVES 6

★

From Start to Finish:
1 hour 25 minutes

Actual Working Time:
45 minutes

Make Ahead: Partially
(see step 2)

Can Be Frozen: Yes
(see step 2)

Best Seasons:
Fall and winter

Shopping Note:
Butternut squash has a tough skin that must be removed with a vegetable peeler or a sharp knife. The grocery store where I shop sells the squash already peeled, a great time-saver. You might want to check your local market to see if squash is available this way.

MADE WITH SIMPLE, UNPRETENTIOUS ingredients, this soup is one of my favorites. The deep golden color comes from butternut squash that has been simmered in broth with onions and herbs and then pureed. A garnish of crisp, thin slices of sautéed kielbasa (the lighter turkey variety) adds a pleasing smoky flavor as well as visual appeal.

2	tablespoons unsalted butter (*divided*)
2	cups chopped onions
8	cups peeled, diced butternut squash (about 2¼ pounds peeled squash or slightly more, if unpeeled; *see Shopping Note*)
6	cups chicken broth
1½	teaspoons dried thyme leaves
½	teaspoon salt, plus more if needed
1	bay leaf, broken in half
¾-1	cup 1% milk
6	ounces turkey kielbasa, cut into ⅛-inch-thick slices (*see Shopping Notes*, page 301)
	Fresh thyme sprigs for garnish (*optional*)

1. Heat 1 tablespoon butter in a large, heavy pan over medium-high heat. When hot, add onions and cook, stirring, for about 4 minutes, or until softened. Add squash and cook, stirring, for 3 to 4 minutes more. Add broth, thyme, ½ teaspoon salt and bay leaf. Bring to a boil, lower heat and simmer, uncovered, until squash is very tender, 35 to 40 minutes. Remove bay leaf pieces.

2. Remove soup from heat and puree in a food processor fitted with a metal blade, a blender or a food mill. Stir in ¾ cup milk. Taste and season with more salt, if needed. (*Soup can be made 1 to 2 days ahead; cool, cover and refrigerate. It can also be frozen; defrost before continuing.*)

3. Reheat soup, stirring. If it seems too thick, stir in remaining ¼ cup milk.

4. Just before serving, heat remaining 1 tablespoon butter in a medium, heavy skillet over medium heat. Add kielbasa slices and cook, stirring constantly, until sausages are lightly browned and somewhat crisp, 2 to 3 minutes. Remove and drain on paper towels.

5. To serve, ladle soup into 6 soup bowls. Top each serving with several slices of kielbasa and garnish with a fresh thyme sprig, if desired.

Menu Suggestion:
"Waldorf of Sorts" Salad (page 254) and this soup make a wonderful meal for cold weather. You might like to include some warm French bread too.

Sweet Potato *and* Leek Soup *with a* Hint *of* Orange

SERVES 12

★

From Start to Finish:
  1 hour 30 minutes

Actual Working Time:
  30 minutes

Make Ahead: Yes
  (see step 4)

Can Be Frozen: Yes
  (see step 4)

Best Seasons:
  Fall and winter

Time-Saver:
  The diced sweet potatoes
can be dotted with butter,
sprinkled with brown sugar
and cooked in a microwave
dish, covered with plastic
wrap, in a microwave oven.
Use high power and cook
them for 5 to 7 minutes.
Cooking times may vary
depending on individual
ovens, so watch carefully.

MY MOTHER LOVED SWEET POTATOES and often served them baked or sautéed, but she never discovered the benefits of making soup with them. Too bad, because they are rich, velvety and robust when pureed. Here they are baked and then cooked in broth with leeks. Orange zest adds a clean splash of flavor at the end. This soup is ideal for Thanksgiving, but you can halve the recipe for smaller gatherings.

3¾	pounds sweet potatoes
6	tablespoons (¾ stick) cold unsalted butter (*divided*)
2	tablespoons light brown sugar
4	cups cleaned chopped leeks (5-6 medium, white part only; *see Cooking Technique*, page 57)
12	cups chicken broth, plus more if needed
2-2½	tablespoons grated orange zest (orange portion of rind), from about 2 large navel oranges
	Salt (*optional*)
12	flat-leaf parsley sprigs or ¼ cup chopped fresh for garnish

1. Preheat oven to 375°F. Peel sweet potatoes and cut into ½-inch dice. Place in 1 large or 2 medium shallow baking pans. Cut 4 tablespoons butter into small dice and dot potatoes with them. Sprinkle brown sugar over potatoes. Bake until tender, 45 to 55 minutes, turning potatoes several times to mix melted butter and sugar.

2. Meanwhile, melt remaining 2 tablespoons butter in a large, heavy nonreactive pot over medium-high heat. Add leeks and sauté, stirring, until softened, about 5 minutes. Add 12 cups broth and bring to a simmer. Reduce heat to low and simmer for 15 minutes; remove from heat.

3. When sweet potatoes are done, add them to broth mixture and re-turn to medium heat. Simmer for 5 minutes.

4. Puree soup in batches in a food processor fitted with a metal blade, a blender or a food mill until very smooth. If soup seems too thick, add more broth. Stir in 2 tablespoons orange zest and taste; add re-maining orange zest for a stronger flavor. Taste and add salt, if desired. (*Soup can be made 1 day ahead. Cool, cover and refrigerate. It can also be frozen; defrost before continuing.*)

5. Reheat over medium heat, stirring constantly. To serve, garnish each serving with a sprig of parsley or with a little chopped parsley.

Menu Suggestion:

Serve as a first course on Thanksgiving, followed by Southern Herb-Roasted Turkey (page 144).

Spicy Tortilla Soup *with* Vegetables

SERVES 6

★

From Start to Finish:
1 hour 10 minutes

Actual Working Time:
50 minutes

Make Ahead: Partially
(see steps 2, 3 and 4)

Can Be Frozen: Yes
(see step 2)

Best Seasons: All year

Shopping Note:
Swanson's makes a very
good canned vegetable
broth.

THIS MILDLY SPICY SOUP with Mexican accents makes a perfect main course. Traditionally, it is made with a tomato-flavored chicken broth, seasoned with spices and topped with crispy fried tortilla strips. I have added red and yellow peppers, carrots, zucchini and tomatoes, along with seasonings of cumin, oregano and red pepper flakes. The tortilla strips on top are baked, not fried. Cilantro-lemon relish, sunflower seeds and grated Jack cheese also garnish the soup. For a more robust version, I sometimes buy ¾ pound smoked turkey breast, cut it into strips and add it to the soup just before serving.

FOR SOUP

1½ tablespoons olive oil

1½ cups chopped onions

1 tablespoon minced garlic

1 28-ounce can Italian-style tomatoes, drained and coarsely chopped

2¼ teaspoons dried oregano leaves

¼ teaspoon crushed red pepper flakes

½ tablespoon ground cumin

½ teaspoon freshly ground black pepper

6 cups vegetable broth (*see Shopping Note*) or chicken broth

1 cup thinly sliced peeled carrots

½ cup finely diced red bell pepper

½ cup finely diced yellow bell pepper

½ cup finely diced celery

1½ cups finely diced zucchini
 Salt

FOR GARNISHES

7 6-inch round corn tortillas, cut into ¼-inch strips

½ cup cleaned packed fresh cilantro leaves (stemmed)

1 tablespoon grated lemon zest
  (yellow portion of rind)
2 teaspoons finely minced garlic
3 teaspoons fresh lemon juice
¾ cup (3 ounces) grated Monterey Jack cheese
6 tablespoons sunflower seeds or pumpkin seeds
  (pepitas; *see Shopping Note*)

Shopping Note:

Pepitas, or pumpkin seeds, can be bought salted, roasted or raw. For this dish, roasted pepitas, either unsalted or lightly salted, work well. The seeds are available in health-food stores, Mexican markets and some supermarkets.

Menu Suggestion:

Mexican Layered Salad with Cumin-Honey Dressing (page 252) is a wonderful accompaniment for a light lunch or supper.

1. **To prepare soup:** Heat oil in a medium, heavy skillet over medium-high heat. When hot, add onions and cook, stirring, until softened, 4 to 5 minutes. Add garlic and cook, stirring, for 1 minute more. Add tomatoes, oregano, red pepper flakes, cumin and pepper. Cook, stirring often, until vegetables are tender, about 10 minutes. Puree in a food processor fitted with a metal blade, a blender or a food mill; set aside.

2. Bring broth to a simmer in a large, heavy pot over high heat. Reduce heat to medium; add carrots, red and yellow peppers and celery. Cook until tender, 6 to 8 minutes. Add zucchini and cook for 3 minutes more. Stir pureed tomato mixture into pot and cook for 1 minute more. Remove from heat; season to taste with salt. (*Soup can be made 1 day ahead. Cool, cover and refrigerate. It can also be frozen; defrost before continuing.*)

3. **To prepare garnishes:** Arrange a rack at center position and preheat oven to 350°F. Spray an aluminum-foil-lined baking sheet with nonstick cooking spray and spread tortilla strips in a single layer. Bake until crisp, about 20 minutes. Stir strips after first 10 minutes and check to see how fast they are crisping. (*Strips can be prepared 1 day ahead; cool and store in a tightly sealed plastic bag. Place on a baking sheet and recrisp in a 350°F oven for 5 to 10 minutes, if necessary.*)

4. Combine chopped cilantro, lemon zest and garlic in a small bowl. (*Topping can be made 1 day ahead; cover and refrigerate.*)

5. When ready to serve, reheat soup and ladle 1 cup into each of 6 individual bowls. Stir ½ teaspoon lemon juice into each bowl. Garnish each serving with tortilla strips, cilantro mixture, cheese and sunflower or pumpkin seeds. Arrange remaining tortilla strips in a basket and serve bowls of garnishes alongside.

Meal-*in*-Itself Vegetable Soup

SERVES 6

From Start to Finish:
1 hour 35 minutes

Actual Working Time:
45 minutes

Make Ahead: Yes
(see step 3)

Can Be Frozen: Yes
(see step 3)

Best Seasons: All year

THIS SOUP IS SO HEARTY AND FILLING that it can easily stand on its own with a loaf of warm bread and a salad. I put in all the traditional vegetables, including leeks, carrots, celery and both yellow and green squash, but I also add some unexpected ones, such as chicory, a slightly bitter green. In the Italian tradition, I shave strips of Parmesan cheese over the soup.

2 tablespoons olive oil

½ cup diced carrots (¼-inch dice)

½ cup cleaned, chopped leeks, white parts only
(*see Cooking Technique*, page 57)

½ cup diced celery (¼-inch dice)

1 tablespoon finely chopped garlic

1½ teaspoons dried thyme leaves, plus more if needed

1¼ teaspoons dried rosemary leaves, crushed,
plus more if needed

1 teaspoon salt, plus more if needed

½ teaspoon crushed red pepper flakes,
plus more if needed

7 cups chicken broth

¼ cup tomato puree

½ cup sun-dried tomatoes (if packed in oil, pat dry),
cut into quarters

2 red bell peppers, cut into ½-inch-wide strips

2 cups cleaned chicory (curly endive), coarsely
chopped (*divided*)

2 small zucchini (¾ pound), cut in half lengthwise,
then cut into ¼-inch-thick slices

2 small yellow squash (¾ pound), cut in half
lengthwise, then cut into ¼-inch-thick slices

1 4-to-6-ounce wedge imported Parmesan cheese,
at room temperature, for garnish
(*see Healthful Variation*)

6 fresh rosemary sprigs for garnish (*optional*)

1. Heat oil in a large, heavy pan over medium-high heat. When hot, add carrots, leeks and celery. Cook, stirring constantly, for about 4 minutes, until vegetables are softened. Add garlic, 1½ teaspoons thyme, 1¼ teaspoons rosemary, 1 teaspoon salt and ½ teaspoon red pepper flakes. Cook, stirring, for 1 minute.

2. Add broth, tomato puree, sun-dried tomatoes, red peppers and 1 cup chicory. Stir to blend. Bring mixture to a simmer. Reduce heat to low, cover and simmer until peppers are tender but not mushy, about 40 minutes. (*Freeze extra tomato puree for another use.*)

3. Remove 1½ cups of soup and puree in a food processor fitted with a metal blade, a blender or a food mill. Stir puree back into soup. Add zucchini, yellow squash and remaining 1 cup chicory. Cook until vegetables are tender, 6 to 10 minutes more. Taste and add more herbs, salt or red pepper flakes, if desired. (*Soup can be made 2 days ahead; cool, cover and refrigerate. It can also be frozen; defrost before continuing. Reheat, stirring often, until hot.*)

4. Ladle soup into 6 individual bowls. Shave strips from Parmesan, using a vegetable peeler. Arrange 4 or 5 cheese strips on top of each bowl and garnish each with a fresh rosemary sprig, if desired.

Healthful Variation: Although the shaved Parmesan strips are delicious, you may omit them to lower the fat without affecting the soup's flavor.

Roasted Garlic *and* White Cheddar Soup

SERVES 6

From Start to Finish:
1 hour 40 minutes

Actual Working Time:
35 minutes

Make Ahead: Yes
(see step 3)

Can Be Frozen: Yes
(see step 3)

Best Season: Winter

I COULD EAT THIS SOUP EVERY DAY during the cold weather and never tire of it. Thick, rich, scented with roasted garlic, sautéed leeks and potatoes and melted cheese, it is equally good served as an opener to a robust winter menu or as a main course with a green salad and fruit for lunch or supper.

3 large garlic heads
½ cup olive oil
2 cups cleaned, chopped leeks, white parts only
   (4-5 leeks; *see Cooking Technique*, page 57)
3 pounds all-purpose potatoes (such as Idahos
   or russets), peeled and cut into ½-inch dice
6 cups chicken broth
¼ teaspoon freshly ground black pepper,
   plus more if needed
½ teaspoon salt, plus more if needed
1½ cups (about 6 ounces) packed grated mild white
   Cheddar cheese, *divided*
2 cups 1% milk
⅓ cup chopped fresh chives or flat-leaf parsley
   for garnish

1. Arrange a rack at center position and preheat oven to 400°F.

2. Smash each head of garlic with your hand to break it into cloves. Lightly smash individual cloves with the back of a large knife so that papery coating is loosened. Peel off papery skin. Place garlic cloves in a medium ovenproof ramekin, soufflé dish or baking dish. Pour oil over cloves; oil should cover them completely. Cover tightly with a double thickness of aluminum foil. Bake until garlic cloves are very tender and light golden brown, 20 to 30 minutes; check after 20 minutes as oven temperatures can vary. If not done, check every 5 minutes.

When the garlic cloves are tender, remove with a slotted spoon and drain; reserve oil.

3. Place 2 tablespoons reserved oil in a large, heavy pot over medium-high heat. (*Save remaining oil, refrigerated, for another use; it is full of flavor and can be used in salad dressings or for sautéing in place of regular olive oil.*) Add leeks and cook, stirring constantly, for 2 minutes. Add potatoes and cook, stirring, for 2 minutes more. Add broth, ¼ teaspoon pepper and ½ teaspoon salt and bring to a simmer over high heat. Reduce heat to low and simmer, uncovered, until potatoes are tender, 25 to 35 minutes. Remove from heat and add roasted garlic. Puree in a food processor fitted with a metal blade, a blender or a food mill. Return to pot and place over low heat. (*If not serving soup immediately, cool, cover and refrigerate for up to 2 days. It can also be frozen; defrost before continuing.*)

4. To serve, reheat soup until hot, stirring constantly, since soup has a tendency to stick to bottom of pan. Stir in 1 cup cheese, a handful at a time, making certain each addition has melted before adding more. Stir in milk. Taste and add more salt and pepper, if needed. Ladle soup into 6 individual bowls or cups. Garnish each serving with a little remaining cheese, some chopped chives or parsley and a grating of pepper, if desired.

Menu Suggestion:
A salad of mixed greens—Boston lettuce, spinach and romaine—in a light red wine vinegar dressing and warm crusty sourdough bread make great accompaniments.

Black *and* White Chili

SERVES 6

From Start to Finish:
1 hour 20 minutes
Actual Working Time:
45 minutes
Make Ahead: Partially
(see steps 3 and 4)
Can Be Frozen: Yes
(see step 3)
Best Seasons:
Fall and winter

Shopping Note:
Mexican oregano has
a stronger taste than
traditional (Mediterranean)
oregano. The Mexican
variety is available, dried,
in some supermarkets.
If you can't find it, use
Mediterranean oregano.

I AM ESPECIALLY FOND OF THIS CHILI, in which boneless chicken breasts, cubed and coated with spices, replace traditional ground beef. White and black beans are used in place of red ones. A sour-cream garnish flavored with orange and cilantro adds another change of taste. (*See photograph, page 47.*)

2½ tablespoons chili powder
2½ teaspoons ground cumin
1½ teaspoons dried oregano leaves,
preferably Mexican oregano (*see Shopping Note*)
¼ teaspoon crushed red pepper flakes
1½ teaspoons salt, plus more if needed
¼ cup all-purpose flour
2 pounds boneless, skinless chicken breasts,
cut into ½-inch cubes
3 tablespoons vegetable oil, plus more if needed
½ cup chopped carrot
½ cup chopped onion
½ cup chopped celery
2 teaspoons chopped garlic
1 28-ounce can plum tomatoes, drained and chopped
5 cups chicken broth
1 15½-ounce can black beans, drained and rinsed
1 15½-ounce can white navy or Great Northern
beans, drained and rinsed
1 cup nonfat sour cream (*see Healthful Variation*)
2 teaspoons grated orange zest
(orange portion of rind)
2 tablespoons fresh orange juice
4 teaspoons chopped fresh cilantro

1. Combine chili powder, cumin, oregano, red pepper flakes and 1½ teaspoons salt in a bowl and mix well. Measure 2 tablespoons spice mixture and combine with flour. Place in a bowl and toss with chicken cubes.

2. Heat 3 tablespoons oil in a large, heavy skillet over medium-high heat. When oil is hot, add enough chicken to fit comfortably in a single layer. Sauté, turning often, until chicken is golden, 3 to 4 minutes. Remove with a slotted spoon and drain on paper towels. Repeat until all chicken is cooked, adding more oil, if necessary. Set aside.

3. Add carrot, onion and celery to skillet and cook, stirring, until just softened, 3 to 4 minutes. Add garlic and cook for 1 minute more. Add remaining 2 tablespoons spice mixture and toss well. Return chicken to skillet along with tomatoes and broth. Bring to a simmer, reduce heat to low and simmer until chicken is tender and soup thickens, 20 to 25 minutes. Add beans and cook for 10 minutes more. Season to taste with salt, if needed. Remove from heat. (*Chili can be made 1 day ahead. Cool, cover and refrigerate. It can also be frozen; defrost before continuing.*)

4. To finish chili, mix together sour cream, orange zest, orange juice and cilantro in a small serving bowl. (*Garnish can be prepared 2 to 3 hours ahead. Cover and refrigerate.*)

5. Reheat chili over medium heat, stirring often. To serve, ladle into 6 bowls. Garnish with a dollop of sour-cream mixture.

Healthful Variation: Although I usually prefer reduced-fat sour cream to the nonfat varieties, nonfat works fine in this recipe because of the strong seasonings of orange and cilantro.

Menu Suggestion:

Mexican Layered Salad with Cumin-Honey Dressing (page 252) and Margarita Cheesecake (page 378) are irresistible accompaniments.

Black Bean Soup
with Fresh Orange Relish

SERVES 6

From Start to Finish:
5 hours (includes 2 hours for soaking beans and 2 hours for simmering soup)

Actual Working Time:
50 to 60 minutes

Make Ahead: Partially (see steps 2 and 3)

Can Be Frozen: Yes (see step 2)

Best Seasons:
Fall and winter

Cooking Technique:
Be careful when working with hot peppers! The tissues around your mouth, nose, eyes and ears are sensitive to the oils and fumes of hot peppers, and if you touch any of these areas with pepper-coated fingers, you will feel unpleasant burning sensations. I use rubber gloves to protect my hands, taking care to remove and wash them as soon as I am finished.

MY GOOD FRIEND CAROLYN CLAYCOMB, who is a talented chef from Columbus, Ohio, created this special black bean soup. What makes it so good and different is the fresh orange relish that is used as a garnish; its bright citrus flavor is a perfect counterpoint to the dense, rich bean broth. This soup takes several hours to assemble and cook, but it improves in flavor if made a day ahead and is a fine main course with corn bread and a salad.

FOR SOUP

3 cups dried black beans
2 tablespoons olive oil
2 cups chopped red onions
1 cup chopped red bell peppers (about 1 large pepper)
1 tablespoon finely chopped garlic
1½ tablespoons seeded, minced jalapeño peppers (about 4 small; *see Cooking Technique*)
2 bay leaves, broken in half
2 tablespoons chili powder
1 tablespoon ground cumin
½ tablespoon dried oregano leaves
½ cup sun-dried tomatoes (*not* packed in oil), chopped
10 cups chicken broth
2 28-ounce cans plum tomatoes, drained well and chopped
Salt and freshly ground black pepper

FOR ORANGE RELISH AND GARNISH

4-5 large oranges (enough to make 2 cups segments)
3 tablespoons chopped red onion
2 teaspoons seeded, chopped jalapeño pepper (*see Cooking Technique*)

2 tablespoons chopped fresh cilantro,
   plus ⅓ cup (*divided*)
1 tablespoon olive oil
⅓ cup reduced-fat sour cream

Menu Suggestion:
This soup can be served with the same accompaniments mentioned for Black and White Chili (page 77).

1. **To prepare soup:** Place beans in a large, heavy pot and cover with 2 inches of water. Bring to a boil over medium-high heat; boil for 2 minutes. Remove from heat and let beans soak for 2 hours. Drain and set aside.

2. Heat oil in a large, heavy pot over medium-high heat. When hot, add onions, red pepper, garlic and jalapeño pepper and sauté, stirring constantly, for 4 to 5 minutes. Add bay leaves, chili powder, cumin, oregano and sun-dried tomatoes; stir well. Add reserved black beans, broth and canned tomatoes. Bring to a simmer, reduce heat to low and simmer, uncovered, for about 2 hours or longer, or until beans are tender. Taste and season soup as desired with salt and pepper. Remove from heat. Discard bay leaves. (*Soup can be made 1 to 2 days ahead; cool, cover and refrigerate. It can also be frozen; defrost before continuing.*)

3. **To prepare orange relish:** With a sharp knife, peel oranges, removing skin and all white flesh underneath. When orange is peeled, you will see the faint outline of membranes with orange segments in between. Cut out orange segments. If any membrane remains on slices, cut off and discard. Cut segments coarsely into large chunks and place in a nonreactive mixing bowl. Add red onion, jalapeño pepper, 2 tablespoons cilantro and oil and toss to mix. (*Relish can be made 1 day ahead. Cover and refrigerate.*)

4. Reheat soup, stirring often, over medium-high heat and stir in remaining ⅓ cup cilantro. To serve, ladle soup into 6 bowls. Garnish each serving with some orange relish and a dollop of sour cream.

Corn *and* Wild Rice Soup *with* Smoked Sausage

MAKES 12
SERVINGS
(EACH 1 CUP)

From Start to Finish:
1 hour 30 minutes

Actual Working Time:
40 minutes

Make Ahead: Yes
(see step 4)

Can Be Frozen: Yes
(see step 4)

Best Seasons:
Fall and winter

Shopping Note:

Wild rice is not a true rice
but, rather, a marsh grass
that grows in wet areas,
especially in the northern
Great Lakes region. It is
expensive, particularly when
purchased boxed. Some
supermarkets and specialty
stores sell it in lower-priced
bulk. There are varying
qualities of wild rice; the
best varieties include long,
slender dark brown grains.

D ARK, SLENDER WILD RICE GRAINS, bits of bright yellow corn and morsels of rust-hued kielbasa sausage combine in an interesting mélange of color, flavor and texture in this soup, which is made with chicken and corn stocks. This makes a special first course for a Thanksgiving dinner, or you might like to serve it with a salad and warm bread for lunch or supper. (*See photograph, page 34.*)

12½	cups chicken broth (*divided*)
1¼	cups wild rice (*see Shopping Note*)
5	tablespoons vegetable oil
10	ounces smoked sausage, preferably turkey kielbasa, cut into ¼-inch dice (*see Shopping Notes*, page 301)
2½	cups chopped onions
1¼	cups diced carrots (¼-inch dice)
10	ears fresh corn, boiled until tender (about 5 minutes), scraped clean of kernels, or 2½ pounds frozen kernels, defrosted
2½	teaspoons salt, plus more if needed
1¼	teaspoons freshly ground black pepper, plus more if needed
1¼	cups half-and-half, plus more if needed
2-3	tablespoons chopped fresh chives or flat-leaf parsley for garnish (*optional*)

1. Place 5 cups broth in a medium, heavy saucepan over medium-high heat. When it just begins to simmer, add wild rice. Reduce heat to medium-low, cover and cook until all liquid is absorbed, 20 to 30 minutes. Remove from heat. You should have 3¾ cups cooked rice.

2. Heat oil in a large, deep-sided pot over medium-high heat. When hot, add sausage and sauté, stirring, until golden, 4 to 5 minutes. Add onions and carrots and cook, stirring, for 3 to 4 minutes more. Add 6 cups broth and bring mixture to a simmer over high heat. Reduce heat to low and simmer for 15 minutes.

3. **Meanwhile, prepare corn broth:** Set aside 2½ cups fresh or frozen corn. In a blender or a food processor fitted with a metal blade, puree remaining corn with remaining 1½ cups broth. Puree well to produce a thick, opaque broth.

4. Add cooked wild rice, corn broth and reserved corn to pot and stir well. Cook for 10 to 15 minutes more. Season with 2½ teaspoons salt and 1¼ teaspoons pepper. Stir in 1¼ cups half-and-half. If soup is too thick, thin with additional half-and-half. Taste and adjust seasonings, adding more salt and pepper, if needed. (*Soup can be made 2 days ahead. Cool, cover and refrigerate. It can also be frozen; defrost before continuing. Reheat, stirring often.*)

5. To serve, ladle into bowls. Garnish each serving with chives or parsley, if desired.

Smoked Turkey Gumbo

SERVES 6

From Start to Finish:
1 hour 45 minutes

Actual Working Time:
40 minutes

Make Ahead: Partially
(see step 3)

Can Be Frozen: Yes
(see step 3)

Best Seasons:
Fall and winter

Shopping Notes:
Liquid smoke is available
in most supermarkets.
Look for it with the
barbecue sauces and other
condiments.

Smoked turkey breast is
available in the deli section
of most supermarkets; buy
a single piece and dice it.

I HAVE MANY CHILDHOOD MEMORIES of eating gumbos made by my mother's family, who lived near New Orleans. Those spicy gumbos were always made with crab or shrimp and served over mounds of fluffy white rice. Central to their preparation was a roux, a fat-and-flour mixture cooked and stirred for a long time and used to thicken the soup. I have eliminated the time-consuming roux and substituted diced smoked turkey breast for the fish and wild rice for white. Okra is a traditional gumbo ingredient (in fact, "gumbo" is the African name for okra), but instead of simmering it until it becomes stringy, I quickly sauté it and use as a garnish.

8 cups chicken broth (*divided*),
  plus 1 cup more if needed
1 cup wild rice (*see Shopping Note*, page 80)
½ teaspoon liquid smoke (*see Shopping Notes*)
2 tablespoons vegetable oil (*divided*)
2 cups cleaned, chopped leeks, white parts only
  (*see Cooking Technique*, page 57)
1 cup chopped celery (¼-inch dice)
1 cup diced red bell pepper (½-inch dice)
½ cup diced green bell pepper (½-inch dice)
½ cup thinly sliced carrots
1 tablespoon finely chopped garlic
1 teaspoon dried basil leaves
1 teaspoon dried thyme leaves
1 28-ounce can crushed tomatoes
  1-to-1½-pound piece smoked turkey breast, skin
    removed, diced to make 2 cups (*see Shopping Notes*)
¼ teaspoon crushed red pepper flakes, plus generous
  pinch more for a spicier taste
⅛ teaspoon cayenne pepper
  Salt and freshly ground black pepper
2 cups (about ½ pound) fresh okra (or frozen,
  defrosted and patted dry), sliced ¼ inch thick,
  for garnish
  Fresh thyme or flat-leaf parsley sprigs for garnish

1. Place 3 cups broth in a medium, heavy saucepan over high heat and bring to a simmer. Reduce heat to low; add wild rice and liquid smoke. Cover and simmer until rice is tender and has absorbed all liquid, about 45 minutes. Set aside.

2. Heat 1½ tablespoons oil in a large nonstick skillet over medium-high heat. When hot, add leeks, celery, red and green peppers, carrots and garlic. Stir well; add basil and thyme. Sauté, stirring constantly, for 5 minutes. Remove from heat and set aside.

3. Place remaining 5 cups broth in a large, heavy, deep-sided pot over medium-high heat. Bring to a simmer, reduce heat to low and add crushed tomatoes. Simmer for 20 minutes. Add wild rice, sautéed vegetables, turkey, ¼ teaspoon or more red pepper flakes and cayenne. Taste and season generously with salt and pepper. Cook for 5 minutes more. (*Gumbo can be made 1 to 2 days ahead. Cool, cover and refrigerate. It can also be frozen; defrost before continuing.*)

4. If gumbo has been made ahead, reheat over medium heat until hot, adding more chicken broth if it seems too thick. Keep warm at a simmer.

5. Meanwhile, heat remaining ½ tablespoon oil in a medium nonstick skillet over high heat. When oil is hot, add okra and sauté, stirring constantly, just until heated through, 3 to 4 minutes. Season lightly with salt and pepper.

6. To serve, ladle gumbo into 6 shallow soup bowls. Garnish each serving with some sautéed okra and thyme or parsley sprigs.

Variation: One-half pound chicken or turkey kielbasa or an equal amount of cooked shrimp or crab can be added to the gumbo with the turkey breast in step 3 for extra flavor.

Menu Suggestion:

For this gumbo, which is a meal in itself, a salad of mixed greens in vinaigrette dressing and a loaf of warm, crusty French bread are perfect accompaniments.

Smoky Peppers Chicken Noodle Soup

SERVES 6

From Start to Finish:
1 hour 20 minutes

Actual Working Time:
30 minutes

Make Ahead: Yes
(see step 4)

Can Be Frozen: Yes
(see step 4)

Best Seasons:
All year, because you
never know when you'll
catch a cold!

Shopping Note:
Chipotle chilies are quite
hot and can be bought
dried, canned or pickled.
For this recipe, buy dried
ones; they have been
smoked and have deep red,
wrinkled skin. They are
available in some
supermarkets and in
specialty-food shops.

CHICKEN SOUP IS GOOD FOR WHATEVER AILS YOU, and this one, renewed with the addition of dried chipotle chile peppers, is a spirited remake of the original. The peppers add a smoky flavor to the chicken broth, while a relish of chopped red onions tossed with lime juice makes a fresh-tasting topping.

2 celery stalks, cleaned, coarsely chopped
2 medium onions, coarsely chopped,
    plus ½ cup chopped (*divided*)
2 carrots, peeled, coarsely chopped,
    plus ½ cup diced (¼-inch dice), *divided*
2 fresh flat-leaf parsley sprigs
8 cups chicken broth, plus more if needed
1 pound boneless, skinless chicken breasts
1 tablespoon olive oil
2 teaspoons chopped garlic
3 whole dried chipotle chile peppers
    (*see Shopping Note*)
¼ pound noodles (preferably fresh fettuccine
    noodles ¼-½ inch wide), cut or broken in half
    Salt and freshly ground black pepper (*optional*)

FOR GARNISH
½ cup chopped red onion
1½ tablespoons fresh lime juice

2 tablespoons chopped fresh cilantro

1. Place celery, 2 coarsely chopped onions, coarsely chopped carrots, parsley and 8 cups broth in a large saucepan or stockpot over medium-high heat. Bring to a simmer, reduce heat to low, cover and simmer for 15 minutes. Add chicken, cover and cook for 12 to 15 minutes.

2. Remove chicken from broth with a slotted spoon; set aside. Strain broth, discard vegetables and measure out broth, adding more, if necessary, to make 8 cups. Set aside.

3. In a large, heavy pot over medium heat, heat oil until hot. Add remaining ½ cup diced carrots and remaining ½ cup chopped onion and sauté, stirring, until softened, 3 to 4 minutes. Add garlic and cook, stirring, for 1 minute more. Add chipotle chilies and reserved 8 cups broth. Bring to a simmer and lower heat. Cook, uncovered, for 10 to 15 minutes. Add noodles and cook until tender, 4 to 5 minutes for fresh, 8 to 12 minutes for dried.

4. While noodles are cooking, cut chicken into ½-to-¾-inch dice. When noodles are done, add chicken to pot and cook just until heated through, about 1 minute. Remove chilies. Taste and season with salt and pepper, if needed. (*Soup can be made 1 day ahead. Cool, cover and refrigerate. It can also be frozen; defrost before continuing. Reheat, stirring often.*)

5. **To prepare garnish:** Toss red onion with lime juice.

6. To serve, ladle soup into 6 individual bowls. Garnish each serving with some red onions and a sprinkling of cilantro.

Menu Suggestion:
   This soup is good with South-of-the-Border Grilled Cheese and Salsa Sandwiches (page 321).

Cream of Smoked Chicken and Apple Soup

SERVES 6

From Start to Finish:
1 hour 10 minutes

Actual Working Time:
40 minutes

Make Ahead: Partially
(see step 2)

Can Be Frozen: Yes
(see step 2)

Best Seasons:
Fall and winter

CREAM OF CHICKEN SOUP has long been a classic, whether homemade or from a can. Smoked chicken (or smoked turkey, if chicken is hard to find) and apples lend an unconventional but pleasing touch to this notable dish. This soup is filling, even though only a little cream is used to enrich it, so it is best served as a meal in itself rather than a first course.

FOR SOUP

2 tablespoons vegetable oil
1 cup chopped onions
1 cup peeled, chopped Granny Smith apples
¼ cup all-purpose flour
5 cups chicken broth
¾ cup paper-thin sliced carrots (1-2 medium)
3 cups diced (¼-to-½-inch dice) smoked chicken
   or turkey breast, skin removed (1¾-2 pounds)
1 teaspoon Dijon mustard
¼ cup whipping cream
   Freshly ground white pepper

FOR GARNISH

1 tablespoon unsalted butter
1 Granny Smith apple, peeled, cored,
   stemmed and cut into paper-thin wedges

2 tablespoons chopped fresh chives or
   flat-leaf parsley

1. **To prepare soup:** Heat oil in a large, heavy, lidded saucepan or pot over medium-high heat. When hot, add onions and apples and sauté until softened, 3 to 4 minutes. Stir in flour and cook, stirring, for 3 to 4 minutes. Add broth and bring to a simmer. Reduce heat to low, cover and cook for 20 minutes.

2. Puree in a food processor fitted with a metal blade, a blender or a food mill. Return to saucepan or pot. Add carrots and cook over medium heat, uncovered, for 10 minutes, or until tender. Add smoked chicken or turkey, mustard, cream and white pepper. Heat just to warm chicken, 2 to 3 minutes more. (*Soup can be make 1 day ahead; cool, cover and refrigerate. It can also be frozen; defrost before continuing. Reheat, stirring, when needed.*) Keep at a simmer while preparing garnish.

3. **To prepare garnish:** Heat butter in a medium skillet over medium-high heat. When hot, add apple slices and cook, tossing, until softened and lightly browned, 2 to 4 minutes.

4. To serve, ladle soup into 6 individual bowls. Garnish each serving with some sautéed apples and sprinkle with chives or parsley.

Menu Suggestion:

A light mixed green salad in a lemon dressing and a loaf of warm whole wheat bread are good side dishes for this soup.

Peppered Salmon *and* Corn Chowder

SERVES 6

★

From Start to Finish:
1 hour 30 minutes

Actual Working Time:
1 hour 15 minutes

Make Ahead: Yes
(see step 4)

Can Be Frozen: No

Best Seasons:
Summer and fall

Shopping Note:

Seafood boil seasonings, such as Old Bay or Zatarain's Crab Boil, are a mixture of strong, aromatic dried spices. These mixtures traditionally are added to the cooking liquid for boiling shellfish, giving an extra burst of flavor. They are located in the spice section of supermarkets.

CLAM CHOWDER is one of America's most celebrated soups. Though I've tried chowders made with other shellfish as well, I had never thought of salmon chowder, until my friend Norma La Moreaux brought me a batch one day. The soup, brimming with salmon, also contained fresh corn, diced red-skin potatoes and roasted red peppers. Colorful, full of flavor and prepared with low-fat milk and yogurt rather than cream, it is a delectable yet healthy main course.

2 salmon steaks (¾-1 inch thick),
   about 1¼-1½ pounds total

1½ tablespoons fresh lemon juice (*divided*)

4½ tablespoons vegetable oil (*divided*)
   Salt and freshly ground black pepper

2 cups cleaned, chopped leeks, white parts only
   (3-4 medium; *see Cooking Technique,* page 57)

1 cup chopped celery

4 teaspoons chopped garlic

⅓ cup all-purpose flour

4 cups chicken broth

1¼ pounds medium-sized red-skin potatoes
   (about 5), peeled and cut into ½-inch dice

1½ cups fresh corn kernels (about 3 ears), preferably
   white corn, or 1½ cups frozen, defrosted and
   patted dry

⅓ cup roasted red pepper (*see Shopping Notes,* page 12),
   cut into ¼-inch-wide strips

½ teaspoon liquid smoke (*see Shopping Notes,* page 82)

½ teaspoon Worcestershire sauce

1 teaspoon dried tarragon leaves

½ teaspoon seafood boil seasonings, preferably
   Old Bay brand (*see Shopping Note*)

5 tablespoons nonfat plain yogurt

⅓ cup 1% or 2% milk, plus up to ¾ cup more milk
 if needed
6 teaspoons chopped fresh dill (*divided*)
⅓ cup sliced green onions (including 2 inches of
 green tops) for garnish

Menu Suggestion:
 Mixed Greens in Orange
Balsamic Dressing (page
247) and warm sourdough
bread taste delicious with
this soup.

1. Place salmon steaks on rack of a broiler pan. Mix 1 tablespoon lemon juice and ½ tablespoon oil in a small bowl. Brush fish on both sides with mixture. Season fish on both sides lightly with salt and generously with pepper. Let stand for 10 minutes.

2. Arrange a rack 4 to 5 inches from heat source and preheat broiler. Broil salmon until flesh is opaque and flakes easily, 3 to 5 minutes per side. Remove and cool. Discard skin, bones and any gray matter; cut into 1-inch chunks. Set aside.

3. Place 1 tablespoon oil in a large nonstick skillet over medium-high heat. When hot, add leeks, celery and garlic and sauté, stirring, for 3 to 4 minutes. Remove from heat; set aside.

4. In a large, heavy pot over medium-high heat, add remaining 3 tablespoons oil. When hot, add flour and cook, stirring, for 1 minute. Add broth and cook, whisking constantly to blend flour and liquid, for about 3 minutes; sauce should be thick enough to coat the back of a spoon. Stir in sautéed leek mixture, then potatoes, corn, roasted pepper, liquid smoke, Worcestershire sauce, tarragon, seafood boil, yogurt and ⅓ cup milk. Bring to a simmer, reduce heat to low, and cook until potatoes are tender, 10 minutes or more. Add remaining ½ tablespoon lemon juice, 2 teaspoons dill and cooked salmon. Cook just to heat salmon, 3 to 4 minutes. If soup seems too thick, thin with more milk. Taste and season with salt and pepper, if needed. (*Soup can be prepared 1 day ahead. Cool, cover and refrigerate. Reheat, stirring, over medium heat.*)

5. Ladle soup into 6 shallow bowls. Garnish each serving with some sliced green onions and remaining 4 teaspoons dill.

Grilled Scallop *and* Tomato Bisque

SERVES 8

From Start to Finish:
1 hour 55 minutes

Actual Working Time:
55 minutes

Make Ahead: Partially
(see step 3)

Can Be Frozen: Yes
(see step 3)

Best Seasons:
Summer and early fall

Cooking Technique:
On each sea scallop, you will see a small piece of connective tissue on the side. Although it can be left on, I always remove it by gently peeling it off with my fingers before cooking the scallops.

A SEAFOOD BISQUE USUALLY IMPLIES A RICH, thick soup base made with fish broth and crustacean shells. Bisques are typically enriched with generous amounts of cream as well. In this lighter version, the bisque is thickened with tomatoes, which are cooked with leeks and herbs and then pureed. Succulent sea scallops are grilled quickly and added at serving time.

4	tablespoons olive oil (*divided*)
2¼	cups cleaned, chopped leeks, including 1 inch of green tops (about 3 medium; *see Cooking Technique,* page 57)
2¼	cups chopped onions (2 medium)
1½	tablespoons finely chopped garlic
1½	tablespoons chopped fresh thyme leaves or 1½ teaspoons dried
1½	tablespoons chopped fresh rosemary or 1½ teaspoons dried
4½	pounds plum tomatoes, stemmed and coarsely chopped, or two 35-ounce cans whole tomatoes, drained and chopped
1½	teaspoons salt, plus more if needed
	Freshly ground black pepper
6	cups chicken broth
	Dash sugar (*optional*)
¼-½	cup whipping cream (*optional*)
1½-1¾	pounds sea scallops (*see Cooking Technique*)
1½	tablespoons fresh lemon juice
	Fresh rosemary sprigs for garnish (*optional*)

1. Heat 2 tablespoons oil in a large, heavy nonreactive pan over medium-high heat. When hot, add leeks and onions and sauté, stirring constantly, until softened, 4 to 5 minutes.

2. Add garlic, thyme and rosemary and cook, stirring, for 2 minutes more. Add tomatoes, 1½ teaspoons salt, several grindings of pepper and broth, and bring mixture to a simmer. Reduce heat to low and simmer until vegetables are quite tender, 25 to 30 minutes.

3. Remove soup from heat and puree, using a food processor fitted with a metal blade, a blender or a food mill. Taste and add more salt and pepper, if desired. If soup seems a little acidic, add sugar. Stir in cream, if desired. (*Soup can be prepared 1 day ahead. Cool, cover and refrigerate. It can also be frozen; defrost before continuing.*)

4. About 1 hour before serving, prepare scallops. Place scallops in a glass or ceramic bowl. Whisk together lemon juice, ½ teaspoon black pepper and remaining 2 tablespoons oil in a small bowl. Pour marinade over scallops and toss well. Cover and refrigerate scallops for 30 minutes, stirring several times.

5. Arrange a rack 5 inches from heat source and preheat grill or broiler. Thread scallops onto metal skewers and grill or broil until opaque and cooked through, 3 to 4 minutes. Watch carefully so scallops do not overcook and become dry.

6. To serve, reheat soup, stirring often, and ladle into 8 bowls. Divide scallops evenly and mound in center of each bowl. Garnish each serving with a rosemary sprig, if desired.

Menu Suggestion:
Mixed Greens in Orange Balsamic Dressing (page 247) and warm French bread are good side dishes to offer with this soup.

Chapter 3

Covered Dishes
Potpies, Cobblers, Stews
and Baked Pasta

Chicken *and* Fennel Potpies

THESE CHICKEN POTPIES BEAR NO RESEMBLANCE to those that came in little cardboard boxes that I was served as a child. They are made with tender chunks of chicken breast, fresh fennel and thin strips of prosciutto, all folded into a lemon-scented white sauce and topped with a golden, flaky crust. They freeze beautifully.

FOR CRUST

3 cups sifted all-purpose flour
¾ teaspoon salt
12 tablespoons (1½ sticks) unsalted butter, well chilled and cut into small chunks
4½ tablespoons vegetable shortening, well chilled and cut into small chunks
6 tablespoons cold water

FOR FILLING

1 large or 2 small fennel bulbs (*see Shopping Note*)
5 cups chicken broth
6 large boneless, skinless chicken breast halves (1¾-2 pounds), cut into 1-inch cubes
½ cup diced carrots (¼-inch dice), blanched in boiling water for 2-3 minutes, drained well
5 tablespoons unsalted butter
5 tablespoons all-purpose flour
2½ cups 2% milk
3 tablespoons fresh lemon juice
2 teaspoons crushed fennel seeds (*see Cooking Technique*, page 108)
½ teaspoon salt, plus more if needed
Freshly ground black pepper
¼ pound thinly sliced prosciutto, cut into 2-by-¼-inch strips
1 egg white, lightly beaten

SERVES 8

From Start to Finish:
2 hours 20 minutes (includes 45 minutes for chilling dough)

Actual Working Time:
1 hour

Make Ahead: Yes (see step 8)

Can Be Frozen: Yes (see step 8)

Best Seasons:
Fall and winter

Shopping Note:
Although I have come to take fennel for granted, I have noticed that my students often hang on every word when I talk about it in class. A thick celery-colored bulb with a long green stalk topped by feathery foliage, fennel has an elusively sweet, slightly licorice flavor. Some markets label it "sweet anise." It can be used raw, sliced in strips in salads or as a crudité for dipping. It can also be cut into wedges and roasted, grilled or sautéed.

1. **To prepare crust:** Process flour, salt, butter and shortening in a food processor fitted with a metal blade, pulsing for 15 seconds. Add water and process until a ball of dough forms, about 30 seconds. Alternatively, by hand, place flour and salt in a mixing bowl. Cut in butter and shortening with a pastry blender or 2 table knives until mixture resembles oatmeal flakes. Gradually add water, mixing just until dough holds together. Gather dough into a ball.

2. Remove dough from bowl and pull off about 3 tablespoons. Smear piece of dough onto a work surface with the heel of your hand. Continue smearing remaining dough, taking 3 tablespoons each time. (This process will ensure that flour and fat are well blended.)

3. Shape dough into a ball, flatten and wrap in plastic wrap. Refrigerate for 45 minutes or longer.

4. **To prepare filling:** Cut leaves and stalks from fennel. Halve bulbs lengthwise and cut out tough triangular cores. Cut fennel halves into 3-by-¼-inch strips; you should have about 3 cups. Set aside.

5. Bring broth to a boil in a large saucepan. Add fennel and cook, uncovered, for 7 minutes. Add chicken and carrots; simmer until tender, about 10 minutes more. Remove and strain chicken and vegetables. Discard broth.

6. Melt butter in a large, heavy saucepan over medium-high heat. Add flour and cook, stirring, for 2 minutes. Gradually whisk in milk and continue to whisk until mixture thickens and coats the back of a spoon, 4 to 5 minutes. Add chicken and vegetables, lemon juice, fennel seeds, ½ teaspoon salt, pepper and prosciutto. Fill eight 1¼-cup soufflé dishes, ramekins or custard cups with filling.

7. Roll out dough on a floured surface to a ¼-inch-thick circle. Cut 8 rounds that are 1 inch larger in diameter than tops of dishes. Cover each dish with a circle of dough and press overlapping portions against sides.

8. If desired, cut leaves or other patterns from scraps of dough to decorate tops. Cut a 1½-inch slit in top of each pie to serve as a vent. (*If not using immediately, cover and refrigerate pies for up to 1 day, or freeze. If frozen, defrost overnight in refrigerator before using.*)

9. Arrange a rack at center position and preheat oven to 375°F. Brush tops of pies lightly with egg white. Bake until pastry is golden brown, 25 to 30 minutes. Serve immediately.

Menu Suggestion:

A seasonal salad of mixed greens tossed in a vinaigrette dressing goes with the potpies. For dessert, serve White Chocolate- and Pecan-Studded Brownies (page 380).

Salmon Potpie
with Buttermilk Crust

SERVES 8 TO 10

★

From Start to Finish:
1 hour 35 minutes

Actual Working Time:
1 hour 10 minutes

Make Ahead: Partially
(see step 5)

Can Be Frozen: No

Best Seasons:
Fall, winter and early
spring

THIS RECIPE MAKES ENOUGH to feed the masses, or at least a large group of friends. Fresh salmon pieces, cubed potatoes and sliced fennel are folded into a white sauce and topped with a buttermilk biscuit crust. The filling can be prepared several hours ahead and the biscuit topping put together and added at baking time. (*See photograph, page 43.*)

FOR FILLING

2   pounds salmon fillets
5   tablespoons vegetable oil (*divided*)
    Salt and freshly ground black pepper
¾   pound Yukon Gold (*see Shopping Note*, page 212)
    or red-skin potatoes
1¾ cups cleaned and thinly sliced leeks, white parts
    only (about 2-3 medium; *see Cooking Technique*,
    page 57)
1½ cups thinly sliced fennel (1-2 bulbs, halved,
    cored and sliced, lacy stalks discarded;
    see Shopping Note, page 93)

FOR SAUCE

5   tablespoons unsalted butter
5   tablespoons all-purpose flour
2½ cups whole or 2% milk
5-6 tablespoons fresh lemon juice
    Salt and freshly ground pepper

FOR BISCUIT TOPPING

2   cups cake flour, sifted
2   teaspoons baking powder
2   teaspoons sugar
½   teaspoon baking soda
½   teaspoon salt
6   tablespoons (¾ stick) cold unsalted butter, diced

**½ cup plus 2 tablespoons buttermilk (*divided*),
plus extra for brushing tops of biscuits**

1. Preheat oven to 425°F. Spray an aluminum-foil-lined baking sheet with nonstick cooking spray.

2. **To prepare filling:** Brush salmon fillets lightly with 1 tablespoon oil and season with salt and pepper. Place on baking sheet. Bake until centers are just cooked, 8 to 12 minutes. Remove from oven and let cool. Remove and discard skin and cut salmon into 1-inch-square pieces.

3. Meanwhile, cook potatoes in boiling, salted water to cover until tender, not mushy, 15 to 20 minutes. Peel and cut into ½-inch dice.

4. Place remaining 4 tablespoons oil in a large, heavy skillet over medium heat. When hot, add leeks and fennel and cook, stirring constantly, until tender, 4 to 6 minutes. Remove from heat and toss with cooked potatoes and salmon pieces; set aside.

5. **To prepare sauce:** Melt butter in a medium saucepan over medium-high heat. Add flour and cook, stirring, until well blended, 1 to 2 minutes. Gradually pour in milk, whisking constantly. When thickened, add lemon juice, a little at a time, tasting after each addition. Season sauce with salt and pepper; add to salmon and vegetables. Spread filling in a large oven-to-table baking dish and cool slightly. (*Filling can be made 1 day ahead; cool, cover and refrigerate.*)

6. When ready to bake potpie, arrange a rack at center position and preheat oven to 400°F.

7. **To prepare biscuit topping:** Combine flour, baking powder, sugar, baking soda and salt in a large bowl. Cut in butter with a pastry blender or 2 table knives until mixture resembles coarse crumbs. Add ½ cup buttermilk and stir until a dough forms. If mixture seems too dry, gradually add 2 tablespoons buttermilk. Roll out dough on a floured work surface to a thickness of ¼ inch. Using a 2-to-3-inch round cookie cutter, cut dough into rounds and arrange in overlapping rows on top of filling. Brush tops of biscuits lightly with buttermilk. Bake until filling is bubbling and biscuits are golden, 20 to 25 minutes. Serve warm.

Menu Suggestion:

A simple salad of Boston lettuce, watercress and green onions tossed in a mustard dressing is all that is needed to go with this potpie. Country Chocolate Loaf Cake (page 366), dusted with confectioners' sugar and served without Warm Chocolate-Coffee Sauce, makes a special ending, especially with fresh fruit.

Chicken *and* Spring Onion Cobbler

SERVES 8

★

From Start to Finish:
2 hours 15 minutes
(includes 65 minutes to
cook chicken and cobbler)

Actual Working Time:
1 hour 5 minutes

Make Ahead: Partially
(see step 3)

Can Be Frozen: No

Best Seasons:
Fall, winter and especially
spring

Shopping Note:
Saffron is made from the
flower stigmas of a variety
of the crocus plant. The
stigmas (each flower
contains only three) are
harvested by hand, and it
takes 1,400 to make an
ounce. You can buy saffron
either powdered or in
threads in the spice section
of the supermarket. Crush
threads slightly before
using. Saffron costs several
dollars per gram, but
fortunately, a tiny amount
of this pungent, aromatic
spice goes a long way.

I LOVE THE FLAVORS AND TEXTURES in this savory cobbler. A saffron-scented sauce enrobes juicy chunks of chicken, chopped green onions, cubed ham and vegetables. The corn bread topping is baked until it is crisp and golden.

FOR FILLING

7	cups canned chicken broth, plus more if needed
3-3½	pounds chicken breasts, bone in, skin left on
⅛	teaspoon crushed saffron threads (*see Shopping Note*)
⅔	cup diced carrots
⅔	cup diced celery
1	cup chopped green onions, including 1 inch of green tops
1	cup tiny green peas (if frozen, defrost and drain)
¼	pound diced smoked ham
⅔	cup chopped onions
3	tablespoons chopped fresh flat-leaf parsley

FOR SAUCE

8	tablespoons (1 stick) unsalted butter
¾	cup all-purpose flour
1	teaspoon salt
½	teaspoon freshly ground black pepper

FOR TOPPING

1	cup milk, plus 2-4 tablespoons more, if needed
1	large egg, lightly beaten
2	tablespoons unsalted butter, melted
1	cup all-purpose flour
1	cup yellow cornmeal
½	cup (2 ounces) grated medium-sharp Cheddar cheese
3	tablespoons chopped fresh flat-leaf parsley (*divided*)
4	teaspoons baking powder

1   teaspoon salt

½   teaspoon freshly ground black pepper

1. **To prepare filling:** Combine 7 cups broth, chicken and saffron in a large, heavy pot. Bring to a boil over high heat. Reduce heat to low, cover and simmer until chicken is cooked through, about 30 minutes. Transfer chicken to a large bowl and cool briefly; set broth aside. Remove skin and bones from chicken. Cut chicken into ¾-inch cubes and place in a large oven-to-table baking dish (a 13-by-9-inch glass dish works well).

2. Bring broth to a boil. Add carrots and celery and cook until crisp-tender, about 5 minutes. Using a slotted spoon, transfer to dish with chicken, reserving broth. Add green onions, peas, ham, onions and parsley to chicken. Stir to mix.

3. **To prepare sauce:** Measure broth, adding more, if necessary, to make 6½ cups. Place butter in a large, heavy saucepan over medium-high heat. When hot, add flour and cook, stirring constantly, for 2 minutes. Add broth and cook, whisking constantly, until sauce thickens and is smooth, about 8 minutes. Add salt and pepper. Remove from heat and pour over vegetable and chicken mixture in baking dish. Stir to mix well. (*Filling can be made 1 day ahead. Cool, cover and refrigerate.*)

4. When ready to bake cobbler, arrange a rack at center position and preheat oven to 400°F.

5. **To prepare topping:** Whisk 1 cup milk, egg and butter together in a bowl. Stir in flour, cornmeal, cheese, 2 tablespoons parsley, baking powder, salt and pepper. Mix well. If mixture is very stiff, add up to 4 tablespoons more milk to loosen it slightly. (Batter should be thick but drop firmly from a spoon.) Drop batter by spoonfuls over cobbler filling. Bake cobbler, uncovered, until filling is hot and crust is crisp and light golden, 30 to 35 minutes. Remove, sprinkle with remaining 1 tablespoon parsley and serve.

Menu Suggestion:

A watercress salad in a light lemon dressing can accompany the cobbler; Dark Chocolate Walnut Layer Cake (page 370) makes a scrumptious dessert.

Shrimp *and* Corn Cobbler

SERVES 6

From Start to Finish:
1 hour 55 minutes

Actual Working Time:
1 hour 5 minutes

Make Ahead: Partially
(see step 4)

Can Be Frozen: No

Best Seasons:
Summer and early fall

Shopping Note:
Evaporated skim milk is
canned unsweetened milk
from which 60 percent of
the water has been removed.
Evaporated milk is available
in both whole and skim
forms; the skim has much
less fat, ½ percent or less.
This canned milk can be
stored on the shelf until
opened; after opening,
refrigerate it, tightly
covered, for up to 1 week.

THE FILLING FOR THIS DELIGHTFUL COBBLER, a combination of fresh corn, onions, bell peppers, tomatoes and shrimp, is encased in a sauce flavored with Jarlsberg cheese and covered with a golden corn bread crust.

FOR FILLING

1	tablespoon olive oil
1½	cups chopped onions
1	teaspoon minced garlic
¼	cup diced red bell pepper
¼	cup diced green bell pepper
1¼	cups corn kernels (scraped from 3-4 ears)
1¼	pounds tomatoes, unpeeled, seeded and chopped
¼	cup all-purpose flour
1½	cups evaporated skim milk (*see Shopping Note*)
1	cup (4 ounces) grated, packed Jarlsberg cheese Salt and freshly ground black pepper
¾	pound large shrimp, peeled, deveined, cut into chunks and patted dry (*see Shopping Notes, page 18*)
2	tablespoons chopped fresh flat-leaf parsley
½	tablespoon chopped fresh chives

FOR CRUST

1	cup all-purpose flour
¾	cup yellow cornmeal
3	teaspoons baking powder
1	teaspoon salt
½	teaspoon freshly ground black pepper
5	tablespoons grated Jarlsberg cheese (1-2 ounces), *divided*
1	large egg
1	cup 2% milk or buttermilk
3	tablespoons unsalted butter, melted
2	tablespoons chopped fresh chives or flat-leaf parsley

1. Arrange a rack at center position and preheat oven to 350°F.

2. **To prepare filling:** Heat oil in a medium skillet over medium-high heat. When hot, add onions and sauté, stirring, until softened, 2 to 3 minutes. Add garlic and cook for 1 minute more. Remove from heat. Stir in bell peppers, corn and tomatoes. Set aside to cool.

3. Place flour in a medium, heavy saucepan. Starting with ¼ cup, gradually whisk in evaporated skim milk. Place sauce over medium heat and whisk constantly until it thickens, 3 to 4 minutes (*see Cooking Technique*, page 52). Gradually whisk in cheese, a handful at a time. Taste and season with salt and pepper. Stir in corn and tomato mixture. Cool completely. Stir in shrimp, parsley and chives.

4. Spray a medium-sized (6-cup) oven-to-table baking pan with non-stick spray. Spread filling evenly in pan. Set aside. (*Filling can be made 1 day ahead. Cool, cover and refrigerate; uncover before baking.*)

5. **To prepare crust:** Combine flour, cornmeal, baking powder, salt, pepper and 4 tablespoons cheese in a large mixing bowl. In another bowl, combine egg, milk or buttermilk, butter and chives or parsley. Gradually stir milk mixture into dry ingredients until a biscuit dough is formed. Drop tablespoons of dough over surface of filling and then smooth and spread dough evenly. Sprinkle remaining 1 tablespoon cheese over dough.

6. Bake until top is light golden brown, 30 to 35 minutes. Cool for 5 minutes before serving.

Menu Suggestion:
Serve with Mixed Greens in Orange Balsamic Dressing (page 247). White Chocolate- and Pecan-Studded Brownies (page 380) with fresh strawberries is a tempting dessert.

Wintertime Sausage *and* Beef Stew

SERVES 6 TO 8

★

From Start to Finish:
3 hours 30 minutes
(includes 2 hours 15
minutes for cooking stew)

Actual Working Time:
1 hour 30 minutes

Make Ahead: Yes
(see step 6)

Can Be Frozen: Yes
(see step 6)

Best Season: Winter

THERE IS NOTHING LIKE A GOOD STEW in the winter months. The combination of beef and kielbasa sausage makes this one more flavorful than traditional versions. The beef is simmered in red wine and beef broth until fork-tender, then the sausage is added, along with sautéed carrots and parsnips. The stew improves in flavor when made a day ahead and is delicious over caraway-scented noodles.

About 4 tablespoons vegetable oil

1 pound turkey kielbasa, cut diagonally into ½-inch-wide slices (*see Shopping Notes,* page 301)

2½ pounds beef stew meat, trimmed, cut into 1½-inch cubes, patted dry

¼ cup all-purpose flour

3½ tablespoons unsalted butter (*divided*)

4 medium onions, sliced

1 tablespoon minced garlic

3 cups beef broth

2 cups dry red wine

3 fresh flat-leaf parsley sprigs

2 bay leaves

1½ teaspoons dried thyme leaves

4 parsnips, peeled, cut diagonally into ½-inch-wide slices (about 1 pound)

5 large carrots, peeled, cut diagonally into ½-inch-wide slices (about 1 pound)

1½ cups water

2 teaspoons sugar

½ teaspoon salt, plus more if needed

1½ tablespoons unsalted butter, softened, mixed with 1½ tablespoons flour, for thickening (*optional*)

Freshly ground black pepper

3 tablespoons chopped fresh flat-leaf parsley for garnish

1. Arrange rack at center position and preheat oven to 325°F.

2. Add enough oil just to coat bottom of a large Dutch oven with a lid. Place over medium-high heat heat until hot. Add sausage and cook until lightly browned, stirring frequently, about 3 minutes. Transfer to paper towels using a slotted spoon. Cool, cover and refrigerate.

3. Add just enough oil to recoat bottom of Dutch oven and add one-fourth of beef; brown on all sides. Transfer to paper towels using slotted spoon. Repeat with remaining beef, cooking it in batches. Pour off fat. Return beef to Dutch oven and sprinkle with flour. Toss to coat well. Bake, uncovered, stirring occasionally, for 10 minutes. Remove from oven; leave oven on.

4. Meanwhile, heat 2½ tablespoons butter in a large, heavy skillet over medium-high heat. Add onions and cook until light brown, stirring frequently, about 8 minutes. Add garlic and cook, stirring, for 1 minute more. Add onion mixture to beef, along with broth, wine, parsley, bay leaves and thyme. Bring to a simmer over medium heat, stirring frequently. Remove from heat, cover and bake in oven until beef is tender, about 2¼ hours. Remove from oven and set aside.

5. While meat is cooking, melt ½ tablespoon butter over medium heat in same skillet used to cook onions. Add parsnips and cook for 3 minutes, stirring frequently. Remove from pan and set aside. Melt remaining ½ tablespoon butter in same skillet, add carrots and cook for 3 minutes, stirring frequently. Add water, sugar and ½ teaspoon salt and bring to a boil. Reduce heat, cover and simmer for 10 minutes; add parsnips. Simmer until vegetables are tender, about 4 minutes more; do not overcook. Drain and set aside.

6. Remove bay leaves and parsley and bring stew to a simmer over medium heat. If sauce is too thin, whisk in 1 teaspoon butter-and-flour paste, mixing well, until sauce thickens. Whisk in additional teaspoons of paste as necessary. Add sausage, carrots and parsnips and cook until heated through, stirring occasionally. Season with additional salt and pepper to taste and serve sprinkled with parsley. (*Stew can be prepared 1 to 2 days ahead. Cool, cover and refrigerate. It can also be frozen; defrost before reheating. Reheat over medium heat when needed.*)

Menu Suggestion:
Serve with Caraway Noodles (page 238) or 1 pound cooked wide noodles. Lightly buttered green beans add color to this menu. Honey and Ginger Roasted Pears (page 352) are a perfect end to this meal.

Chicken *and* Spring Vegetable Stew

SERVES 6 TO 8

★

From Start to Finish:
2 hours

Actual Working Time:
50 minutes

Make Ahead: Partially
(see step 3)

Can Be Frozen: Yes
(see step 3)

Best Seasons:
Spring and early summer

Shopping Note:
Uncle Ben's quick brown rice, which cooks in 10 minutes, is excellent. To make 6 cups, bring 3¼ cups chicken broth to a boil over high heat in a large, heavy saucepan. Add 3 cups brown rice. Reduce heat to low, cover and simmer for 10 minutes, or until broth is absorbed. Remove from heat and fluff with a fork. Taste and add salt, if necessary. (If you use a brand other than Uncle Ben's, follow the instructions on the package, replacing the water with chicken broth.)

WHAT I LIKE BEST ABOUT THIS subtly flavored ragout, in which chicken breasts and thighs are simmered with leeks and carrots in broth and white wine, is that it can be almost completely made two days ahead.

6 chicken breast halves, plus 6 chicken thighs
(about 4½ pounds total; *see Healthful Variation*)
Salt and freshly ground black pepper
1½ tablespoons vegetable oil, plus more if needed
4½ tablespoons unsalted butter, softened,
plus more if needed (*divided*)
3 cups cleaned, chopped leeks, white parts only
(about 2-3 large; *see Cooking Technique*, page 57)
3 large garlic cloves, smashed and peeled
¾ pound carrots, peeled and cut into sticks
2 inches long by ½ inch wide
1 tablespoon dried tarragon leaves
3½ cups dry white wine
1¾ cups chicken broth
1¾ cups beef broth
¼ cup all-purpose flour
1 10-ounce package frozen tiny peas, thawed
6 ounces snow peas, ends trimmed on diagonal
and strings removed
3-4 tablespoons chopped fresh tarragon leaves,
plus sprigs for garnish
6 cups cooked brown rice (*see Shopping Note*)
or white rice

1. Remove excess fat from chicken; pat dry. Season generously with salt and pepper. Heat 1½ tablespoons oil and 1½ tablespoons butter over medium-high heat in a large, heavy, deep-sided casserole with a lid. When oil is hot, add enough chicken pieces to fit comfortably in

a single layer. Sauté, turning frequently, until pieces are lightly browned, about 5 minutes. Remove and repeat with remaining chicken, adding more butter and oil in equal amounts, if needed. Set aside.

2. Check oil in casserole; there should be a thin coating on bottom. If not, add a little more oil and heat until hot. Add leeks and sauté, stirring, for about 3 minutes. Add garlic and carrots and cook, stirring, for 3 minutes more. Stir in dried tarragon.

3. Return chicken to casserole, placing pieces on top of vegetables. Add wine and broths. Bring to a simmer over medium-high heat. Cover, reduce heat to low and simmer until chicken is very tender, about 50 minutes. Remove from heat; cool, cover and refrigerate if not using immediately. (*Chicken can be prepared 1 day ahead to this point. It can also be frozen; defrost before continuing.*)

4. To reheat and finish dish, place casserole, uncovered, over medium-high heat and bring to a boil. Lower heat and simmer, stirring, until chicken is completely warmed, 10 to 15 minutes.

5. Strain chicken and vegetables and arrange on a warm serving tray. Return strained liquid to casserole and skim off any fat. Bring to a simmer. Mix remaining 3 tablespoons softened butter with flour to form a paste. Gradually whisk, by spoonfuls, into simmering liquid. Stir until sauce has thickened, 3 to 4 minutes. Taste and season generously with salt and pepper.

6. Add peas and snow peas and cook for only 1 minute so vegetables do not lose their bright green color.

7. To serve, use a slotted spoon to ladle some snow peas and peas over chicken and carrots. Ladle remaining snow peas and peas as a border. Top with some sauce and garnish chicken with chopped fresh tarragon. Garnish plates with tarragon sprigs. Pass remaining sauce separately. Serve with brown or white rice.

Healthful Variation: Substitute 3 pounds of boneless, skinless chicken breasts, cut into 1½-inch pieces, for breasts and thighs. Use 1½ cups each of broths; the cooking time will be shorter, about 15 minutes.

Menu Suggestion:

This stew is also delicious served over lightly buttered noodles. Plan on 1¼ pounds of fresh or 1 pound of dried for 6 servings. A watercress salad tossed in lemon dressing could complete the main course. A bowl of strawberries topped with Honey-Cream Sauce (page 345) is a light dessert.

Shrimp, Tomato and Artichoke Stew

SERVES 6

From Start to Finish:
1 hour 30 minutes

Actual Working Time:
30 minutes

Make Ahead: Partially
(see step 1)

Can Be Frozen: Yes
(see step 1)

Best Seasons:
All year, especially
summer and early fall

THIS WONDERFUL LIGHT STEW is one I serve to my friends who are watching their weight and fat grams. Canned Italian-style tomatoes, cooked with broth and white wine, form the base. Artichoke hearts and large fresh shrimp are added just before serving. Fresh basil and shaved Parmesan garnish the dish.

2	tablespoons olive oil
⅓	cup chopped onion
⅓	cup finely chopped carrot
⅓	cup finely chopped celery
4	teaspoons minced garlic
6	tablespoons all-purpose flour
1	28-ounce can Italian plum tomatoes plus a 16-ounce can, drained, coarsely chopped
4	cups canned reduced-sodium chicken broth
1	cup dry white wine
2¼	teaspoons dried basil leaves
¼	teaspoon crushed red pepper flakes
1	9-ounce package frozen artichoke hearts, defrosted
1¼	pounds fresh fettuccine or 1 pound dried
2¼	pounds uncooked large shrimp, peeled, deveined (*see Shopping Notes*, page 18)
	Salt and freshly ground black pepper
6	tablespoons sliced fresh basil leaves for garnish
1	4-to-6-ounce piece imported Parmesan cheese, shaved into strips with a vegetable peeler, for garnish (*see Healthful Variation*)

1. Heat oil in a large, heavy Dutch oven over medium-high heat. Add onion, carrot and celery and sauté for 2 minutes. Add garlic and sauté for 1 minute more. Sprinkle flour over vegetables and cook, stirring, for 2 minutes. Stir in tomatoes, broth, wine, basil and red pepper flakes and bring to a boil. Reduce heat to medium and cook until thickened to a thin-sauce consistency, stirring frequently, about 45 minutes. Add artichoke hearts and cook until tender, stirring occasionally, about 8 minutes. (*Stew can be prepared 1 day ahead. Cool, cover and refrigerate. It can also be frozen; defrost before continuing.*)

2. Cook fettuccine in a pot of boiling, salted water until tender but firm to the bite, 3 to 4 minutes for fresh, about 12 minutes for dried.

3. Meanwhile, bring stew to a simmer. Add shrimp and simmer until cooked through, stirring occasionally, about 5 minutes. Season with salt and pepper.

4. Drain fettuccine and divide among 6 plates. Spoon stew over pasta. Sprinkle with sliced basil leaves and Parmesan shavings and serve.

Healthful Variation: Although the shaved Parmesan is attractive and delicious in this dish, you can omit it to reduce fat.

Menu Suggestion:
Spinach Salad with Brown Mushrooms in Lemon-Garlic Dressing (page 250), made without the water chestnuts, can accompany this stew. Fresh peach slices and raspberries, served with a scoop of vanilla ice cream or frozen yogurt and sprinkled with crushed chocolate or plain biscotti crumbs, make a colorful finale.

Fennel-Scented Veal Stew

SERVES 6

★

From Start to Finish:
2 hours 45 minutes
(includes 1 hour
30 minutes for
simmering stew)

Actual Working Time:
1 hour

Make Ahead: Yes
(see step 5)

Can Be Frozen: Yes
(see step 5)

Best Seasons:
Fall and winter

Cooking Technique:
Oval, greenish brown
fennel seeds can be used in
both savory and sweet
foods. They are found in
the spice section of the
grocery store. Crushing the
seeds releases more flavor.
Simply place the seeds in a
small plastic bag, and, using
a meat pounder or a rolling
pin, crush them until they
resemble a very coarse
powder.

THIS IS A PERFECT MAKE-AHEAD DISH for a crowd. It can be frozen or simply refrigerated for a day or two before serving. In fact, the flavors improve when the stew has had a chance to sit. Its unique flavor comes from crushed fennel seeds, which are added to the sautéed veal and onions along with wine, broth and tomatoes. The stew is best over buttered noodles.

6	tablespoons olive oil (*divided*), plus more if needed
3	pounds veal stew meat, trimmed of all fat, cut into 1½-inch cubes, patted dry with paper towels
	Salt and freshly ground black pepper
4	cups sliced onions (about 4 medium)
1-1½	tablespoons chopped garlic
6	tablespoons flour (*divided*)
2	teaspoons fennel seeds, crushed (*see Cooking Technique*)
1½	teaspoons dried basil leaves
1	teaspoon dried thyme leaves
1	teaspoon crushed dried rosemary leaves
	Generous ½ teaspoon crushed red pepper flakes
1	28-ounce can Italian-style tomatoes, drained and coarsely chopped
3	cups beef broth
1	cup dry white wine
1¼	pounds fresh fettuccine or 1 pound dried
1½	tablespoons unsalted butter
	Several fresh thyme, rosemary or basil sprigs for garnish (*optional*)

1. Heat 4 tablespoons oil in a large, heavy, deep-sided pan with a lid over medium-high heat. Season veal pieces with salt and pepper to taste. When oil is hot, add enough veal to fit comfortably in a single layer and sauté, turning, until browned, 3 to 4 minutes.

2. Remove with a slotted spoon and drain on paper towels. Repeat until all meat has been browned, adding more oil, if necessary.

3. Add remaining 2 tablespoons oil to pan and heat over medium-high heat. When hot, add onions and cook, stirring, until lightly browned, about 5 minutes. Add garlic; cook, stirring, for 1 minute more.

4. Return meat to pan. Toss with 2 tablespoons flour and cook, stirring, for 2 minutes. Add fennel seeds, basil, thyme, rosemary, red pepper flakes, tomatoes, broth and wine. Bring to a simmer, reduce heat to low and simmer, covered, until meat is tender, about 1 hour.

5. Remove ½ cup liquid to a small bowl and mix with remaining 4 tablespoons flour to make a loose paste. Stir into stew and cook, uncovered, for 30 minutes more. (*Stew can be made 2 days ahead; cool, cover and refrigerate. It can also be frozen; defrost before using. Reheat, stirring often, over medium heat.*)

6. When ready to serve, bring 6 quarts water to a boil. Add 1½ tablespoons salt and fettuccine and cook until pasta is tender but still firm, about 3 to 4 minutes for fresh, 12 minutes for dried. Drain well and toss with butter.

7. Divide pasta evenly among 6 dinner plates and ladle stew over pasta. Garnish with sprigs of thyme, rosemary or basil, if desired.

Menu Suggestion:

Lightly buttered green beans and warm French bread are fitting accompaniments. Apple-Date Strudels with Honey Sauce (page 362) make a memorable ending.

Out-of-the-Ordinary
Spicy Tomato *and* Cheese Macaroni

MAKES 4 LARGE OR
6 SMALL SERVINGS

★

From Start to Finish:
1 hour 25 minutes

Actual Working Time:
1 hour

Make Ahead: Partially
(see steps 2 and 5)

Can Be Frozen: No

Best Seasons:
Fall, winter and early
spring

Shopping Note:
Havarti is a mild Danish
cheese with a creamy
smooth texture. It is sold
plain or flavored with
caraway seeds or herbs. Use
plain Havarti in this recipe.
It melts easily, and its flavor
complements the spicy
tomato sauce.

I AM CRAZY ABOUT THIS GLORIOUS BAKED PASTA DISH. To make it, I toss large pasta tubes—macaroni or rigatoni or penne—with a very simple but exceptionally good tomato sauce seasoned liberally with red pepper flakes. Then I add creamy Havarti and imported Parmesan cheeses along with slivered black olives. This is a main-course pasta; all you need to go with it is a salad and warm, crusty Italian bread. (*See photograph, page 44.*)

6	tablespoons olive oil (*divided*)
1½	cups chopped onions
1	teaspoon finely chopped garlic
3	28-ounce cans Italian-style tomatoes, drained and coarsely chopped
2	teaspoons dried basil leaves
	Scant 1½-2 teaspoons crushed red pepper flakes
¼	teaspoon freshly ground black pepper
	Salt
2	cups chicken broth
1	pound large macaroni, rigatoni or penne pasta
2½	cups (about 10 ounces) shredded Havarti cheese (*see Shopping Note*)
⅓	cup (1-2 ounces) freshly grated imported Parmesan cheese
⅓	cup pitted slivered black olives
¼	cup finely chopped fresh basil or flat-leaf parsley for garnish

1. Heat 3 tablespoons oil in a large, heavy skillet over medium-high heat. When oil is hot, add onions and garlic and sauté, stirring, for about 3 minutes. Add tomatoes, basil, scant 1½ teaspoons red pepper flakes, pepper and 1 teaspoon salt and stir well. Add broth and bring to a low boil.

2. Cook until liquid has reduced and mixture is chunky, about 25 minutes. Remove from heat. Taste and add more red pepper flakes, if desired. (*Sauce can be made ahead 1 day in advance. Cool, cover and refrigerate. Reheat until warm before combining with cooked pasta.*)

3. To cook pasta, bring 5 quarts water to a boil and add pasta and 1 tablespoon salt. Bring water back to a boil and cook until pasta is just tender to the bite, 8 to 10 minutes, depending on type of pasta used (watch carefully, because cooking times vary).

4. When pasta is cooked, drain well in a colander. Place in a greased 2½-to-3-quart gratin or baking dish that can be used for serving. Toss pasta with remaining 3 tablespoons oil. Taste and, if needed, add more salt.

5. Add warm tomato sauce to pasta and toss well to combine. Add Havarti and toss again. Sprinkle Parmesan over top. Arrange olives, shiny black sides up, over pasta. (*Pasta can be prepared several hours ahead to this point. Cool, cover and refrigerate until needed.*)

6. Arrange a rack at center position and preheat oven to 350°F. Bake pasta, uncovered, until hot and bubbly, about 25 minutes. Remove and sprinkle with basil or parsley. Serve hot.

Menu Suggestion:

Spinach Salad with Brown Mushrooms in Lemon-Garlic Dressing (page 250) is a perfect match for this pasta. For dessert, put scoops of coffee ice cream or frozen yogurt in wine glasses and drizzle with Warm Chocolate-Coffee Sauce (page 366).

Santa Fe "Lasagna"

SERVES 10

★

From Start to Finish:
2 hours

Actual Working Time:
1 hour

Make Ahead: Partially
(see step 3)

Can Be Frozen: Yes
(see step 3)

Best Seasons: All year

CORN TORTILLAS REPLACE LASAGNA NOODLES in this striking dish. The tortillas are spread with black bean dip and then topped with smoked turkey and spicy vegetables. Ricotta, Cheddar and pepper Jack cheeses add robust flavors to this lasagna, which is perfect for a crowd.

2 tablespoons vegetable oil

1½ cups thinly sliced onions

2 tablespoons chopped garlic

2 cups zucchini, sliced into ¼-inch-thick rounds
(about 2 medium)

7 ounces roasted red peppers, cut into ¼-inch strips
(*see Shopping Notes*, page 12), or 2-3 medium red
bell peppers, roasted, peeled, seeded, membranes
removed, cut into ¼-inch strips
(*see Cooking Technique*, page 13)

3 teaspoons chili powder

2 teaspoons ground cumin

2 teaspoons dried oregano leaves

2 cups reduced-sodium chicken broth

10-12 ounces boneless smoked turkey breast
(or 3 smoked chicken breast halves, skin
and bones removed), cut into ½-inch chunks

11-12 ounces mild black bean dip, preferably fat-free style
(*see Shopping Note*, page 30)

12 6-inch corn tortillas

8 plum tomatoes, sliced into ¼-inch-thick rounds

2 cups reduced-fat ricotta cheese

1 cup (4 ounces) grated medium-sharp
Cheddar cheese

1 cup (4 ounces) grated pepper Jack cheese

2-3 tablespoons chopped fresh cilantro for garnish

1. Spray a 13-by-9-inch or similar-sized oven-to-table baking dish with nonstick cooking spray.

2. Place a large, heavy skillet over medium-high heat and add oil. When hot, add onions and sauté for 3 to 4 minutes, until softened. Add garlic, zucchini and roasted peppers. Cook for 2 to 3 minutes more. Add chili powder, cumin and oregano, and stir. Add broth and turn heat to high. Cook for 5 minutes; add turkey or chicken. Continue to cook until all liquid evaporates, 10 to 15 minutes more. Remove from heat and set aside.

3. Spread half of bean dip evenly over one side of each of 6 tortillas. Arrange tortillas, bean side up, slightly overlapping, in baking dish. Arrange half of tomato slices over tortillas; drop dollops of half of ricotta over tomatoes. Sprinkle one-third each of Cheddar and pepper Jack cheeses over ricotta. Spread half of vegetable-turkey mixture over cheeses. Repeat layering in this way, using tortillas, dip, tomatoes, ricotta, one-third each of Cheddar and pepper Jack cheeses and vegetable-turkey mixture. Finish by sprinkling remaining one-third of Cheddar and pepper Jack cheeses over lasagna. (*Dish can be prepared 2 to 3 hours ahead; cover and refrigerate until needed. It can also be frozen; defrost before continuing.*)

4. Arrange a rack at center position and preheat oven to 350°F. Bake until hot and bubbling and cheese is golden, about 35 minutes. Cool for 5 minutes. Sprinkle with cilantro. Cut into 10 servings.

Menu Suggestion:
Serve with Mexican Layered Salad with Cumin-Honey Dressing (page 252) and, for dessert, Margarita Cheesecake (page 378).

Chapter 4

Prize Catches

SHELLFISH SPECIALS

FISH FROM SEA AND STREAM

Lobsters *with* Apricot-Rosemary Mayonnaise

THIS FLAVORED MAYONNAISE makes a delicious alternative to the melted butter that typically accompanies boiled lobsters. The sauce, which takes only minutes to assemble, is prepared with light mayonnaise to which apricot spread, fresh rosemary, Dijon mustard and lemon are added.

Apricot-Rosemary Mayonnaise (page 191)
4   live lobsters, 1¼-1½ pounds each
    Salt
1   lemon, cut into 8 wedges (*optional*)
1   bunch watercress, cleaned and patted dry (*optional*)

1. Prepare Apricot-Rosemary Mayonnaise. (*Sauce can be prepared 1 day ahead; cover and refrigerate until ready to use.*)

2. To cook lobsters, bring at least 6 quarts of water to a boil over high heat in an extra-large stockpot or lobster pot. Add ½ to 1 tablespoon salt for each quart water. When water returns to a boil, add lobsters, reduce heat to medium, cover and simmer for 10 to 12 minutes. Test for doneness by removing a lobster from pot and twisting one thin leg on body. If leg pulls off easily and quickly, lobster should be done.

3. Drain lobsters. Arrange lobsters on a large platter and surround with lemon wedges and watercress, if desired. Divide mayonnaise into 4 small serving bowls and serve each lobster with its own bowl of mayonnaise.

SERVES 4

From Start to Finish:
35 minutes
Actual Working Time:
10 minutes
Make Ahead: Partially
(see step 1)
Can Be Frozen: No
Best Seasons:
All year, especially
summer

Menu Suggestion:
Summer Corn and Tomato Pudding (page 202) and fresh green beans go well with the lobsters. For dessert, try Best-Ever Plum Upside-Down Cake (page 364) or Lemon Cheesecake (page 376), served with fresh strawberries, raspberries or blueberries to replace the cranberry topping.

New Orleans Shrimp Baked *with* Sourdough Bread Crumbs *and* Herbs

SERVES 4 TO 6

★

From Start to Finish:
1 hour 15 minutes

Actual Working Time:
50 minutes

Make Ahead: Partially
(see step 2)

Can Be Frozen: No

Best Seasons: All year

Shopping Note:
Andouille, a spicy Cajun-style sausage, is sold in many parts of our country. Aidells Sausage Company, based in California, makes a good andouille that is distributed nationally. Turkey kielbasa can be substituted if andouille is not available.

THIS IS A GREAT MAKE-AHEAD DISH. Large shrimp are butterflied with tails left intact and nestled into a stuffing made with sourdough bread crumbs, spinach and andouille sausage. The shrimp can be placed in a pan with the stuffing several hours ahead and baked just before serving.

3 tablespoons unsalted butter (*divided*)
3 tablespoons olive oil (*divided*)
¼ pound andouille or smoked sausage,
    cut into ¼-inch cubes (*see Shopping Note*)
½ cup chopped green onion, including
    2 inches of green tops
1 tablespoon minced garlic
½ cup frozen spinach, defrosted, squeezed dry and
    coarsely chopped (half of a 10-ounce package)
½ teaspoon red pepper sauce, preferably Tabasco
2 cups fresh sourdough or French bread crumbs
¼ cup chicken broth
   Salt
¼ teaspoon freshly ground black pepper
1 pound large or extra-large unshelled shrimp,
    shelled and deveined, with tails left on
    (*see Shopping Notes*, page 18)
3 tablespoons chopped fresh flat-leaf parsley
    for garnish

1. Heat 2 tablespoons butter and 2 tablespoons oil in a large, heavy skillet over medium-high heat. When hot, add sausage and sauté, stirring constantly, for about 2 minutes. Add green onion and garlic and cook, stirring, for 1 minute more. Add spinach and red pepper sauce and cook, stirring, for 2 to 3 minutes more. Remove from heat and stir in bread crumbs and broth. Mix well and season with salt to taste and pepper.

2. Spray a 10-inch round or similar-sized oven-to-table baking dish with nonstick cooking spray. Spread half of filling in baking dish. Butterfly shrimp on their undersides (*see Cooking Technique*), leaving tails intact. Arrange them, cut sides down, with tails upright over stuffing. Loosely pack remaining stuffing around shrimp to keep them erect. (*Dish can be prepared 2 to 3 hours ahead; cover and refrigerate.*)

3. When ready to bake, arrange a rack at center position and preheat oven to 350°F.

4. Melt remaining 1 tablespoon butter with remaining 1 tablespoon oil in a small saucepan and brush over shrimp. Bake until shrimp are pink and bread crumbs are slightly crispy on top, about 20 minutes.

5. Remove and cool for 5 minutes. Sprinkle with parsley and serve.

Cooking Technique:

To butterfly a shrimp, make a lengthwise slit down the center of the underside, without cutting all the way through.

Menu Suggestion:

A simple salad like Mixed Greens in Orange Balsamic Dressing (page 247) is all that is needed to accompany the shrimp. Fresh fruit and a plate of White Chocolate- and Pecan-Studded Brownies (page 380) are perfect for dessert.

Shrimp Sautéed *with* Fresh Fennel *and* Tomatoes

SERVES 6

★

From Start to Finish:
45 minutes

Actual Working Time:
45 minutes

Make Ahead: No

Can Be Frozen: No

Best Seasons:
Summer and early fall

LARGE SHRIMP, FENNEL—both fresh bulbs and crushed fennel seeds—and fresh chopped tomatoes are combined into this robustly flavored dish. The shrimp and fennel are sautéed, then simmered in wine, and the fresh tomatoes are added at the last minute. This colorful main course is delicious served over white rice.

4   medium fennel bulbs (3 cups chopped; *see Shopping Note*, page 93)
5   tablespoons olive oil
2¼ pounds large or extra-large shrimp, peeled and deveined (*see Shopping Notes*, page 18)
2   teaspoons finely chopped garlic
½   cup dry white wine
2   teaspoons fennel seeds, crushed (*see Cooking Technique*, page 108)
    Salt
1   teaspoon freshly ground black pepper
2½ cups peeled, seeded, diced ripe tomatoes (½-inch dice), drained (about 6 medium)
3   tablespoons chopped fresh flat-leaf parsley for garnish

1. Cut off and discard lacy stalks from fennel bulbs. Slice bulbs lengthwise and remove hard triangular cores. Cut bulbs into ½-inch cubes; set aside.

2. Heat oil in a large, heavy nonreactive skillet over medium heat. Add fennel cubes and sauté, stirring frequently, until softened, about 10 minutes.

3. Add shrimp and garlic to skillet and sauté, stirring, until shrimp are pink, just 2 minutes. (Do not overcook.) Add wine and cook, stirring, until all liquid evaporates, about 3 minutes. Add fennel seeds, salt to taste and pepper and mix well.

4. Add tomatoes and cook, tossing, for 1 to 2 minutes, just to warm through. Taste mixture and add more salt, if desired.

5. Arrange mixture on a serving plate and sprinkle with parsley. Serve hot.

Variation: You can substitute sea scallops for the shrimp in this recipe. Use about 2 pounds sea scallops and cook for the same amount of time. Scallops are done when opaque and cooked all the way through.

Menu Suggestion:
White rice and Mixed Greens in Orange Balsamic Dressing (page 247) complement this dish admirably. Ginger and Brown Sugar Grapefruit Compotes with Vanilla Ice Cream (page 346) make a fine dessert.

Scallops *with* Orange *and* Sherry

SERVES 6

★

From Start to Finish:
50 minutes

Actual Working Time:
50 minutes

Make Ahead: Partially
(see step 2)

Can Be Frozen: No

Best Seasons: All year

Shopping Note:

To save time, you can buy freshly squeezed orange juice at most markets. If you are squeezing your own, 3 large oranges yield about 1 cup juice; you'll need 9 oranges.

ONE OF MY STUDENTS told me that she and her husband did not like scallops but that this recipe had changed their minds. It was the orange sauce that did the trick. To make it, fresh orange juice is reduced to intensify its flavor, and then chopped shallots that have been simmered in sherry are stirred in for a subtle finish.

3	cups freshly squeezed orange juice (*see Shopping Note*)
6	tablespoons finely chopped shallots
6	tablespoons dry sherry
6	tablespoons water
⅜	teaspoon ground coriander
	Pinch cayenne pepper
	Salt
3	tablespoons olive oil, plus more if needed
2½-3	pounds sea scallops, rinsed and patted dry, with connective tissue removed and discarded (*see Cooking Technique, page 90*)
1	tablespoon grated orange zest (orange portion of rind) for garnish
2	tablespoons chopped fresh flat-leaf parsley or chives for garnish

1. Place orange juice in a medium nonreactive saucepan over medium-high heat and bring to a boil. Cook until juice has reduced to 1 cup, 5 minutes or more. Remove from heat and set aside.

2. Place shallots, sherry and water in a small saucepan over medium-high heat and cook until all liquid evaporates, 2 to 3 minutes or more, watching constantly. Remove and stir shallots into orange juice. Add coriander, cayenne and a sprinkle of salt; stir well. Set aside. (*Sauce can be made 1 day ahead. Cool, cover and refrigerate. Reheat, stirring, when needed.*)

3. When ready to cook scallops, heat 3 tablespoons oil in a large, heavy skillet over medium-high heat. When hot, add enough scallops to fit comfortably in a single layer. Quickly sauté, turning once, until lightly browned and cooked through, 3 to 4 minutes or more. (Do not over-cook.) Remove to a platter to keep warm and continue cooking re-maining scallops, adding more oil, if necessary.

4. Place scallops on a heated serving plate; season lightly with salt. Drizzle with sauce and sprinkle with orange zest and parsley or chives.

Variation: This sauce is good with baked pork chops or grilled chicken.

Menu Suggestion:

Serve these scallops with Wild Rice with Red and Green Grapes (page 228), omitting the grapes and adding the optional 2 tablespoons extra butter called for in the recipe, and steamed snow peas or sugar snap peas.

Scallop Popover
with Tomato-Orange Sauce

SERVES 6

★

From Start to Finish:
2 hours

Actual Working Time:
55 minutes

Make Ahead: Partially
(see step 1)

Can Be Frozen:
Sauce only (see step 1)

Best Seasons: All year

THIS IS A SPECTACULAR DISH I discovered when I moved to New England several years ago. Fellow cooking teacher and good friend Charlotte Turgeon first told me about it, explaining that a popover batter is poured into a baking dish and baked with any combination of seafood and vegetables in it. While the popover batter bakes, it rises up around the sides of the pan, forming a shell. The seafood and vegetables cooked in it serve as a filling. I added the light tomato-orange sauce, which can be prepared several days ahead. (*See photograph, page 37.*)

FOR TOMATO-ORANGE SAUCE

2 tablespoons olive oil

¾ cup chopped onions

1 teaspoon chopped garlic

1 28-ounce can Italian-style tomatoes, drained and coarsely chopped

1 teaspoon dried basil leaves

¼ teaspoon crushed red pepper flakes

1 teaspoon grated orange zest (orange portion of rind)

Dash sugar

½ teaspoon salt, plus more if needed

¾ cup chicken broth

⅓ cup dry white wine

FOR POPOVER

1 medium carrot, peeled

4 large eggs or 1 cup egg substitute

1¼ cups skim milk

½ teaspoon salt, plus more if needed

1¼ cups all-purpose flour

Generous sprinkle of cayenne pepper

1 pound sea scallops, washed, with connective tissue removed and discarded (*see Cooking Technique,* page 90)

¾ cup green onions (including 2 inches of
    green tops), cut diagonally into ½-inch pieces
    Freshly ground black pepper
½ cup frozen green peas, defrosted and drained
½ cup (2 ounces) grated Gruyère cheese
1-2 tablespoons chopped fresh flat-leaf parsley
    or chives for garnish (optional)

1. **To prepare sauce:** Heat oil in a medium, heavy skillet over medium-high heat. When hot, add onions and garlic. Cook, stirring, for 2 to 3 minutes. Stir in tomatoes, basil, red pepper flakes, orange zest, sugar and ½ teaspoon salt. Add broth and wine and simmer until tomatoes are soft and mushy, 12 to 15 minutes. Puree mixture in a food processor fitted with a metal blade, a blender or a food mill. Taste and season with more salt, if needed. (*Sauce can be made up to 2 days ahead. Cool, cover and refrigerate. The sauce can be frozen; defrost before continuing. Reheat, stirring, when needed.*)

2. **To prepare popover:** Arrange a rack at center position and preheat oven to 375°F. Coat a 13-by-9-inch oven-to-table baking dish with nonstick cooking spray. Cut carrot into 2-by-⅛-inch strips. Blanch carrots in boiling, salted water to cover, for 5 minutes. Drain and set aside.

3. Whisk eggs or egg substitute and milk together in a bowl. In another bowl, stir together ½ teaspoon salt, flour and cayenne. Gradually whisk egg mixture into dry ingredients. Pour batter into baking dish. Scatter scallops in center of batter, leaving a 2-inch border of batter. Sprinkle carrots and green onions over scallops. Season with salt and pepper. Bake for 40 minutes, or until batter rises up around sides and becomes golden and lightly crusty. Leaving popover in oven, sprinkle peas and cheese over filling. Bake to heat peas and melt cheese, about 7 minutes more. Serve hot. Cut into 6 portions and top each with warm tomato-orange sauce and, if desired, a sprinkling of parsley or chives.

Variation: Leftover tomato-orange sauce is a wonderful topping for pizza. The sauce is also good on grilled swordfish (see page 170) or served over fresh cooked pasta.

Menu Suggestion:

This dish is a meal in itself, so I serve a mixed green salad with a light dressing and warm French bread with it. For dessert, try Lemon Cheesecake (page 376) with fresh strawberries piled on top and dusted with powdered sugar in place of the cranberry topping.

Honey *and* Lime Scallops

SERVES 6

★

From Start to Finish:
1 hour 35 minutes

Actual Working Time:
35 minutes

Make Ahead: No

Can Be Frozen: No

Best Seasons: All year

Menu Suggestion:
Cumin Corn Rice
(page 224) and sliced ripe
summer tomatoes sprinkled
with herbs, or green beans
sautéed in a little butter can
accompany the scallops.
Fresh raspberries or
strawberries topped with
Honey-Cream Sauce (page
345) are a simple dessert.

MY FRIEND CAROLYN CLAYCOMB, a member of my cooking school staff for many years and a gold medalist on the 1988 U.S. Culinary Olympics team, gave me the idea for this simple dish. Sea scallops are marinated in lime juice, honey and olive oil and then sautéed until golden. Fresh strips of lime zest make a colorful garnish.

2½-3 pounds sea scallops, rinsed and patted dry,
    with connective tissue removed and discarded
    (*see Cooking Technique*, page 90)
½ cup fresh lime juice
4 tablespoons honey
6 tablespoons extra-virgin olive oil (*divided*),
    plus more if needed
½ teaspoon Dijon mustard
2 tablespoons finely chopped shallots
    Salt and freshly ground black pepper
1 tablespoon lime zest (green portion of rind),
    cut into fine strips for garnish

1. Place scallops in a shallow nonreactive dish. Combine lime juice, honey, 4 tablespoons oil, mustard and shallots in a mixing bowl and whisk well to blend. Pour mixture over scallops and marinate for about 1 hour, covered and refrigerated.

2. Drain scallops and pat as dry as possible with a clean kitchen towel. Heat remaining 2 tablespoons oil in a heavy skillet over medium-high heat. When hot, add enough scallops to cover bottom of pan and sauté, turning often, until opaque, 3 to 4 minutes. Remove cooked scallops to a side dish and cover loosely with foil. Continue cooking scallops, using more oil as needed.

3. Salt scallops to taste and add a generous amount of pepper. Arrange servings on dinner plates, garnish with lime zest and serve.

Broiled Trout *with* Sesame Seeds *and* Chives

IN THIS RECIPE, I love to use salmon trout, which are a pale coral hue (almost like salmon) and are thin and sleek but slightly larger than regular trout. If they are not available, rainbow, brook or other trout fillets can be substituted. The cooking method is simplicity itself. The fish are marinated briefly in soy sauce, rice wine vinegar and sesame oil, then broiled and garnished with chopped chives and toasted sesame seeds. (*See photograph, page 36.*)

6 tablespoons soy sauce

6 tablespoons rice wine vinegar

2 tablespoons plus 1 teaspoon dark Asian
    sesame oil

6 salmon trout fillets (about 8 ounces each),
    see *Shopping Note and Variation*
    Salt (*optional*)

1½ tablespoons toasted sesame seeds
    (*see Cooking Technique*, page 195)

1½ tablespoons chopped fresh chives

1. Combine soy sauce, vinegar and sesame oil in a bowl and mix well to blend. Place fillets, skin side down, in a nonreactive dish that will hold them comfortably. Pour soy-sauce mixture over top and refrigerate, covered, for 1 to 2 hours, turning several times.

2. When ready to cook, arrange a rack 5 to 6 inches from heat source and preheat broiler. Remove fillets from marinade and place, flesh side up, on a rack in a broiler pan. Broil until flesh flakes easily when pierced with a knife, 4 to 5 minutes; watch carefully.

3. When done, remove from oven. Cut a small piece from 1 fillet and taste. If necessary, salt fish. (Because soy sauce is salty, you probably will not need additional salt.) Arrange fillets on a heated platter and sprinkle with sesame seeds and chives.

SERVES 6

From Start to Finish:

1 to 2 hours 15 minutes (includes 1 to 2 hours for marinating)

Actual Working Time:

15 minutes

Make Ahead: No

Can Be Frozen: No

Best Seasons:

Spring and summer

Shopping Note:

Salmon trout has pale pink flesh and is usually available during the summer months in some fish markets. You can substitute other trout of similar size.

Menu Suggestion:

For accompaniments, serve fresh asparagus, steamed until tender and tossed with butter and lemon juice, and Roasted New Potato and Watercress Salad (page 258). Ginger and Brown Sugar Grapefruit Compotes with Vanilla Ice Cream (page 346) make a light and refreshing dessert.

Variation: Salmon fillets (6 to 8 ounces each) are equally good prepared this way. Since the salmon is usually thicker than trout (about ½ to ¾ inch thick), you will probably need to broil them for 2 to 3 minutes more.

Swordfish *with* Tomato-Lime Salsa

I LIKE TO SERVE THIS DISH IN WARM WEATHER because it is light but filling. Swordfish steaks are marinated in lime juice and olive oil and then broiled and served with a fresh salsa made with tomatoes, cucumber and jalapeño pepper. The salsa can be prepared ahead, so all you have to do at serving time is broil the fish.

Tomato-Lime Salsa (page 190)
6 swordfish steaks, cut about ¾ inch thick (6-7 ounces each), *see Variation*
4 teaspoons grated lime zest (green portion of rind)
⅓ cup fresh lime juice
⅓ cup olive oil
Salt and freshly ground black pepper

1. Prepare Tomato-Lime Salsa. (*Salsa can be made ahead, covered and refrigerated for up to 1 day. Bring to room temperature 30 minutes before serving and drain well.*)

2. Place fish in a large, shallow glass, ceramic or other nonreactive pan. Combine lime zest, lime juice and oil in a bowl and whisk to blend. Pour mixture over fish, cover and marinate for 2 hours, turning several times.

3. When ready to cook, arrange a rack 5 to 6 inches from heat source and preheat broiler. Remove fish from marinade and place on a rack in a broiler pan. Broil for 4 minutes per side, turning once, or until flesh is opaque and flakes easily when pierced with a knife. Remove from pan and lightly salt and pepper fish. To serve, garnish each serving with about 2 tablespoons salsa.

Variation: You can substitute individual salmon fillets or steaks the same weight as the swordfish. Broiling time is about the same: broil until the fish is opaque and flakes easily.

SERVES 6

From Start to Finish:
2 hours 40 minutes
(includes 2 hours for
marinating)
Actual Working Time:
40 minutes
Make Ahead: Partially
(see step 1)
Can Be Frozen: No
Best Seasons:
Summer and early fall

Menu Suggestion:
Simple Saffron Rice (page 225) and fresh tender green beans are good with the swordfish. Fresh store-bought strawberry sorbet topped with sliced strawberries and sprigs of mint is a fast dessert.

Salmon Fillets *with* Ginger *and* Pepper Butter

SERVES 6

★

From Start to Finish:
3 to 6 hours 25 minutes
(includes 3 to 6 hours for
marinating)

Actual Working Time:
25 minutes

Make Ahead: Partially
(see step 1)

Can Be Frozen:
Butter only (see step 1)

Best Seasons: All year

HAVE USED THIS DISH TIME AND AGAIN for entertaining because there is so little last-minute cooking involved. The flavorful ginger butter can be made a day ahead, and the salmon is marinated several hours in advance. All that is necessary at serving time is to broil the fish for a few minutes.

FOR GINGER AND PEPPER BUTTER

6   tablespoons (¾ stick) unsalted butter, softened
¼   teaspoon salt
¼   teaspoon cayenne pepper
2   tablespoons peeled and finely chopped gingerroot
2   teaspoons balsamic vinegar or red wine vinegar

FOR SALMON

½   cup olive oil
2   tablespoons soy sauce
¼   cup chopped shallots
1   teaspoon grated lemon zest
     (yellow portion of rind)
     Freshly ground black pepper
6   salmon fillets (6-7 ounces each)

1. **To prepare butter:** Combine all ingredients in a small bowl and mix until well blended. Place in a small soufflé dish or glass bowl; cover and refrigerate until needed. (*Butter can be prepared 1 day in advance. Remove from refrigerator 30 minutes before using. It can also be frozen; wrap tightly in plastic wrap, then in foil, and freeze. Defrost and bring to room temperature before using.*)

2. **To prepare salmon:** Combine oil, soy sauce, shallots, lemon zest and several grinds pepper in a small mixing bowl and mix well. Remove any bones from fillets with clean tweezers and arrange fillets, skin side down, in a shallow glass or ceramic dish that will hold them comfortably in a single layer. Pour marinade over salmon and marinate in refrigerator for 3 to 6 hours, turning several times.

3. When ready to cook fillets, arrange a rack 4 to 5 inches from heat source and preheat broiler. Remove salmon from marinade and arrange, skin side down, on a rack in a broiler pan. Broil until flesh is opaque and fish springs back when touched with your fingers, 5 to 10 minutes; cooking time will vary according to thickness of fillets.

4. To serve, arrange fillets on a warm serving plate and top each portion with a generous dollop of ginger and pepper butter.

Menu Suggestion:

Sesame Asparagus (page 195) and Mustard-Scented Scalloped Potatoes (page 217) are terrific side dishes. Warm Spiced Plums with Honey-Cream Sauce (page 345) make a tempting ending.

Baked Salmon *with* Goat Cheese *and* Fresh Herbs

SERVES 6

From Start to Finish:

2 hours 30 minutes
(includes 2 hours for
marinating)

Actual Working Time:

30 minutes

Make Ahead: No

Can Be Frozen: No

Best Seasons:

All year, especially spring
and summer

SURPRISINGLY, SALMON AND GOAT CHEESE are complementary flavors. In this dish, fillets are marinated in lemon juice and olive oil and baked briefly in a hot oven. Each serving is then garnished with a generous dollop of soft, creamy goat cheese seasoned with fresh tarragon and chives.

6	salmon fillets (6-7 ounces each)
¼	cup fresh lemon juice
¼	teaspoon salt, plus more to taste
¼	teaspoon freshly ground black pepper, plus more to taste
6	tablespoons olive oil
2	garlic cloves, crushed
6	ounces soft, creamy goat cheese, at room temperature (*see Shopping Note,* page 28)
3	tablespoons minced fresh tarragon leaves (*divided*)
3	tablespoons snipped fresh chives (*divided*)

1. Place salmon fillets in a shallow glass baking dish just large enough to accommodate them. Remove any bones with clean tweezers. Mix lemon juice, ¼ teaspoon salt and ¼ teaspoon pepper in a small bowl. Gradually whisk in oil. Mix in garlic and pour over fish. Cover and refrigerate for 2 hours, turning fish several times.

2. Arrange a rack at center position and preheat oven to 450°F. Cover a heavy baking sheet with aluminum foil. Spray lightly with nonstick cooking spray and place fish, skin side down, on foil. Bake until opaque, 9 to 12 minutes.

3. Meanwhile, beat cheese until soft and smooth. Mix with 1½ tablespoons each of tarragon and half of chives.

4. Remove fillets from oven and remove and discard skin. Transfer fish to a platter; season with salt and pepper to taste. Place a generous dollop of cheese mixture on top of each fillet. Sprinkle with remaining herbs.

Menu Suggestion:

Serve with steamed green beans and Potato and Sweet Red Pepper Gratin (page 220), and for dessert, Vanilla and Chocolate Layered Cheesecake (page 374).

Striped Bass *with* Country-Mustard Chive Butter

SERVES 6

From Start to Finish:
40 minutes

Actual Working Time:
20 minutes

Make Ahead:
Partially (see step 1)

Can Be Frozen:
Butter only (see step 1)

Best Seasons: All year

IN MY EARLY DAYS AS A FOOD WRITER, I became a fan of striped bass, but for quite a few years, the fish almost disappeared from the marketplace because the supply was depleted. Fortunately, the striped bass population has been protected, and today, they are back at the store. In this recipe, small bass are sprinkled with lemon juice and baked with a coating of stone-ground mustard, chives and butter. As the butter melts, sinking into the flesh of the fish, the dark mustard seeds and flecks of green chives remain on top, adding visual appeal.

1½ tablespoons stone-ground country Dijon mustard
1½ teaspoons grated lemon zest
      (yellow portion of rind)
3½ tablespoons fresh lemon juice (*divided*)
 ¾ teaspoon salt, plus more if needed
 ¼ teaspoon freshly ground black pepper,
      plus more if needed
 8 tablespoons (1 stick) unsalted butter, softened
 5 tablespoons finely chopped fresh chives (*divided*)
 3 striped bass fillets (about 1 pound each
      and about ¾ inch thick)

1. Place mustard, lemon zest, 1½ tablespoons lemon juice, ¾ teaspoon salt, ¼ teaspoon pepper, butter and 3 tablespoons chives in a small glass or ceramic mixing bowl. Mix well with a wooden spoon to blend. (*If not using immediately, cover and refrigerate; butter can be prepared 2 days ahead. It can also be frozen; wrap tightly in plastic wrap and then in foil. Defrost and bring to room temperature 45 minutes before using.*)

2. When ready to bake fish, arrange a rack at center position and preheat oven to 450°F.

3. Line a rimless baking sheet with aluminum foil. Spray generously with nonstick cooking spray. Spray skin side of bass fillets with nonstick spray. Place fillets, skin side down, on foil. Run your fingers over flesh sides of fish. If you feel any bones, remove them with clean tweezers. Brush each fillet with about 2 teaspoons remaining lemon juice; then salt and pepper each fillet well. Spread about 2 to 2½ tablespoons softened mustard-chive butter over each fillet to coat evenly.

4. Bake until fish is opaque and flakes easily when pierced with a small paring knife, about 14 minutes or more. Remove fillets from oven.

5. Transfer fish, using 2 spatulas, to a serving plate. Brush any remaining softened mustard-chive butter over fillets while they are hot; butter will melt immediately. Sprinkle fillets with remaining 2 tablespoons chives. To serve, cut into 6 portions.

Variation: You can substitute two 1½-pound salmon fillets for the bass. The cooking time will be about the same. You can also substitute about 3 pounds red snapper fillets. The snapper fillets are smaller, however, and will cook in less time. Watch carefully and cook until flesh is opaque and flakes easily.

Menu Suggestion:

Corn on the cob, steamed fresh green beans and sliced tomatoes are great summer side dishes. In the winter, serve with Potato and Sweet Red Pepper Gratin (page 220) and zucchini sautéed in a little olive oil. Fresh Fruit in Red Wine and Ginger Sauce (page 347) is a perfect dessert.

Chapter 5

Well-Seasoned Birds
and Meats

Roast Chicken *and* Potatoes *with* Rosemary, Thyme *and* Lemon

THE SIMPLEST OF INGREDIENTS—a cut-up chicken and new potatoes—are baked under a blanket of fresh herbs and paper-thin lemon slices. The result is an exceptionally aromatic and attractive main course, great for a family meal but memorable enough to serve to company as well.

¼	cup olive oil
1	4½-to-5-pound roasting chicken, cut into 8 pieces, patted dry (*see Time-Saver*)
1½	pounds new potatoes, unpeeled, cut into ½-inch-wide wedges
	Salt and freshly ground black pepper
7	tablespoons fresh lemon juice
2	tablespoons red wine vinegar
12	large fresh thyme sprigs, plus more for garnish
10	large fresh rosemary sprigs, plus more for garnish
2	lemons, cut into ⅛-inch-thick slices, plus 6 wedges for garnish

1. Preheat oven to 400°F.

2. Heat oil in large, heavy skillet over medium-high heat. When hot, add chicken pieces in batches and brown on all sides, about 8 minutes. Transfer chicken to large roasting pan and add potato wedges, scattering them around chicken. Season with salt and pepper. Mix lemon juice with vinegar. Pour over chicken and potatoes. Top with 12 thyme sprigs and 10 rosemary sprigs. Make a layer of lemon slices over herbs. Bake until chicken and potatoes are tender, about 1 hour.

3. Discard lemon slices and herbs. If chicken breasts are too large for a single serving, halve them lengthwise. Transfer chicken and potatoes to a heated platter. Garnish with lemon wedges, thyme and rosemary.

SERVES 6

★

From Start to Finish:
1 hour 45 minutes
Actual Working Time:
35 minutes
Make Ahead: No
Can Be Frozen: No
Best Seasons:
All year, especially summer and fall

Time-Saver:
Ask the butcher to cut the chicken into 2 breasts, 2 wings, 2 thighs and 2 legs to save time. Extra chicken parts can be frozen to use in making chicken broth.

Menu Suggestion:
Sliced zucchini sautéed in a little olive oil and sprinkled with Parmesan cheese is a good vegetable to serve with the chicken and potatoes. Honey and Ginger Roasted Pears (page 352) rounds out the menu.

Cider-Roasted Chicken

SERVES 6

★

From Start to Finish:
2 hours 35 minutes
(includes 2 hours of
roasting)

Actual Working Time:
35 minutes

Make Ahead: No

Can Be Frozen: No

Best Seasons:
Fall and winter

IN THE FALL, WHEN FRESH CIDER APPEARS at markets and roadside stands, I am reminded of this recipe. Chicken with an apple tucked into the cavity is roasted on a bed of diced apples and aromatic vegetables, then basted with cider and chicken broth. The cooked bird is tender and moist, with dark, crispy skin. To accompany it, the pan drippings and roasted vegetables are turned into a rich sauce.

4 tablespoons unsalted butter, softened (*divided*)

1 tablespoon vegetable oil

2 medium leeks, cleaned, white parts coarsely chopped (about 2 cups; *see Cooking Technique, page 57*)

2 medium carrots, sliced ½ inch thick

1 Granny Smith apple, unpeeled, cut into ½-inch dice, plus 1 whole Granny Smith apple, unpeeled

1 4-to-4½-pound roasting chicken

½ teaspoon salt, plus more if needed

¼ teaspoon freshly ground black pepper, plus more if needed

½ teaspoon dried sage leaves, crumbled

2 cups chicken broth

1¼ cups cider

Fresh sage leaves for garnish (*optional*)

1. Preheat oven to 375°F.

2. Heat 1 tablespoon butter and oil in a large, heavy, flameproof roasting pan over medium-high heat. When hot, add leeks and carrots and sauté, stirring constantly, until just softened, about 5 minutes. Add diced apple and cook, stirring, for 1 minute more. Remove from heat.

3. Remove package of giblets and neck from cavity of chicken; discard or save for another use. Rinse chicken well and pat dry. Combine ½ teaspoon salt, ¼ teaspoon pepper and dried sage and rub

mixture in cavity. Place whole apple inside cavity. Rub chicken with 1 tablespoon softened butter. Set chicken on top of vegetable mixture in roasting pan.

4. Combine broth and cider in a bowl and pour ⅓ cup over chicken. Roast for 1¾ to 2 hours, basting every 30 minutes with ⅓ cup cider mixture and brush with ½ tablespoon softened butter. Chicken is done when juice runs clear when flesh is pierced with a knife and when a thermometer inserted in thigh registers 175°F to 180°F. When done, remove chicken to warm serving platter and cover loosely with aluminum foil.

5. Place roasting pan with vegetables and juices over medium heat. Add remaining cider mixture. Whisk well to scrape any brown particles in pan into liquid. Remove pan from heat and strain out vegetables. Return liquid to pan, then puree vegetables in a food processor fitted with a metal blade, a blender or a food mill and return to pan. Continue to cook sauce, stirring constantly, until it reduces slightly, 3 to 4 minutes. Swirl in any remaining softened butter. Taste and season with salt and pepper as needed.

6. To serve, cut chicken into serving pieces and arrange on a serving plate. Top with some sauce. Garnish with sage leaves, if desired. Pass extra sauce separately.

Menu Suggestion:
  Yukon Gold Mashed Potatoes with Buttermilk (page 212) and Green Beans with Roasted Onions (page 206) make great partners for the chicken. Prince Albert Pumpkin Brownies (page 382) are a scrumptious ending.

Lemon *and* Dill Chicken Cutlets

SERVES 4

★

From Start to Finish:
50 minutes

Actual Working Time:
35 minutes

Make Ahead: Partially
(see step 1)

Can Be Frozen: No

Best Seasons: All year

Shopping Note:

Be certain to buy ground chicken or turkey that does not include the skin (which adds a high amount of fat). Check the package label or ask the butcher.

MY MOTHER USED TO FLOUR CUBE STEAKS, brown them, then simmer them with onions for an hour or two until they were fork-tender and covered with a rich pan gravy. I loved the wonderful aroma that this dish gave to our kitchen and could hardly wait for dinner on those days. My updated version is lighter and takes much less time to prepare. It is made with ground chicken or turkey combined with chopped onion, lemon and dill. Once the meat is shaped into patties, floured and quickly sautéed, it is ready. The only thing left to do then is to make a quick sauce by adding lemon juice and broth to the pan.

1 pound ground chicken or turkey (*see Shopping Note*)
½ cup very finely chopped onion
1½ teaspoons grated lemon zest
   (yellow portion of rind)
1½ tablespoons lemon juice (*divided*)
1½ teaspoons dried dill
¾ teaspoon salt, plus more if needed
   Scant ⅛ teaspoon freshly ground black pepper,
      plus more if needed
¼ cup all-purpose flour
1-2 tablespoons vegetable oil, plus more if needed
1 cup reduced-sodium chicken broth
1 tablespoon unsalted butter, softened,
   mixed with 1 tablespoon flour to form a paste
   Fresh dill sprigs for garnish (*optional*)
4 very thin wedges of lemon for garnish (*optional*)

1. Place ground chicken or turkey, onion, lemon zest, ½ tablespoon lemon juice, dried dill, ¾ teaspoon salt and ⅛ teaspoon pepper in a large mixing bowl and mix well with a spoon to combine. Divide into 4 equal portions and shape into patties about ½ inch thick. (*Patties can be prepared several hours ahead. Cover with plastic wrap and refrigerate until needed.*)

2. When ready to sauté patties, spread flour on a dinner plate. Lightly dredge each patty in flour. Place a large, heavy skillet over medium-high heat and add enough oil to coat pan lightly. When oil is hot, place patties in pan and sauté until golden on both sides, 3 to 4 minutes per side. Lower heat to medium, cover pan and cook patties for 5 minutes more. Transfer to a warm plate and cover loosely with aluminum foil.

3. Keep heat on medium. Add broth to skillet and whisk well to scrape up pan drippings. Gradually whisk in butter and flour paste until sauce thickens. Stir in remaining 1 tablespoon lemon juice. Season sauce to taste with salt and pepper and remove from heat.

4. To serve, arrange chicken patties on a warm serving platter. Top each with sauce and garnish with dill sprigs and lemon wedges, if desired.

Menu Suggestion:

Yukon Gold Mashed Potatoes with Buttermilk (page 212) and Honey and Brandy Carrots (page 209) are excellent dishes to serve with the cutlets. Country Chocolate Loaf Cake with Warm Chocolate-Coffee Sauce (page 366) makes a special dessert.

Cajun-Style Cornish Hens
with Rosemary Bacon Rice

SERVES 6

★

From Start to Finish:

3 hours (includes 1 hour
30 minutes for marinating
hens and for making
Rosemary Bacon Rice)

Actual Working Time:

1 hour 10 minutes

Make Ahead: Partially
(see step 1)

Can Be Frozen: No

Best Seasons:

Fall and winter

L ITTLE CORNISH HENS, those specially bred birds that weigh about 1½ pounds, are fairly mild in flavor and, in my opinion, profit from assertive seasonings. They certainly get an infusion of flavor in this preparation. The hens are stuffed under the breast skin with a spicy butter and then coated with a cayenne pepper and mustard glaze. They can be assembled 1½ hours ahead and need only to be roasted 1 hour before serving. Rosemary Bacon Rice, a colorful mélange of white rice, red peppers and yellow squash seasoned with rosemary, is an admirable accompaniment to the birds.

Rosemary Bacon Rice (page 223)
3   Cornish hens (about 1½ pounds each)
7   tablespoons unsalted butter, softened (*divided*)
2   teaspoons chopped garlic
2¼   teaspoons cayenne pepper (*divided*)
5   drops red pepper sauce, preferably Tabasco
½   teaspoon dried thyme leaves
½   teaspoon salt (*divided*), plus more for seasoning
¼   cup Dijon mustard
2   teaspoons red wine vinegar
½   teaspoon garlic powder
   Freshly ground black pepper
⅔   cup chicken broth
   Fresh rosemary sprigs for garnish (*optional*)

1. Prepare Rosemary Bacon Rice. (*Rice can be prepared 2 to 3 hours ahead; cool, cover and refrigerate until needed.*)

2. Rinse and dry outside and cavities of hens. Combine 6 tablespoons butter, garlic, 1¼ teaspoons cayenne, red pepper sauce, thyme and ¼ teaspoon salt in a food processor fitted with a metal blade. Process until smooth, 30 to 40 seconds, or mix ingredients with a wooden spoon in a bowl.

3. Remove butter mixture and divide into 3 equal portions. With your fingers, gently loosen skin over entire breast area of 1 hen. Place one-third of seasoned butter between skin and flesh and pat over entire breast area. Repeat with other hens.

4. Combine mustard, vinegar, remaining 1 teaspoon cayenne, garlic powder and remaining ¼ teaspoon salt; mix well to form a paste. Brush mixture evenly over outside surface of hens. Cover and refrigerate and marinate for 1½ hours. Bring hens to room temperature for 20 minutes before roasting.

5. Arrange a rack at center position and preheat oven to 450°F. Salt and pepper cavities of hens. Place hens breast side up on a rack in a roasting pan. Roast for 15 minutes.

6. Reduce heat to 350°F. Brush hens with remaining 1 tablespoon butter and roast for 45 minutes or a little longer, basting with ⅓ cup broth every 15 minutes, until juices run clear when hens are pierced with a knife. About 20 minutes before hens are done, rewarm rice, covered, in oven until heated through.

7. Remove birds and let stand for 5 minutes. Strain pan juices into a saucepan and skim to remove fat. Keep warm on very low heat. With kitchen scissors or a sharp knife, halve birds. Cut away backbones so you have pieces of equal size. Arrange birds on a bed of rice and spoon over pan juices. Garnish with rosemary sprigs, if desired.

Menu Suggestion:

This dish is really a meal in itself with the hens and the rice studded with vegetables. A basket of warm crusty sourdough bread and a mixed green salad in a light dressing are all that is needed to fill out the main course. For dessert, serve Ginger and Brown Sugar Grapefruit Compotes with Vanilla Ice Cream (page 346).

Thyme-Scented Chicken Meat Loaf

SERVES 4 TO 6

★

From Start to Finish:
1 hour 30 minutes

Actual Working Time:
45 minutes

Make Ahead: Partially
(see steps 2 and 5)

Can Be Frozen: No

Best Seasons:
Fall and winter

WHEN I PREPARED THIS MEAT LOAF in a winter cooking class, my students were wild about it. Made with ground chicken or turkey in place of beef, mixed with grated apples to add flavor and moisture and seasoned generously with thyme, it is delicious with a quickly made mushroom gravy. I served it with mashed potatoes and salad, and at the end of the class, after most people had helped themselves to seconds, not one single plate had a morsel left on it!

FOR MEAT LOAF

2 tablespoons unsalted butter (*divided*)

⅓ cup finely diced carrots (¼-inch dice)

⅓ cup finely diced leeks (¼-inch dice),
   white parts only (*see Cooking Technique*, page 57)

⅓ cup finely diced celery (¼-inch dice)

1 pound ground chicken or turkey
   (*see Shopping Note*, page 138)

1¼ cups fresh bread crumbs

1½ teaspoons dried thyme leaves

1 teaspoon salt

½ teaspoon freshly ground black pepper

1 medium unpeeled tart apple (such as
   Granny Smith), cleaned and grated

2 egg whites

FOR GRAVY

2 tablespoons unsalted butter (*divided*)

1½ cups finely chopped green onions
   (including 3 inches of green tops)

4 ounces shiitake mushrooms, cleaned,
   stems discarded, cut into ¼-inch strips

4 ounces white cultivated mushrooms, cleaned
   and sliced thinly through stems
   Salt

2 tablespoons all-purpose flour

1½ cups chicken broth
2   teaspoons reduced-sodium soy sauce

1. **To prepare meat loaf:** Melt 1 tablespoon butter in a medium, heavy skillet over medium-high heat. When hot, add carrots, leeks and celery and sauté, stirring, until softened, 4 to 5 minutes. Cool.

2. Place ground chicken or turkey, bread crumbs, thyme, salt, pepper, apple and cooled sautéed vegetables in a mixing bowl and stir well to blend. Add egg whites and mix well; mixture will be quite wet. Divide in half and shape into 2 oval loaves. Spray a roasting pan generously with nonstick cooking spray and put loaves in pan. Dot loaves with remaining 1 tablespoon butter. (*Meat loaves can be prepared 1 day ahead to this point; cover and refrigerate.*)

3. When ready to bake, arrange a rack at center position and preheat oven to 350°F. Bake meat loaves for 40 to 45 minutes, until cooked completely through. Remove and cool for 5 minutes.

4. **To prepare gravy:** Heat 1 tablespoon butter in a medium, heavy skillet. When hot, add green onions and cook, stirring, for about 2 minutes. Add mushrooms and cook, stirring, until mushrooms are tender, 4 to 5 minutes. Season with salt to taste, remove from heat and set aside.

5. Melt remaining 1 tablespoon butter in a medium, heavy saucepan. When hot, add flour and cook, stirring, for 2 minutes. Add broth and whisk until sauce is smooth and just thickened, 2 to 3 minutes. Whisk in soy sauce. Stir in mushroom mixture. Taste and, if desired, add more salt. (*Gravy can be prepared 1 day ahead; cover and refrigerate; reheat to serve.*)

6. To serve meat loaves, cut into ½-inch-thick slices and arrange on a heated serving platter. Ladle some mushroom gravy over slices. Pass any extra gravy separately.

Variation: My students like the sliced, cold leftovers (if there are any!) in sandwiches with lettuce and mayonnaise on sourdough bread.

Menu Suggestion:
Yukon Gold Mashed Potatoes with Buttermilk (page 212) and steamed green beans are ideal side dishes for the meat loaf. Deep-Dish Apple and Cream Cheese Pie (page 354), Honey and Ginger Roasted Pears (page 352) or fresh fruit and White Chocolate- and Pecan-Studded Brownies (page 380) are dessert possibilities.

Southern Herb-Roasted Turkey

BASTED WITH THYME- AND ROSEMARY-seasoned butter as well as broth, this turkey is a deep golden brown and incredibly moist and tender after roasting. The pan drippings, enriched with some of the herb butter, are turned into a delectable gravy.

SERVES 10

★

From Start to Finish:

3 hours 55 minutes
(includes 2 hours 45
minutes for roasting)

Actual Working Time:

40 minutes, plus basting
every 30 minutes

Make Ahead: Partially
(see step 1)

Can Be Frozen:

Herb butter only
(see step 1)

Best Seasons:

Fall and winter

Cooking Technique:

Birds are trussed so
they keep their shape and
roast evenly. Years ago, I
learned how to truss a bird
from cooking authority
Jacques Pépin:

1. Remove tips (which
burn easily) from wings and
tuck first section of wing
under the other.

2. Holding a long (2-to-
2½-foot) piece of heavy
kitchen string or twine in
both hands, slide string
under tail section (where
legs are). Bring string up
around bases of the legs

12	tablespoons (1½ sticks) unsalted butter, softened
1¾	teaspoons dried rosemary leaves, crumbled
1¾	teaspoons dried thyme leaves, crumbled
	Salt
1	14-pound turkey, neck and giblets reserved
	Freshly ground black pepper
1	large leek (white and pale green parts only), cleaned and coarsely chopped (*see Cooking Technique*, page 57)
1	medium carrot, sliced
3	fresh rosemary sprigs or 1 teaspoon dried leaves, crumbled
3	fresh thyme sprigs or 1 teaspoon dried leaves, crumbled
5	cups reduced-sodium chicken broth (*divided*), plus more if needed
	Fresh rosemary sprigs for garnish (*optional*)
	Fresh thyme sprigs for garnish (*optional*)

1. Blend butter, dried rosemary and dried thyme in a small bowl. Season herb butter generously with salt. (*Herb butter can be prepared 2 days ahead. Cover tightly and refrigerate. It can also be frozen; wrap carefully in plastic wrap, then in foil. Defrost before using. Bring to room temperature before continuing.*)

2. Preheat oven to 350°F. Season turkey cavity with salt and pepper. Place leek, carrot, rosemary and thyme inside cavity. Truss turkey to hold shape (*see Cooking Technique*). Wipe skin dry with paper towels. Set aside 6 tablespoons herb butter for sauce. Rub 2 tablespoons herb butter over turkey skin. Place turkey on a rack set in a flameproof roasting pan. Arrange neck and giblets around turkey.

3. Roast turkey, uncovered, until meat thermometer inserted into thickest part of thigh registers 175°F to 180°F, basting with ⅓ cup broth and brushing with herb butter every 30 minutes, about 2 hours 45 minutes. Transfer turkey to a platter and discard neck and giblets. Tent loosely with aluminum foil.

4. Pour pan juices into a large (6-to-8-cup) glass measuring cup and skim off any fat. Set measuring cup aside. Pour 2 cups remaining broth into roasting pan. Set pan over high heat and bring to a boil. Using a whisk, scrape up any brown bits from bottom of pan and cook, whisking, for 1 to 2 minutes. Pour hot broth into measuring cup with reserved pan juices. If necessary, add enough additional broth to measure 6 cups. Strain contents of measuring cup into a heavy, medium saucepan. Boil over high heat until reduced by half to 3 cups, about 30 minutes. Whisk reserved 6 tablespoons herb butter into reduced liquid to finish sauce. Taste and season, if needed, with salt.

5. To serve, garnish turkey with bouquets of rosemary and thyme, if desired, and carve at table, or carve turkey, arrange on a serving tray and garnish with fresh rosemary and thyme sprigs. Pass sauce separately.

and tie them together so that one leg slightly overlaps the other. Slide string under drumstick and pull it tight. Pull string along both sides of bird, tightly, pushing breast up and pulling legs toward body. Lay turkey on one side and bring one end of string around wings on both sides. When you bring string around front of bird (between 2 wings), make certain loose neck skin is secured with string. Tie with a firm knot and cut off excess string.

Menu Suggestion:

Corn Bread and Sweet Pepper Dressing (page 240), Grated Sweet Potatoes with Honey and Orange (page 210), Green Beans with Roasted Onions (page 206) and Spiced Cranberries (page 184) all go with the turkey. Cream Cheese Pumpkin-Pecan Pie (page 360) makes a special ending.

Roast Turkey Breast
with Sage Butter

SERVES 8 TO 10

★

From Start to Finish:
2 hours 30 minutes to 3
hours (includes 1½ to 2
hours for roasting turkey)
Actual Working Time:
1 hour, plus basting every
20 minutes
Make Ahead: Partially
(see steps 1 and 3)
Can Be Frozen: No
Best Seasons:
Fall and winter

Shopping Note:
Ask your butcher to bone
a 5-to-6-pound whole
turkey breast but to leave
the skin on. Then ask the
butcher to cut the breast
into two halves, which will
each weigh about 2 to 2½
pounds. Occasionally, you
can find boned turkey
breast halves, about 2½
pounds each, at the market.
If these are available, buy
two for this recipe.

I F YOU DON'T LIKE CARVING A TURKEY and your guests only like white meat, roast breast of turkey is the answer. For this recipe, a whole breast is cut into halves, and each half is spread with sage butter, then topped with sautéed leeks. The breasts are fitted together, enclosing the leeks and herb butter, creating a rolled boneless roast, which becomes permeated by the flavor of its savory stuffing during the cooking. Delicious gravy is made from the pan drippings.

¾ cup unsalted butter, softened
2 tablespoons chopped fresh sage leaves
    or 2 teaspoons dried leaves, crumbled
6 strips lean or turkey bacon, fried or microwaved
    until crisp, then finely crumbled
    (*see Shopping Note,* page 335)
    Salt and freshly ground black pepper
1½ tablespoons vegetable oil
1½ cups cleaned chopped leeks, white parts only
    (about 2 medium; *see Cooking Technique,* page 57)
1 5-to-6-pound fresh whole turkey breast, split,
    boned and trimmed, skin left on (*see Shopping Note*)
4 cups reduced-sodium chicken broth,
    plus more if needed
    Fresh sage leaves or flat-leaf parsley sprigs
    for garnish

1. Combine butter, sage and bacon in a mixing bowl. Season with salt and pepper and mix well to blend. Set aside. (*Sage butter can be prepared 1 to 2 days ahead. Cover and refrigerate; bring to room temperature before using.*)

2. Heat oil in a medium, heavy skillet over medium-high heat. When hot, add leeks and cook, stirring constantly, until softened, about 4 minutes. Remove from heat and cool completely.

3. Place 1 boned turkey breast half, skin side down, on a work surface. If still attached, remove small fillet (*see Cooking Technique*) and save for another use. Spread half of sage butter over breast and top with cooled sautéed leeks. Season generously with salt and pepper. Also remove fillet from second breast half. Position second breast half, skin side up, over leeks so that tapered end of it covers broad end of breast already on work surface. (This will produce a roast of equal thickness at each end, allowing for even roasting.) With kitchen twine, tie breast halves together at 1-inch intervals. (*Breast can be prepared 1 day ahead. Cover and refrigerate.*)

4. When ready to roast turkey breast, arrange a rack in bottom third of oven and preheat oven to 350°F. Spread 1½ tablespoons sage butter over surface of breast and place breast on a rack set in a flameproof roasting pan. Pour ⅓ cup broth over bird. Tent breast with aluminum foil.

5. Roast turkey for 1½ to 2 hours, basting with ⅓ cup broth every 20 minutes. Remove foil after 1 hour. Turkey is done when juices run clear when flesh is pierced with a knife and when a meat thermometer inserted into thickest part of breast registers 175°F.

6. Remove breast from pan and set aside. Remove rack and place roasting pan with pan drippings over medium-high heat. Add remaining broth and cook until sauce reduces and thickens slightly, 4 to 5 minutes or more, stirring constantly. Whisk in remaining sage butter. Taste sauce and season with salt and pepper. To serve, remove strings and slice turkey into ¾-inch-thick slices. Arrange in overlapping rows on a serving platter. Garnish with fresh sage or parsley sprigs. Spoon over a little sauce and pass remaining sauce separately.

Menu Suggestion:

Sourdough Bread Stuffing with Mushrooms and Leeks (page 244) or Wild Rice with Red and Green Grapes (page 228), Baked Butternut Squash and Apples with Maple Syrup (page 213), Green Beans with Roasted Onions (page 206) and Honeyed Cranberry Sauce (page 185) complement the turkey breasts. Fresh fruit and Prince Albert Pumpkin Brownies (page 382) or Golden Pumpkin Roll with Toffee Cream Filling and Warm Caramel Sauce (page 372) can end this menu.

Cooking Technique:

Boned breasts sometimes have a small elongated piece of meat on the underside. This piece, which has a white tendon running lengthwise through its center, is called a fillet or tender. I usually pull it off to create a flat surface. Save the fillet for another use; it is good for stir-fries, or it can be poached and used in chicken or turkey salads.

Pot Roast *with* Rich Root Vegetable Sauce

SERVES 6 TO 8

★

From Start to Finish:
3 to 4 hours (includes 2½ to 3 hours of roasting)

Actual Working Time:
40 minutes, plus basting every 30 minutes

Make Ahead: Yes
(see step 6)

Can Be Frozen: Yes
(see step 6)

Best Seasons: All year

Shopping Note:
You can try other cuts of beef (rump or chuck, for example) in this dish, but my favorite is a boneless beef sirloin tip.

I THINK JUST ABOUT EVERYONE HAS MEMORIES of a favorite pot roast they sampled during their youth. The one I remember best had a rich dark sauce and was generously seasoned with onions. The following recipe, the creation of my talented friends and fellow cooks Rich Terapak and Steve Stover, is reminiscent of my childhood recollection. The roast is browned and then braised French-style with aromatic vegetables and tomatoes in broth and wine. A hint of allspice and cloves adds subtle flavoring. The sauce, thickened by pureeing the braising vegetables, is lighter than traditional pot roast gravies, which are thickened with flour. This roast tastes even better when made a day ahead so the seasonings meld.

2 tablespoons olive or vegetable oil
1 4-pound boneless beef sirloin tip roast
    (*see Shopping Note*)
    Salt and freshly ground black pepper
1 cup thinly sliced onions
1 cup chopped celery
1 cup chopped carrots
3 teaspoons fresh thyme leaves or 1 teaspoon dried
    Generous pinch (1/16 teaspoon) ground allspice
    Generous pinch (1/16 teaspoon) ground cloves
3 fresh flat-leaf parsley sprigs
2 bay leaves, broken in half
3 large garlic cloves, peeled and crushed
1 28-ounce can Italian-style tomatoes,
    drained and coarsely chopped
3 cups beef broth
2 cups dry red wine
    Sugar
1-2 teaspoons unsalted butter (*optional*)
    Fresh flat-leaf parsley sprigs and/or fresh
    thyme sprigs for garnish (*optional*)

1. Preheat oven to 350°F.

2. In a 4-to-5-quart heavy, ovenproof, deep-sided pot with a lid, heat oil over medium-high heat until hot. Pat roast dry, then add to pan and brown evenly on all sides, about 5 minutes. Remove roast to a plate and salt and pepper meat generously on all sides.

3. Add onions, celery and carrots to pan and cook, stirring constantly, until vegetables are just tender, about 5 minutes. Add thyme, allspice, cloves, 3 parsley sprigs, bay leaves, garlic, tomatoes, broth and wine to pan and stir to mix well. Return roast to pan and bring liquid to a simmer. Cover pan tightly with aluminum foil and then with a lid.

4. Bake, basting and turning roast every 30 minutes to ensure even cooking, until a sharp knife can be inserted easily, about 2½ to 3 hours. This slow and long cooking will make meat more tender and flavorful.

5. When done, remove pan from oven and meat from pan. Strain vegetables from liquid in pan. Remove and discard bay leaves. Puree vegetables in a food processor fitted with a metal blade, a blender or a food mill. Return pureed vegetables and liquid to pan. Taste, and if sauce seems too acidic, add a pinch or two of sugar.

6. Over medium-high heat, reduce sauce by one-third to about 4 cups. The sauce should just coat the back of a spoon lightly. Taste and season with salt and pepper, if needed. (You may not need to add any salt if you used salted beef broth.) To make sauce smoother and richer, whisk in optional butter. If not serving immediately, return roast to pan. (*Cool, cover and refrigerate for up to 3 days. Roast can also be frozen; defrost before continuing. Reheat in a preheated 350°F oven for 30 minutes or longer to warm through.*)

7. To serve, remove meat and cut into thin slices. Arrange slices on a warm serving platter and spoon over some sauce. Garnish meat, if desired, with a bouquet of parsley and thyme sprigs. Place extra sauce in a bowl and pass separately.

Menu Suggestion:
Yukon Gold Mashed Potatoes with Buttermilk (page 212) and buttered carrots sprinkled with brown sugar or a simple salad with a light dressing are appropriate side dishes. Deep-Dish Apple and Cream Cheese Pie (page 354) makes an all-American dessert.

Fillet of Beef Stuffed *with* Red Peppers, Spinach *and* Goat Cheese

SERVES 8

From Start to Finish:
1 hour 45 minutes

Actual Working Time:
45 minutes

Make Ahead: Partially
(see step 3)

Can Be Frozen: No

Best Seasons: All year

A BEEF FILLET IS CERTAINLY "company" fare. But because it is an expensive cut of meat, cooks want assurance that a recipe calling for it will work. This fillet, stuffed with roasted red peppers and a creamy mixture of spinach, herbs and goat cheese, is truly foolproof. The roast can be filled and tied well in advance so that all that is necessary is to roast the meat for an hour or less before serving. When cut, the slices reveal the red, green and white filling that give this dish its striking appearance.

1¼ pounds spinach, stemmed and cleaned (*divided*)

8 ounces soft, creamy goat cheese
(*see Shopping Note,* page 28)

½ teaspoon dried rosemary leaves, crushed

½ teaspoon dried thyme leaves
Freshly ground black pepper

1 3-pound trimmed beef tenderloin
Salt

4 medium roasted red bell peppers
(*see Cooking Technique,* page 13), peeled,
seeded and cut into quarters

3 tablespoons olive oil
Fresh snipped chives or chopped flat-leaf parsley
for garnish (*optional*)

1. Set aside 10 to 12 large spinach leaves. Blanch remaining leaves in boiling water until just wilted, about 2 minutes. Run under cold water in a strainer to cool. Drain well and place in a clean kitchen towel. Squeeze and wring out until all excess water is removed. Coarsely chop. Mix spinach, goat cheese, rosemary, thyme and ¼ teaspoon black pepper in a mixing bowl until well blended.

2. Make a slit lengthwise down center of tenderloin, cutting two-thirds of the way through meat. Spread meat open and pound to a ½-inch thickness with a meat pounder. Season with salt and pepper.

3. Lay reserved uncooked spinach leaves over meat, leaving a 1-inch border all around and making an overlapping layer over meat. Next, make a layer of overlapping red peppers. Shape cheese and spinach mixture into a log the same length as meat and place over peppers. Roll tenderloin as tightly as possible into a cylinder. Tuck in tail and tie meat tightly at 1-inch intervals with kitchen string. (*Meat can be prepared several hours ahead to this point. Cover and refrigerate.*)

4. Preheat oven to 375°F.

5. Heat oil in a large, heavy skillet over medium-high heat and brown tenderloin well on all sides, about 5 minutes. Transfer meat to a rack set in a roasting pan. Salt and pepper generously.

6. Roast until meat registers 145°F on a meat thermometer, about 45 minutes. Meat should be pink inside. If necessary, make a slit with a small knife to check for doneness.

7. When done, remove from oven and let meat stand for 15 minutes. Cut and remove strings. Cut meat into 1-inch-thick slices. Arrange on a warm serving platter. Garnish with a sprinkling of chives or parsley, if desired.

Menu Suggestion:

Mustard-Scented Scalloped Potatoes (page 217) and steamed or sautéed zucchini are good side dishes for the roast. Vanilla and Chocolate Layered Cheesecake (page 374) makes a fitting finale.

Baked Pork Chops *with* Caramelized Onions *and* Smoked Gouda

SERVES 8

From Start to Finish:
1 hour 45 minutes

Actual Working Time:
45 minutes

Make Ahead: Yes
(see step 4)

Can Be Frozen: Yes
(see step 4)

Best Seasons:
Fall and winter

MY MOTHER, LIKE MANY SOUTHERN COOKS, loved to prepare smothered pork chops. She floured the meat and sautéed it along with sliced onions. Then she added broth and simmered the mixture until the chops were fork-tender. A little smoked Gouda added at the end of the baking time is my variation on this Southern classic. Although the pork chops need an hour in the oven, they improve in flavor when made a day ahead and can be quickly reheated.

8   lean center-cut pork chops, cut ¾-1 inch thick
      (7-8 ounces each), trimmed of excess fat
      Salt and freshly ground black pepper
1   cup all-purpose flour
4   tablespoons vegetable oil (*divided*),
      plus more if needed
8   cups sliced onions
1   teaspoon sugar
4   teaspoons chopped garlic
      About 4 cups beef broth, plus more if needed
¾   cup (3 ounces) grated smoked Gouda
      (grated with rind), *see Healthful Variation*
3   tablespoons chopped fresh flat-leaf parsley
      for garnish

1. Arrange a rack at center position and preheat oven to 350°F.

2. Season chops generously with salt and pepper and dredge in flour. Pour 2 tablespoons oil into a large, heavy skillet and set over medium-high heat. Add half of pork chops or as many as will fit comfortably in a single layer. Brown well, about 4 minutes per side. Place browned chops in large oven-to-table baking dish. Repeat with remaining chops, using more oil, if needed.

3. Add remaining 2 tablespoons oil to skillet or enough to coat bottom with a thin layer and heat until hot. Add onions and cook slowly, stirring over medium heat until onions start to brown, about 6 minutes. Sprinkle with sugar and continue to cook, stirring, until onions are well browned, about 10 minutes. Add garlic and cook for 1 minute more. Arrange onions on top of chops and add 4 cups broth. Chops should be just covered with liquid. If necessary, add more broth or water.

4. Cover dish with a lid or with aluminum foil. Bake until tender when pierced with a knife, 45 to 60 minutes. (*Pork chops can be prepared 1 day ahead to this point; cool, cover and refrigerate. They can also be frozen. Defrost before continuing. Reheat, covered, in a preheated 350°F oven until hot, 15 to 20 minutes.*)

5. To finish dish, remove lid and sprinkle cheese over chops. Bake, uncovered, for about 5 minutes more, or until cheese is melted and slightly crusty. Sprinkle chops with parsley before serving.

Healthful Variation: Although the cheese adds a wonderful flavor to this dish, you can reduce the fat content by using half the amount or omitting it entirely.

Menu Suggestion:

These pork chops are delicious with Caraway Noodles (page 238) and Honey and Brandy Carrots (page 209). Try Prince Albert Pumpkin Brownies (page 382) for a special dessert.

Smothered Pork Chops
with Apricots *and* Prunes

SERVES 8

★

From Start to Finish:
1 hour 45 minutes

Actual Working Time:
40 minutes

Make Ahead: Yes
(see step 4)

Can Be Frozen: Yes
(see step 4)

Best Seasons:
Fall and winter

THESE SMOTHERED PORK CHOPS are cooked on top of the stove rather than in the oven. I use red wine as well as broth to braise the meat and include dried apricots and prunes, which add a hint of sweetness. (*See photograph, page 45.*)

8	lean center-cut pork chops, about ½ inch thick (total weight 3 pounds), trimmed of excess fat
	Salt and freshly ground black pepper
⅓	cup all-purpose flour
¼	cup vegetable oil (*divided*)
4½	cups sliced onions (about 2 large)
5	cups chicken broth
1½	cups dry red wine
16	pitted prunes (about ¾ cup)
16	dried apricots (about ½ cup)
3	tablespoons chopped fresh flat-leaf parsley for garnish

1. Pat pork chops dry with paper towels and sprinkle well with salt and pepper on each side. Spread flour on a dinner plate and dredge each chop in flour. Shake off excess.

2. Heat 2 tablespoons oil in a large, heavy skillet with a lid (cast-iron works well) over medium-high heat. When oil is hot, add enough pork chops to fit comfortably in a single layer. Brown well, about 4 minutes per side. Remove and drain on paper towels. Continue, adding remaining 2 tablespoons oil, until all chops are browned and drained.

3. Pour off all but 2 tablespoons oil. Add onions and cook, stirring, until lightly browned, 4 to 5 minutes. Place chops over onions and add broth and wine. Bring mixture to a simmer, reduce heat, cover and cook for 15 minutes.

4. Stir prunes and apricots into pan. Cover and cook until pork chops are very tender when pierced with a knife, 45 to 50 minutes or more. (*Pork chops can be cooked 1 day ahead; cool, cover and refrigerate. They can also be frozen. Defrost before continuing. Reheat in a preheated 350°F oven until hot, 15 to 20 minutes.*)

5. When ready to serve, remove chops with a slotted spoon and place on a serving platter. Use a slotted spoon to arrange onions and fruit over meat. If sauce is not thick enough, cook it over high heat for a few minutes until it reduces slightly. Ladle sauce over chops and sprinkle with parsley.

Menu Suggestion:

Lightly buttered white or brown rice sprinkled with parsley or Yukon Gold Mashed Potatoes with Buttermilk (page 212) and steamed green beans are tempting side dishes. For dessert, serve White Chocolate- and Pecan-Studded Brownies (page 380).

Orange-Glazed Crown Roast of Pork

From Start to Finish:

3 hours (includes 2 hours roasting)

Actual Working Time:

30 minutes, plus basting every 20 to 25 minutes

Make Ahead: No

Can Be Frozen: No

Best Seasons:

Fall, winter and early spring

Shopping Note:

A crown roast of pork is almost always a special order. Ask the butcher to tie together two racks of pork (trimmed of as much fat as possible) to total about 8 pounds. Depending on the size of the racks, you will have about 14 to 16 ribs. Also ask the butcher to trim away the fat between the rib bones so that the bones are exposed to give the roast an attractive appearance.

THIS DISH IS A SHOW-STOPPER, definitely a main course you make for a special occasion. The pork is studded with garlic and basted, while roasting, with orange juice. Tall, regal and impressive, this crown roast can be served with or without a filling in its center.

1 8-pound crown roast of pork (*see Shopping Note*)
   Salt and freshly ground black pepper
4 large garlic cloves, cut into thin slivers
3½ tablespoons unsalted butter, softened (*divided*)
1 6-ounce can frozen orange juice concentrate, defrosted (*divided*)
1 cup reduced-sodium chicken broth, plus more if needed
   Sugar
1½ tablespoons all-purpose flour
1 bunch watercress, cleaned and dried, for garnish (*optional*)
1 thick-skinned orange, cut into 10 wedges, for garnish

1. Arrange a rack at center position and preheat oven to 350°F.

2. Trim and discard any excess fat both inside and outside roast. Salt and pepper roast generously on all sides. Using a sharp paring knife, make small incisions both outside and inside of roast and insert a garlic sliver in each incision. Place roast on a rack set in a large, flame-proof roasting pan. Rub roast all over with 2 tablespoons butter. Brush it all over with 2 tablespoons orange juice concentrate. Place roast in oven.

3. Combine remaining orange juice concentrate with an equal amount of water in a bowl and mix well. Baste roast every 20 to 25 minutes with about 4 teaspoons orange-juice mixture. Roast should be done in about 2 to 2½ hours; a meat thermometer should register 170°F. If bones seem to be browning too quickly, wrap them in aluminum foil.

4. Transfer roast to a serving platter, cover loosely with aluminum foil and let stand for 20 minutes before carving.

5. To prepare sauce, place roasting pan with dark pan drippings over medium heat. Remove and discard any fat (not drippings). Add remaining orange juice from basting and 1 cup broth. Use a whisk to scrape pan drippings into sauce and bring to a simmer. Taste and if sauce is bitter, add pinches of sugar to taste; season sauce with salt and pepper to taste. Mix remaining 1½ tablespoons butter and flour together to form a paste and gradually whisk into sauce and stir until it thickens.

6. To serve, garnish platter with watercress, if desired, and orange wedges. Slice roast into chops and serve topped with sauce.

Menu Suggestion:

Wild Rice with Red and Green Grapes (page 228) can be used as a filling for the roast after baking. Or you might like to try Corn Bread Dressing Loaf with Bacon and Sage (page 242); bake the loaf as directed in a bread pan, but crumble and place in the center of the roast before serving. Serve with fresh green beans or broccoli lightly sautéed in butter and, for dessert, Golden Pumpkin Roll with Toffee Cream Filling and Warm Caramel Sauce (page 372).

Roast Pork Tenderloins
with Fall Fruit Stuffing

SERVES 10

★

From Start to Finish:
2 hours

Actual Working Time:
50 minutes

Make Ahead: Partially
(see step 4)

Can Be Frozen: No

Best Seasons:
Fall and winter

Shopping Notes:

Apricot fruit spread
is sweetened only with
concentrated fruit juices.
It is available in the jam
and jelly section of most
supermarkets.

Dried sour cherries are
available in specialty-food
stores, health-food stores
and many supermarkets.

THESE TENDERLOINS ARE WORTHY of a special celebration. Butterflied and stuffed with a mixture of dried fruits, sautéed shallots, fresh bread crumbs and herbs, they are roasted, then sliced and topped with a delicious sauce. The tenderloins can be prepared several hours ahead.

3¾ cups reduced-sodium chicken broth (*divided*),
     plus more if needed
½   cup dried sour cherries (*see Shopping Notes*)
⅓   cup dried apricots, cut into ¼-inch dice
⅓   cup dried apples, cut into ¼-inch dice
2   tablespoons dried currants
3   tablespoons unsalted butter (*divided*)
½   cup chopped shallots
½   cup fresh bread crumbs
¾   teaspoon dried thyme leaves
¾   teaspoon dried sage leaves, crumbled
4   pork tenderloins (about 14 ounces each),
     fat trimmed
     Salt and freshly ground black pepper
1   tablespoon vegetable oil
1   cup dry white wine
½   cup apricot fruit spread (*see Shopping Notes*)
     or apricot preserves
2   tablespoons cornstarch, dissolved in
     2 tablespoons water
     Fresh thyme and sage sprigs for garnish (*optional*)

1. Bring ¾ cup broth to a boil in a medium, heavy saucepan. Add cherries, apricots, apples and currants. Remove from heat and let stand for 20 minutes. Strain fruit mixture in a sieve set over a bowl, pressing down on fruit with the back of a spoon to extract as much liquid as possible. Transfer fruit to a bowl, and reserve liquid.

2. Melt 2 tablespoons butter in a large, heavy skillet over medium heat. Add shallots and sauté for 3 minutes, until softened. Add bread crumbs, thyme and sage and sauté for 1 minute. Add to fruit mixture.

3. Place pork on a work surface. Using a sharp knife, make a lengthwise cut down center of 1 tenderloin, cutting two-thirds of the way through. Open it like a book. Make a lengthwise cut down center of each flap, cutting ⅓ inch deep to open up meat slightly, making it easier to pound. Using a meat mallet or rolling pin, pound pork to a ¼-inch thickness. Season with salt and pepper. Repeat with remaining tenderloins.

4. Preheat oven to 350°F. Spread one-fourth of the stuffing over 1 tenderloin, leaving a ½-inch border on all sides. Starting with a long side, roll up meat, jellyroll-style. Tie with kitchen string at 1½-inch intervals to hold shape. Repeat with remaining tenderloins and filling. (*Roasts can be prepared 1 day ahead; cover and refrigerate.*)

5. Melt remaining 1 tablespoon butter with oil in a large, heavy, flameproof roasting pan over medium-high heat. Add pork and brown on all sides, about 7 minutes. Remove pork from pan; do not clean pan. Place a rack in same roasting pan and set pork on rack. Mix reserved fruit-soaking liquid and remaining 3 cups broth. Pour mixture over pork. Roast until a meat thermometer inserted into center of pork registers 150°F, basting every 10 minutes with pan juices, about 35 minutes. Transfer pork to a platter and tent with aluminum foil to keep warm.

6. Strain liquid from roasting pan into a measuring cup. Add more broth, if necessary, to make 2 cups. Place roasting pan over medium-high heat. Add wine and 2 cups cooking liquid; bring to a boil, scraping up brown bits. Boil until reduced to 2 cups, about 15 minutes. Mix in apricot spread or preserves. Add cornstarch mixture and bring to a boil, stirring constantly. Taste and season with salt and pepper.

7. Remove strings from pork. Slice pork and overlap slices on a platter. Spoon some sauce over and garnish with thyme and sage sprigs, if desired. Pass remaining sauce separately.

Menu Suggestion:

Honey and Brandy Carrots (page 209) and Yukon Gold Mashed Potatoes with Buttermilk (page 212) are good accompaniments. Prince Albert Pumpkin Brownies (page 382) are a stellar ending.

Chapter 6

Great Barbecuing
and Grilling

1-2-3 Marinade *for* Chicken, Beef, Lamb *and* More

THIS MARINADE, which takes its name from its three ingredients—red wine, orange juice and soy sauce—used in equal amounts, has been in my repertoire for as long as I have been cooking. It is quick to assemble and is perfect for marinating chicken, beef, pork or lamb. It's also delicious on shrimp.

MAKES 1 CUP

★

From Start to Finish:
5 minutes
Actual Working Time:
5 minutes
Make Ahead: Yes
Can Be Frozen: No
Best Seasons: All year

FOR EVERY 1-1½ POUNDS CHICKEN,
BEEF, PORK, LAMB OR SHELLED SHRIMP

⅓ cup dry red wine
⅓ cup orange juice
⅓ cup soy sauce, preferably not
    reduced-sodium soy sauce

1. To prepare sauce, combine wine, orange juice and soy sauce in a bowl and whisk to blend.

2. Marinate meat of choice, turning occasionally to ensure even marinating, in a nonreactive dish or pan in refrigerator, using the time suggestions that follow.

Suggested Times for Marinating Individual Meats
Chicken (individual pieces or boneless breasts): 1½ to 2 hours
Beef (steaks or kabobs): 2 to 3 hours or overnight
Pork (chops or tenderloins): 6 hours or overnight
Lamb (chops, butterflied leg or shoulder, or kabobs): 6 hours or overnight
Shrimp (shelled): 1 hour

Classic Coke Texas Barbecue Sauce

MAKES 1¾ TO
2 CUPS

★

From Start to Finish:
20 minutes

Actual Working Time:
10 minutes

Make Ahead: Yes
(see step 2)

Can Be Frozen: No

Best Seasons: All year

MY GOOD FRIEND JIM BUDROS, a talented cook, was given this recipe by his Great-Aunt Dorothy, who lived in Dallas in the 1950s. She sent it to him years ago written on lined school paper. Since that time, Jim has used this sauce as a spicy glaze that he brushes on meat and chicken in the final minutes of grilling. It is best used in this way because the sugar in the sauce will burn if placed on the meat early in the cooking.

1	cup Coca-Cola (do not use Diet Coke)
1	cup ketchup
¼	cup Worcestershire sauce
¼	cup A-1 sauce
½	teaspoon onion powder
½	teaspoon garlic powder
1	tablespoon white vinegar
½	teaspoon liquid smoke (*see Shopping Notes,* **page 82**)

1. Combine all ingredients except liquid smoke in a medium, heavy saucepan over medium-high heat. Stir to mix and bring to a gentle boil. Cook until sauce has thickened slightly, 8 to 10 minutes.

2. Remove from heat, cool, and stir in liquid smoke. (*If not using immediately, cover and refrigerate. Sauce will keep for 2 weeks.*)

3. Brush on grilled chicken, pork or beef during the last 5 minutes of cooking. Pass extra sauce separately.

Ginger Barbecue Sauce

THIS BARBECUE SAUCE INCLUDES many familiar ingredients: soy sauce for a touch of saltiness, molasses for sweetness and balsamic vinegar for a hint of acid. But it is the fresh chopped ginger and garlic used in copious amounts that make it distinctive. The sauce is thin, rather than thick and syrupy like some barbecue sauces. Its robust flavors make it ideal for basting cuts of pork, such as spareribs (see page 179) and chops that are cooked slowly.

1 cup reduced-sodium soy sauce
⅔ cup molasses, preferably unsulfured
  (*see Shopping Notes*, page 18)
¼ cup balsamic vinegar
6 tablespoons chopped garlic
6 tablespoons chopped peeled gingerroot

1. To prepare sauce, combine all ingredients in a nonreactive bowl and whisk well to blend. (*Sauce can be made 1 day ahead; cover and refrigerate.*)

2. Use sauce to baste and glaze pork chops, pork tenderloins or spareribs.

MAKES ABOUT
2 CUPS

From Start to Finish:
15 minutes
Actual Working Time:
15 minutes
Make Ahead: Yes
(see step 1)
Can Be Frozen: No
Best Seasons: All year

Grilled Plum Chicken

SERVES 6

From Start to Finish:
3 hours 25 minutes
(includes 3 hours for
marinating)
Actual Working Time:
25 minutes
Make Ahead: No
Can Be Frozen: No
Best Seasons: All year

Shopping Note:
Plum sauce is a thick
blend of plums mixed with
chili and spices. Because of
its consistency and sweet,
spicy flavor, it makes a fine
barbecue sauce. It is
available in the Asian-
foods section of many
supermarkets and in Asian
grocery stores. Refrigerate
after opening.

I FIRST TASTED THIS DISH at a beautiful outdoor summer party. I asked the hostess for the recipe and learned it was the specialty of my friends Sharon Reiss and Suzanne Karpus, gifted caterers in Columbus, Ohio. Wasting no time, I called my pals to get directions. I was surprised to learn how uncomplicated this recipe was to prepare. Boneless chicken breasts are marinated overnight in balsamic vinegar, olive oil and Dijon mustard, then quickly grilled. During the last minute of grilling, Asian plum sauce is brushed on the chicken pieces, giving them a lovely caramelized glaze and a fruity, spicy flavor.

6   **boneless, skinless chicken breast halves**
    (about 6 ounces each)
3   **tablespoons balsamic vinegar**
1   **tablespoon Dijon mustard**
½   **teaspoon salt**
¼   **teaspoon freshly ground black pepper**
⅓   **cup olive oil**
6   **tablespoons plum sauce** (*see Shopping Note*)
1   **bunch green onions, cleaned, roots and all but**
    2 inches of green tops cut off on diagonal

1. Remove fat from chicken and place in a resealable plastic bag or a shallow nonreactive dish or pan. Place vinegar, mustard, salt and pepper in a mixing bowl and whisk to blend. Gradually whisk in oil. Pour mixture over chicken and marinate, covered, in refrigerator for 3 to 6 hours or overnight. Turn several times.

2. When ready to cook, arrange a rack about 5 inches from heat source, spray with nonstick cooking spray and preheat grill. When grill is hot, grill chicken, turning several times, until chicken springs back when touched with your fingers and juices run clear when chicken is pierced with a paring knife. (Watch carefully: total time should be 8 to 10 minutes but may vary depending on type of grill and intensity of heat.) Brush tops of each chicken breast with plum sauce and cook for 1 minute more.

3. To serve, arrange chicken in an overlapping pattern on a serving plate and garnish each end of platter with a cluster of green onions.

Menu Suggestion:

Wild Rice, Asparagus and Pecan Salad (page 278) and steamed green beans are good side dishes for the chicken. Serve Gingerbread Ice Cream Sandwiches (page 388) for dessert.

Grilled Chicken
with Pineapple Salsa

SERVES 8

★

From Start to Finish:
3 hours 20 minutes
(includes 2 hours for
marinating)

Actual Working Time:
1 hour 20 minutes

Make Ahead: Partially
(see step 1)

Can Be Frozen: No

Best Season: Summer

THE FRESH PINEAPPLE SALSA is what makes this grilled chicken dish so special. My friend Jim Budros shared the recipe with me. Pineapple, mango, sweet and hot peppers, plus the flavors of lime and cilantro impart an assertive yet refreshing flavor to the salsa. It is wonderful on chicken but can be used on grilled fish as well. (*See photograph, page 40.*)

Pineapple Salsa (page 189)
8 large chicken breast halves (*see Healthful Variation*)
⅓ cup fresh lime juice
⅓ cup olive oil
1 teaspoon salt
¼ teaspoon freshly ground pepper
Several fresh cilantro sprigs for garnish

1. Prepare Pineapple Salsa, and if not using immediately, cover and refrigerate. (*Salsa can be prepared 1 day ahead. Cover and refrigerate. Bring to room temperature 30 minutes before using.*)

2. Place chicken breasts in a shallow nonreactive pan large enough to hold pieces comfortably in a single layer. Combine lime juice, oil, salt and pepper in a small bowl and whisk to blend. Pour marinade over chicken and marinate in refrigerator for 2 hours or, for a more intense flavor, 6 to 8 hours, turning several times.

3. When ready to grill, arrange a rack 5 inches from heat source, spray with nonstick cooking spray and preheat grill. Cook chicken for 10 to 12 minutes per side over hot coals, until golden and crisp outside and juices run clear when chicken is pierced with a knife. (Watch carefully, as cooking times vary with intensity of heat and type of grill.)

4. Arrange chicken on serving platter. Using a slotted spoon, top each piece with some salsa and garnish with cilantro sprigs.

Healthful Variation: In place of chicken breast halves with skin and bones, you can use boneless, skinless chicken breasts. Marinate for 2 to 4 hours and grill, turning, about 8 to 10 minutes total.

Menu Suggestion:
Simple white rice sprinkled with fresh chives and steamed green beans are my suggestions for accompaniments to the chicken. Serve fresh strawberries topped with Honey-Cream Sauce (page 345) for dessert.

Grilled Salmon
with Roasted Garlic

SERVES 8

★

From Start to Finish:
1 hour

Actual Working Time:
20 minutes

Make Ahead: Partially
(see steps 2 and 3)

Can Be Frozen: No

Best Seasons: All year

Shopping Note:
A new, useful gadget
called the "E-Z-Rol" garlic
peeler removes the papery
skin from garlic cloves in
just seconds, leaving them
whole. To use it, place the
clove in the rubber tube and
roll back and forth. This
tool sells for about $7 in
specialty shops.

WHENEVER I PREPARE THIS DISH in cooking
classes, my students are surprised by how well
sweet roasted garlic complements grilled salmon.
For this dish, soft, tender roasted garlic cloves
are pureed and combined with a little butter and oil, then brushed
on the salmon before grilling.

2 **medium garlic heads**
   About ½ cup extra-virgin olive oil
3 **tablespoons unsalted butter**
   Salt and freshly ground black pepper
8 **salmon fillets (6-7 ounces each),**
   with skin left on
4 **teaspoons fresh lemon juice**
4 **teaspoons chopped fresh rosemary leaves,**
   chives or flat-leaf parsley for garnish

1. Arrange a rack at center position and preheat oven to 400°F.

2. Smash each head of garlic with your hand to break it into cloves.
Lightly smash individual cloves with the back of a large knife so that
papery coating is loosened. Peel off papery skin (*see Shopping Note*).
Place garlic in a small, ovenproof ramekin. Pour oil over top to cover
cloves completely. Cover tightly with a double thickness of aluminum
foil and bake for 20 minutes or more, until cloves are very tender and
just light golden, but not brown. (If cloves are not done after 20
minutes, check every 5 minutes until done.) Remove from oil with a
slotted spoon and place in a food processor fitted with a metal blade
or a blender with 1 tablespoon hot oil. (*Remaining garlic-flavored oil can
be saved for 1 to 2 days. Cover and refrigerate; bring to room temperature before
using. Use in salad dressings or for sautéing in place of regular olive oil.*)

3. Add butter to garlic and oil. Puree for 45 to 60 seconds. Transfer puree to a small bowl and season with salt and pepper. (*If not using immediately, cool, cover and refrigerate for up to 2 days.*)

4. Run your fingers over salmon and remove any bones with clean tweezers. Salt and pepper salmon and drizzle ½ teaspoon lemon juice over each fillet. Spread some garlic puree over top of each fillet.

5. Arrange a rack 5 inches from heat source, spray with nonstick cooking spray and preheat grill. Cook salmon until flesh flakes easily, about 10 minutes. (Watch carefully, since cooking time may vary depending on intensity of heat and type of grill.) Alternatively, you can also bake salmon. Arrange a rack in center position and preheat oven to 450°F. Bake salmon until flesh flakes easily, about 15 minutes.

6. To serve, arrange on a serving platter and sprinkle with fresh herbs and more pepper.

Menu Suggestion:
Mustard-Scented Scalloped Potatoes (page 217) and Sesame Asparagus (page 195) complement this fish. Blueberry Sour Cream Pie (page 358) can end the menu.

Grilled Swordfish *with* Tomato-Orange Sauce

SERVES 6

★

From Start to Finish:
50 minutes

Actual Working Time:
35 minutes

Make Ahead: Partially
(see step 1)

Can Be Frozen: No

Best Seasons: All year

MY FRIENDS IN MASSACHUSETTS have made me aware of how good fresh swordfish is, especially when cooked simply. In this preparation, the fish is brushed with a little olive oil and balsamic vinegar and grilled. A light tomato-orange sauce is the perfect topping.

	Tomato-Orange Sauce (page 122)
6	swordfish steaks (6-7 ounces each)
2	tablespoons balsamic vinegar
2	tablespoons olive oil
	Salt and freshly ground black pepper
1½	teaspoons chopped fresh basil leaves, plus basil sprigs for garnish

1. Prepare Tomato-Orange Sauce, and if not using immediately, cover and refrigerate. (*Sauce can be made up to 2 days ahead. Reheat, stirring, when needed.*)

2. Arrange a rack 5 inches from heat source, spray with nonstick cooking spray and preheat grill. Sprinkle fish with vinegar and brush with oil. Season lightly with salt and pepper. Grill fish for 3 to 4 minutes per side, until fish flakes easily when pierced with a knife. (Watch carefully, since cooking time will vary depending on type of grill, intensity of heat and thickness of fish.) Alternatively, you can also broil swordfish. Arrange a rack 5 to 6 inches from heat source and preheat broiler. Coat broiler pan with cooking spray and place seasoned swordfish on a rack in pan. Broil until fish flakes easily when pierced with a knife, 3 to 4 minutes per side.

3. To serve, arrange swordfish on a warm serving platter and top with warm sauce. Sprinkle with chopped basil and garnish with basil sprigs.

Variation: You can substitute salmon fillets for the swordfish. Cook salmon, skin side down, without turning, until flesh is opaque and flakes easily when pierced with a knife, about 8 minutes.

Menu Suggestion:
Simple Saffron Rice (page 225) adds a splash of color to the plate. A mixed green salad with a simple dressing and a hot crusty loaf of French bread can complete the main course. Gingerbread Ice Cream Sandwiches (page 388) are a special dessert.

Mustard *and* Pepper Flank Steaks

SERVES 6

★

From Start to Finish:
6 hours 30 minutes
(includes 6 hours for
marinating)

Actual Working Time:
30 minutes

Make Ahead: Partially
(see step 1)

Can Be Frozen: No

Best Seasons: All year

THE TESTERS FOR THIS BOOK loved this recipe because the marinade can be made the day before, the meat put in it and then left in the refrigerator overnight. They pointed out in their reviews that they came home the next evening, removed the steaks from the marinade and quickly grilled them, with excellent results. Dijon mustard, crushed black peppercorns and fresh ginger are the dominant flavors in the marinade; use a smaller amount of the peppercorns for a milder taste or a larger amount for a spicy flavor. A little soy sauce adds a salty touch, and a few tablespoons of cream contribute sweetness.

⅔ cup Dijon mustard
¼ cup soy sauce
2 tablespoons whipping cream
2 teaspoons dried thyme leaves
2 teaspoons chopped peeled gingerroot
1-1½ teaspoons coarsely crushed black peppercorns
2 flank steaks (about 1¼ pounds each)
1 small bunch watercress, cleaned and dried, for garnish

1. Combine mustard, soy sauce, cream, thyme, ginger and peppercorns in a small mixing bowl and stir well to mix thoroughly. Brush both sides of flank steaks with mustard mixture, coating generously. Place steaks on a plate and cover loosely with plastic wrap. Marinate for 6 hours or, even better, overnight. Refrigerate while marinating, but bring to room temperature 1 hour before grilling.

2. When ready to cook steaks, arrange a rack 5 inches from heat source, spray rack with nonstick cooking spray and preheat grill. When hot, place flank steaks on grill and cook for 6 to 8 minutes per side. Check meat by making a small incision in the thickest part. Meat should be medium-rare when done. (Watch carefully, since cooking times will vary depending on thickness of steaks and type of grill. Flank steak is best cooked medium-rare, or pink inside.) Alternatively, broil steaks 4 to 5 inches from heat for about 6 minutes per side.

3. Remove steaks from grill and slice on diagonal and against the grain into ¼-to-⅜-inch-thick slices. Arrange meat in overlapping layers on a serving plate. Garnish platter with several clusters of watercress.

Menu Suggestion:

Mashed Potatoes with Goat Cheese and Fresh Herbs (page 200), a plate of sliced tomatoes, and zucchini sautéed in a little olive oil can be served with the steaks. Lemon Cheesecake (page 376), mounded with fresh strawberries and blueberries instead of the cranberry topping, makes a refreshing conclusion.

Grilled Sirloin Steaks
with Blue Cheese-Walnut Relish

SERVES 6

From Start to Finish:
35 minutes

Actual Working Time:
35 minutes

Make Ahead: Partially
(see step 1)

Can Be Frozen: No

Best Seasons: All year

THE UNUSUAL RELISH, made with crumbled blue cheese, chopped walnuts and seasonings of lemon, green onions and parsley, is what makes these grilled steaks different. The relish is added while the steaks are piping hot so that the cheese just starts to melt as you serve them.

6	ounces best-quality blue cheese, preferably Roquefort, crumbled
3	tablespoons chopped walnuts
3	tablespoons chopped green onions, including 2 inches of green tops
2	tablespoons chopped fresh flat-leaf parsley
1½	teaspoons grated lemon zest (yellow portion of rind)
2½-3	pounds best-quality boneless sirloin or strip steaks, cut ½-¾ inch thick, trimmed of all excess fat
1½	teaspoons dried thyme leaves
2¼	teaspoons salt
2¼	teaspoons freshly ground black pepper

1. Place cheese, walnuts, green onions, parsley and lemon zest in a bowl and mix well. Set aside. (*Blue cheese relish can be made 1 day ahead. Cover and refrigerate; bring to room temperature 30 minutes before serving.*)

2. Place meat on a work surface. Combine thyme, salt and pepper in a small bowl and mix well. Rub both sides of meat with mixture. Set aside.

3. When ready to cook steaks, arrange a rack 5 inches from heat source, spray rack with nonstick cooking spray and preheat grill. Grill steaks until medium-rare, about 3 to 5 minutes per side. (Watch carefully, since cooking time will vary depending on thickness of meat and intensity of heat.) Alternatively, broil steaks 4 to 5 inches from heat for 3 to 5 minutes per side.

4. Remove and arrange steaks on a warm serving plate. Cut steaks into 6 serving portions and top each serving with a generous tablespoon or more of relish.

Menu Suggestion:

Summer Corn and Tomato Pudding (page 202) and fresh green beans sautéed with chopped garlic in olive oil are great side dishes. A bowl of fresh strawberries, blueberries and raspberries served with Honey-Cream Sauce (page 345) can follow the main course.

Michael's Grilled Rosemary Steaks

SERVES 6

From Start to Finish:
2 hours 20 minutes
(includes 2 hours for
marinating)
Actual Working Time:
20 minutes
Make Ahead: No
Can Be Frozen: No
Best Seasons:
All year, but especially
summer

Menu Suggestion:
Potato and Sweet Red
Pepper Gratin (page 220)
and zucchini and yellow
squash sautéed in olive oil
are good dishes to serve
with the steaks. Slices of
store-bought pound cake,
topped with scoops of
vanilla ice cream or frozen
yogurt and garnished with
fresh sliced peaches and
blueberries, are an easy
dessert.

Y SON MICHAEL, who fancies himself a cook in only two areas, grilled dishes and breakfast fare, thought of studding sirloin steaks with fresh rosemary. The succulent steaks, marinated in garlic and lemon juice, are seasoned subtly with the flavor of the herb.

2   boneless sirloin steaks (each about 1½ pounds
    and ¾ inch thick), trimmed of all excess fat
1   small bunch fresh rosemary
6   medium garlic cloves, peeled and smashed
1   teaspoon salt
½   teaspoon freshly ground black pepper
2   tablespoons lemon juice
6   tablespoons extra-virgin olive oil

1. With a sharp paring knife, make small slits about every inch over both surfaces of steaks. Remove leaves from 2 or 3 rosemary sprigs and insert 1 to 2 leaves into each slit.

2. Place steaks in a shallow nonreactive pan that will hold them in a single layer. Combine garlic, salt, pepper and lemon juice in a small bowl and mix well. Stir in oil and pour over meat. Cover with plastic wrap and marinate for 2 to 6 hours or overnight, turning several times.

3. To cook meat, remove from marinade. Arrange a rack 5 inches from heat source, spray rack with nonstick cooking spray and preheat grill. When grill is ready, cook steaks until medium-rare, 3 to 5 minutes per side. (Watch carefully, since cooking times will vary with type of grill and intensity of heat.) Alternatively, broil steaks 4 to 5 inches from heat for 3 to 5 minutes per side.

4. To serve, place steaks on a warm serving plate and garnish with a cluster of remaining rosemary sprigs. Cut each steak into 3 portions.

California Lamb Chops

ALTHOUGH I DIDN'T DISCOVER THE RECIPE for these lamb chops in the Golden State, I gave them this name because the ingredients are reminiscent of California cuisine, which has taught us to grill all kinds of food. In this recipe, red bell peppers and dried figs are skewered and grilled along with lamb chops. Served with bright golden-hued saffron rice, the chops, peppers and figs add vibrant colors to any table.

SERVES 6

From Start to Finish:
2 hours 50 minutes (includes 2 hours for marinating)
Actual Working Time:
50 minutes
Make Ahead: No
Can Be Frozen: No
Best Seasons:
All year, especially summer

Shopping Note:
Mission (or Black Mission) figs are purple-black in color and have extremely small seeds. They are available dried in most supermarkets.

    1   cup dry red wine
    ⅓   cup olive oil
    3   large garlic cloves, peeled and crushed
    3   bay leaves, broken in half
    ½   teaspoon ground cumin
    ½   teaspoon whole black peppercorns, coarsely crushed
    ½   teaspoon salt
   12   lamb loin chops (about 4-6 ounces each),
          cut 1 inch thick, trimmed of excess fat
   24   dried Mission figs (7-8 ounces; *see Shopping Note*)
    3   red bell peppers, stems, seeds and membranes
          removed, cut into strips ½ inch wide
          by 2-3 inches long

1. Combine wine, oil, garlic, bay leaves, cumin, peppercorns and salt in a bowl and mix well. Reserve ⅓ cup marinade; cover and refrigerate. Arrange lamb chops in a shallow nonreactive dish and pour remaining marinade over them. Cover and marinate in refrigerator for 2 to 6 hours or overnight.

2. About 1 hour before cooking, remove lamb from marinade and bring to room temperature. Remove reserved ⅓ cup marinade from refrigerator. Place figs in a pan of boiling water to cover and boil gently until softened, about 10 minutes. Drain figs and place in a bowl with reserved marinade; add red pepper. Marinate figs and peppers for 30 to 45 minutes.

Menu Suggestion:

Simple Saffron Rice (page 225) and Spinach Salad with Brown Mushrooms in Lemon-Garlic Dressing (page 250) are ideal dishes to accompany the lamb. A bowl of fresh sliced apricots topped with Honey-Cream Sauce (page 345) and sprinkled with toasted almond slices is a quick and refreshing dessert choice.

3. When ready to cook lamb, arrange a rack 5 inches from heat source, spray with nonstick cooking spray and preheat grill. When grill is hot, place figs and peppers on separate metal skewers. Arrange lamb chops, figs and peppers on grill and cook until done. Lamb is best cooked until just pink inside. Chops will take 4 to 5 minutes per side, but watch carefully, since times may vary depending on type of grill and intensity of heat. Figs and peppers should be turned several times and grilled until they are hot and just lightly charred on the outside, 6 to 8 minutes total. (Alternatively, lamb, figs and peppers can be broiled. Arrange a rack 4 to 5 inches from heat source and preheat broiler. Arrange chops, figs and peppers on a rack in a roasting pan and broil for 4 to 5 minutes per side for chops, 6 to 8 minutes total for figs and peppers, turning several times.)

4. To serve, place lamb chops on a warm serving plate. Arrange a border of grilled figs and peppers around chops.

Variation: Twelve rib chops can be substituted for the loin chops. Rib chops are not as meaty, so 12 rib chops serve 4, rather than 6.

Mahogany Spareribs

THESE BARBECUED RIBS are baked, rather than grilled. Coated with ginger- and garlic-flavored barbecue sauce, they are baked until tender, juicy and a rich dark mahogany brown. The sweet aroma of the ribs roasting makes them irresistible even before they come out of the oven.

Ginger Barbecue Sauce (page 163)
6 pounds pork ribs, preferably baby back ribs (*see Shopping Note*), trimmed of excess fat
5-6 tablespoons balsamic vinegar
Salt and freshly ground black pepper
Cayenne pepper
1 bunch green onions, roots and all but 2 inches of green tops trimmed, for garnish (*optional*)

1. Prepare Ginger Barbecue Sauce. (*Sauce can be made 1 day ahead; cover and refrigerate.*)

2. Drop ribs in boiling water to cover and blanch for 4 minutes. Remove and pat dry. Score white membrane on undersides with a knife. Place ribs on a rack in a large roasting pan. (Or use 2 racks and pans.) Brush ribs generously on both sides with balsamic vinegar. Season on both sides lightly with salt and pepper and more generously with cayenne. Let rest for 15 minutes.

3. About 10 minutes before baking ribs, preheat oven to 325°F.

4. Reserve ¾ cup Ginger Barbecue Sauce for glaze and set aside. Brush ribs generously on both sides with about one-third of remaining sauce. Place ribs in oven and bake, basting every 30 minutes with remaining sauce, until they are a rich dark brown and are tender when pierced with a knife, about 1½ hours. When done, remove and mound on a serving tray. Place reserved sauce in a heavy saucepan over medium-high heat. Cook, stirring, until sauce is reduced and has a syrup-like consistency, 3 to 4 minutes. Remove from heat and brush ribs with glaze. Garnish with green onions, if desired.

SERVES 6

From Start to Finish:
2 hours 15 minutes (includes 1½ hours for baking ribs)
Actual Working Time:
45 minutes, plus basting every 30 minutes
Make Ahead: Partially (see step 1)
Can Be Frozen: No
Best Seasons: All year

Shopping Note:
Baby back ribs are cut from the loin (rear) section of the pig, rather than from the breast, as are standard spareribs. Baby back ribs are shorter and easier to handle, but ordinary spareribs can be used interchangeably.

Menu Suggestion:
Serve with Fresh Cole Slaw with Fennel Seed Dressing (page 248), sliced summer tomatoes with fresh chives and/or corn on the cob. For dessert, try Blueberry Sour Cream Pie (page 358) or Caramel Peach Pie (page 356).

Chilied Ribs

SERVES 8 TO 10

From Start to Finish:
5 hours 25 minutes
(includes 2 hours for
marinating and 2 hours for
roasting ribs)
Actual Working Time:
40 minutes
Make Ahead: Partially
(see step 1)
Can Be Frozen: No
Best Seasons: All year

THE BARBECUE SAUCE, with its blend of sweet and hot flavors, gives these ribs a sensational spicy finish. Like the ribs in the preceding recipe, they are baked until succulent and tender. (*See photograph, page 38.*)

FOR SAUCE

4 teaspoons olive oil
1 cup minced onions
1½ cups water
1 cup ketchup
⅔ cup packed light brown sugar
⅔ cup cider vinegar
¼ cup molasses, preferably unsulfured
(*see Shopping Notes,* page 18)
2 tablespoons Worcestershire sauce
2 tablespoons instant coffee granules
2 teaspoons bottled yellow mustard
2 teaspoons chili powder
1 teaspoon ground cumin
¼ teaspoon ground cinnamon
¼ teaspoon cayenne pepper

FOR RIBS

6 slabs baby back pork ribs (about 9 pounds
total weight; *see Shopping Note,* page 179)
½ cup cider vinegar
4 teaspoons liquid smoke (*see Shopping Notes,* page 82)
6 tablespoons chili powder
3 tablespoons ground cumin
1 tablespoon packed light brown sugar
1½ teaspoons onion powder
¼ teaspoon cayenne pepper
Salt and freshly ground black pepper

1. **To prepare sauce:** Place oil in a heavy, medium saucepan over medium heat. When hot, add onions and sauté until translucent, about 5 minutes. Whisk in remaining ingredients. Bring to a boil. Reduce heat; simmer, stirring occasionally, until reduced to approximately 3 cups, about 30 minutes. Remove from heat. (*Sauce can be prepared 1 week ahead; cool, cover and refrigerate. Bring to room temperature before using.*)

2. **To prepare ribs:** Score white membrane on underside of ribs with a knife. Combine vinegar and liquid smoke in a small bowl and brush on both sides of ribs. Cover with plastic wrap and let marinate in refrigerator for 2 hours.

3. When ready to cook ribs, preheat oven to 350°F. Mix together chili powder, cumin, brown sugar, onion powder and cayenne and blend well. Rub mixture evenly on both sides of each slab of ribs. Season with salt and pepper.

4. Use 2 shallow baking pans and place a rack in each. Place ribs, meaty side up, on rack. Roast for 1¾ hours and cover loosely with aluminum foil if they start to brown too quickly.

5. Brush liberally with sauce and return to oven for 10 to 15 minutes. Remove from oven. Cover ribs loosely with foil and let rest for 15 minutes.

6. To serve, cut each slab into 3 or 4 rib sections. Mound ribs on a large serving plate or a wooden board. Pass extra sauce separately.

Menu Suggestion:

Pinto Beans with Tortilla Cheese Crust (page 236) and Mexican Layered Salad with Cumin-Honey Dressing (page 252) have just the right flavors to complement the ribs. Margarita Cheesecake (page 378) makes a striking finale.

Chapter 7

A Pantry *of* Practical Relishes, Chutneys, Salsas *and* Sauces

Dried Cranberry *and* Apple Relish

TALENTED CHEF JONATHAN MAROHN, who owns Sienna, a superb restaurant in South Deerfield, Massachusetts, offered this unusual relish with roast duck one fall evening. When I asked how it was made, he invited me out to his kitchen to see firsthand how easy and quick it was to assemble. In only a few minutes, he sautéed together diced apples, red onion and dried cranberries, then seasoned the mixture lightly with lemon and vinegar. The relish is good with any poultry and with baked ham and roast pork.

MAKES 1½ CUPS

★

From Start to Finish:
35 minutes

Actual Working Time:
35 minutes

Make Ahead: Yes
(see step 2)

Can Be Frozen: No

Best Seasons:
Fall and winter

Shopping Note:
Dried cranberries are available in specialty-food stores, in some health-food shops and in some supermarkets.

¾ cup boiling water
½ cup dried cranberries (*see Shopping Note*)
1 tablespoon unsalted butter
4 teaspoons sugar
1½ cups diced unpeeled tart apples,
   such as Granny Smith (¼-inch dice)
3 tablespoons chopped red onion
3 tablespoons chopped red bell pepper
2 teaspoons fresh lemon juice
2 teaspoons red wine vinegar
   Salt
3 tablespoons minced green onion tops

1. Combine water and cranberries in a small bowl and let stand until cranberries are softened, about 5 minutes. Drain and pat dry.

2. Melt butter in a medium, heavy skillet over medium-high heat. Add sugar and stir until it dissolves, about 1 minute. Stir in apples and cook until they begin to brown lightly and juices evaporate, about 4 minutes. Add red onion and red pepper and sauté until just tender, about 2 minutes. Mix in cranberries, lemon juice and vinegar; simmer for 1 minute more. Season with salt. Transfer to a bowl and cool. Stir in green onions. (*Relish can be made 2 days ahead; cover and refrigerate.*)

3. Serve at room temperature.

Spiced Cranberries

MAKES ABOUT
4 CUPS

★

From Start to Finish:
20 minutes

Actual Working Time:
5 minutes

Make Ahead: Yes
(see step 1)

Can Be Frozen: No

Best Seasons:
Fall and winter

Shopping Note:

Cardamom has a pungent aroma and a slightly sweet taste. The seeds are enclosed in small pods about the size of a cranberry. When crushed or ground just before using, they have a more intense flavor than commercially ground cardamom. Crush the pods and seeds with a mortar and pestle, or place them in a small plastic bag and pound them with a meat pounder or rolling pin. If you have a small electric coffee or spice grinder, grind them in that. If you can't find cardamom pods, substitute ground cardamom.

ERE'S A NEW TWIST ON A CLASSIC holiday condiment. Freshly grated nutmeg, crushed cardamom and ground allspice add new flavorings to this favorite standby.

2	cups sugar
¾	cup water
4	cups fresh cranberries, washed and picked over
1	teaspoon freshly grated nutmeg
½	teaspoon crushed cardamom pods and seeds (*see Shopping Note*)
½	teaspoon ground allspice

1. Cook sugar and water in medium, heavy saucepan over medium heat, stirring until sugar dissolves. Increase heat to medium-high and bring to a boil. Add cranberries, nutmeg, cardamom and allspice. Cook until cranberries pop, about 10 minutes. (*Cranberries can be prepared 2 days ahead; cover and refrigerate.*)

2. Serve at room temperature.

Honeyed Cranberry Sauce

THE SWEET TASTE OF HONEY COMBINES ADMIRABLY with the tart flavor of cranberries in this sauce. In addition to cinnamon and coriander, unexpected seasonings, such as black and cayenne pepper and bay leaf, spice things up further.

1¾ cups cranberry juice (*divided*)
¾ cup honey
1 tablespoon grated orange zest
 (orange portion of rind)
2 whole cloves
1 stick cinnamon
1 bay leaf, broken in half
¾ teaspoon ground coriander
½ teaspoon salt (kosher, if possible)
½ teaspoon freshly ground black pepper
 Scant ⅛ teaspoon cayenne pepper
1 ⅛-inch-thick nickel-sized piece peeled
 gingerroot, chopped
12 ounces fresh cranberries, washed and picked over

MAKES 2½
TO 3 CUPS

From Start to Finish:
35 minutes
Actual Working Time:
20 minutes
Make Ahead: Yes
(see step 2)
Can Be Frozen: No
Best Seasons:
Fall and winter

1. Place 1½ cups cranberry juice, honey and orange zest in a medium, heavy saucepan over medium heat. Bring to a simmer and cook for 3 to 4 minutes. Add cloves, cinnamon stick, bay leaf pieces, coriander, salt, black and cayenne pepper and ginger. Simmer mixture for 2 to 3 minutes; add cranberries. Simmer until cranberries pop and sauce is thick, 10 to 15 minutes.

2. Remove from heat and stir in remaining ¼ cup cranberry juice. (*Sauce can be made 4 to 5 days ahead; cool, cover and refrigerate.*)

3. To serve, bring to room temperature. If desired, remove bay leaves and cinnamon stick and place in a clear glass bowl.

Spicy Corn Relish

MAKES ABOUT
3 CUPS

★

From Start to Finish:
1 hour 10 minutes

Actual Working Time:
35 minutes

Make Ahead: Yes
(see step 1)

Can Be Frozen: No

Best Season: Summer

THIS RELISH, BRIGHTLY COLORED with flecks of yellow corn and red bell pepper, is seasoned with green chilies, mustard and garlic. It will keep up to five days in the refrigerator and can be used with hamburgers, grilled chicken or as a dip offered with hot corn-bread slices or tortilla chips.

2 cups fresh corn (about 4 ears, scraped well)
   or frozen kernels, defrosted and patted dry
1 cup chopped red onions
1 cup chopped red bell peppers
1 4-ounce can drained, chopped mild green chilies
½ cup finely chopped celery
1 cup cider vinegar
6 tablespoons light brown sugar
2 tablespoons dry mustard (preferably Colman's)
¾ tablespoon kosher salt
¾ tablespoon mustard seeds
2 teaspoons finely chopped garlic

1. Mix all ingredients in a large, heavy saucepan over medium-high heat. Bring slowly to a boil. Lower heat to a simmer and cook, uncovered, until almost all liquid has evaporated, 30 to 40 minutes; watch carefully. If you taste relish while it is still warm, flavor may seem extremely sharp or acid. Do not worry: cooled relish will become milder. Transfer to a serving bowl. (*Relish can be made 4 to 5 days ahead; cover and refrigerate.*)

2. Serve at room temperature.

Fall Fruit Chutney

THIS RICH CHUTNEY, with its sweet, tart taste, showcases three fall fruits: pears, apples and cranberries. It is perfect with roast pork or as a spread for smoked turkey sandwiches. You can also serve it as an appetizer mounded on toasted croutons topped with thinly sliced Cheddar cheese.

MAKES ABOUT
3 CUPS

From Start to Finish:
1 hour 40 minutes
Actual Working Time:
25 minutes
Make Ahead: Yes
(see step 2)
Can Be Frozen: No
Best Season: Fall

1 cup cider vinegar
¼ cup water
½ medium onion, finely chopped
½ tablespoon ground ginger
1 teaspoon grated orange zest
   (orange portion of rind)
¾ teaspoon salt
¼ teaspoon ground cinnamon
⅛ teaspoon crushed red pepper flakes
1 small garlic clove, minced
1½ cups firmly packed light brown sugar
1 small Bartlett pear, cored and diced
   (about ½-inch dice)
1 small Granny Smith apple, cored and diced
   (about ½-inch dice)
1 cup fresh cranberries, washed and picked over
¼ cup dried currants

1. Combine vinegar, water, onion, ginger, orange zest, salt, cinnamon, red pepper flakes and garlic in a medium, heavy saucepan over medium-high heat. Bring to a boil, stirring frequently. Reduce heat to low and cook for 15 minutes, stirring occasionally.

2. Add brown sugar, pear, apple, cranberries and currants and stir until sugar dissolves. Cook until fruits are soft and liquid thickens slightly, stirring occasionally, about 1 hour. Cool to room temperature. Chutney will thicken as it cools. (*Chutney can be prepared 4 days ahead. Cover and refrigerate.*)

3. Serve at room temperature.

Lemon-Apricot Chutney

MAKES 2 CUPS

★

From Start to Finish:
1 hour 10 minutes

Actual Working Time:
25 minutes

Make Ahead: Yes
(see step 3)

Can Be Frozen: No

Best Seasons: All year

THIS CHUTNEY is a glistening combination of dried apricots, tart apples and fresh lemon. The sweet fruits are balanced with the tangy flavor of lemon, chopped whole with its rind. The chutney makes a delicious topping for a ham and cream cheese sandwich. Try it with grilled lamb chops or as an accompaniment to baked ham.

1	medium lemon with firm rind
2	small Granny Smith apples (about ¾ pound total)
6	ounces dried apricots, cut into small pieces
⅔	cup golden raisins
⅓	cup coarsely chopped shallots
1	cup light brown sugar
⅔	cup cider vinegar
2½	teaspoons minced garlic
½	teaspoon ground ginger
¼	teaspoon ground cinnamon
¼	teaspoon chili powder
⅛	teaspoon salt
	Pinch ground coriander
	Pinch ground cloves
	Pinch freshly ground black pepper
	Pinch crushed red pepper flakes

1. Cut ends from lemon and discard. Cut lemon into 8 wedges, discarding seeds. Very thinly slice each wedge crosswise so that you have small lemon pieces. Place in a large, heavy saucepan.

2. Peel and core apples; cut into small dice. Add to saucepan.

3. Add all remaining ingredients and place over very low heat. Cook until mixture is quite thick, 30 to 40 minutes. Stir frequently to prevent burning. When chutney is done, remove and cool. (*Chutney can be made 4 to 5 days ahead; cover and refrigerate.*)

4. Bring to room temperature before serving.

Pineapple Salsa

I LIKE THE BRIGHT, REFRESHING TASTE of this salsa, which includes fresh diced pineapple and mango, as well as both sweet and hot peppers. It is delicious on grilled chicken (see page 166) or on grilled fish.

1   1¼-pound peeled fresh pineapple, core removed,
      cut into ½-inch dice (*see Shopping Notes*)
1   mango, peeled, pitted and cut into
      ½-inch dice (*see Shopping Notes*)
1   red bell pepper, seeds and membranes
      removed, cut into ¼-inch dice
1   green bell pepper, seeds and membranes
      removed, cut into ¼-inch dice
1   jalapeño pepper, stems and seeds removed,
      finely chopped (*see Cooking Technique*, page 78)
1   bunch green onions (white part and
      2 inches of green tops), finely chopped
3   medium garlic cloves, finely chopped
¼   cup chopped fresh cilantro
½   cup fresh lime juice
¼   cup honey

1. Combine pineapple, mango, peppers, green onions, garlic and cilantro in a medium nonreactive mixing bowl. Stir to combine. Add lime juice and honey and mix well to blend. (*Salsa can be prepared 1 day ahead. Cover and refrigerate.*)

2. Bring to room temperature 30 minutes before serving.

MAKES 1½ TO
2 CUPS

From Start to Finish:
45 minutes
Actual Working Time:
45 minutes
Make Ahead: Yes
(see step 1)
Can Be Frozen: No
Best Seasons:
Spring and summer

Shopping Notes:
If available, fresh peeled pineapple packaged in plastic containers will save time. Look for it in the supermarket produce department.

Mangoes are oblong in shape and, when ripe, have a yellow skin blushed with red. The soft, juicy flesh is a bright orange color and tastes sweet and tart. To remove the large seed inside, use a sharp knife and carve away the flesh. Mangoes are in season from May to September and can be found in the produce section of many supermarkets.

Tomato-Lime Salsa

MAKES ABOUT
1½ CUPS

★

From Start to Finish:
50 minutes

Actual Working Time:
20 minutes

Make Ahead: Yes
(see step 1)

Can Be Frozen: No

Best Seasons:
All year, especially
summer

TOMATOES, CUCUMBERS, JALAPEÑO PEPPERS, lime, cilantro and mint are a winning combination. This fresh salsa takes only a few minutes to assemble and adds a burst of flavor and color to grilled chicken or fish dishes. It is particularly good with broiled swordfish (see page 127).

1   cup seeded and finely chopped tomatoes,
     preferably plum or Roma
⅓   cup peeled, seeded and finely chopped cucumber
1   tablespoon finely chopped and seeded jalapeño
     pepper (*see Cooking Technique*, page 78)
1   tablespoon grated lime zest
     (green portion of rind)
1   tablespoon fresh lime juice
2   teaspoons finely chopped garlic
3   tablespoons chopped fresh cilantro
1½ tablespoons chopped fresh mint
¼   teaspoon salt, plus more if needed
¼   teaspoon freshly ground black pepper,
     plus more if needed

1. Place all ingredients in a glass or ceramic bowl and mix well. Let stand for 30 minutes. Taste and add more salt and pepper, if needed. (*Salsa can be made 1 day ahead; cover and refrigerate.*)

2. Drain salsa well and serve at room temperature.

Apricot-Rosemary Mayonnaise

MADE WITH store-bought reduced-fat mayonnaise and seasoned with apricot spread, Dijon mustard and fresh rosemary, this quick sauce is a wonderful accompaniment to shellfish, especially lobster (see page 115). It could also be used as a spread for roast chicken or turkey sandwiches.

**MAKES ABOUT
1¼ CUPS**

From Start to Finish:
5 minutes

Actual Working Time:
5 minutes

Make Ahead: Yes
(see step 1)

Can Be Frozen: No

Best Seasons: All year

Shopping Note:
Fresh rosemary is important in this recipe; the dried does not work as well.

 1   cup reduced-fat mayonnaise
     (*see Shopping Notes*, page 12)
 3   tablespoons apricot fruit spread
     (*see Shopping Notes*, page 158)
 3½ teaspoons chopped fresh rosemary leaves
     (*see Shopping Note*)
 2   teaspoons Dijon mustard
 ¾   teaspoon grated lemon zest
     (yellow portion of rind)
 ½   teaspoon fresh lemon juice

1. Combine all ingredients in a small nonreactive mixing bowl. Mix to blend. (*Sauce can be prepared 1 day ahead; cover and refrigerate.*)

2. Serve cold.

Mustard-Maple Mayonnaise

From Start to Finish:
5 minutes

Actual Working Time:
5 minutes

Make Ahead: Yes
(see step 1)

Can Be Frozen: No

Best Seasons: All year

THIS QUICK SAUCE TAKES ONLY FIVE MINUTES to assemble and has a lively taste. Whole-grain Dijon mustard, horseradish and a little maple syrup are mixed with store-bought reduced-fat mayonnaise. I make chicken salad with sliced apples, celery and pecans with this sauce, and it is equally good served with grilled salmon or on ham or turkey sandwiches.

1 cup reduced-fat mayonnaise
(*see Shopping Notes,* page 12)
¼ cup whole-grain Dijon mustard (with seeds)
¼ cup pure maple syrup
2 teaspoons prepared horseradish

1. Combine mayonnaise, mustard, maple syrup and horseradish in a small bowl and whisk well to blend. (*Dressing can be prepared 1 day ahead. Cover and refrigerate until needed.*)

2. Serve cold.

Horseradish Sauce *with* Grated Apple

GRATED APPLE AND CRUSHED CARAWAY SEEDS flavor this horseradish sauce. I like to serve the sauce with corned beef sandwiches (see page 340). It is also good on roast beef sandwiches or with grilled smoked sausages, such as kielbasa.

- ½ cup reduced-fat sour cream
- ¼ cup prepared horseradish
- ⅓ cup grated peeled Granny Smith apple
- ½ teaspoon crushed caraway seeds
  (*see Cooking Technique,* page 238)

MAKES ¾ CUP

From Start to Finish:
  10 minutes
Actual Working Time:
  10 minutes
Make Ahead: Yes
  (see step 1)
Can Be Frozen: No
Best Seasons: All year

1. To prepare dressing, place all ingredients in a small mixing bowl and mix well to blend. If not using immediately, cover and refrigerate. (*Sauce can be prepared 2 days ahead.*)

2. Serve cold or use as a spread for sandwiches.

Chapter 8

Fresh Vegetables *for* Every Season

Sesame Asparagus

THE NEXT TOWN WEST of where I live in Massachusetts is Hadley, known in our area as the asparagus capital of the U.S. because of its large crops of that vegetable. Everyone looks forward to the appearance of the first harvest, around the third week in May. This simple recipe, in which cooked asparagus spears are tossed in rice vinegar and sesame oil and garnished with toasted sesame seeds and orange zest, is perfect for when the first bundles of this vegetable appear.

3 teaspoons rice wine vinegar, plus more if needed
  (*see Shopping Notes*, page 266)

4 tablespoons dark Asian sesame oil
  Salt

2¼ pounds medium asparagus spears,
  tough ends trimmed and discarded

2 tablespoons toasted sesame seeds
  (*see Cooking Technique*)

2½ tablespoons grated orange zest
  (orange portion of rind)

1. Mix vinegar and sesame oil in a small glass or other nonreactive bowl and set aside.

2. Bring 4 quarts water to a boil in a large, deep-sided skillet or a large saucepan. Add 1 tablespoon salt and asparagus. Cook until asparagus spears are just tender, 3 to 4 minutes. Time will vary depending on thickness of spears. When done, remove asparagus and drain well in a colander. Pat dry with a clean kitchen towel.

3. Transfer warm asparagus to a large bowl and toss well with vinegar-oil mixture. Taste asparagus and, if needed, add more salt and/or a little extra rice vinegar. Arrange spears on a serving plate and sprinkle with toasted sesame seeds and orange zest. Serve warm.

SERVES 6

From Start to Finish:
40 minutes

Actual Working Time:
40 minutes

Make Ahead: No

Can Be Frozen: No

Best Season: Spring

Menu Suggestion:
This dish is good with grilled lamb chops, roast chicken or baked ham.

Cooking Technique:
To toast sesame seeds, place seeds in a heavy skillet set over medium-high heat. Shake pan back and forth until seeds are light golden, 3 to 4 minutes. Remove from heat and cool.

Double Asparagus Gratin

SERVES 8

★

From Start to Finish:
1 hour 30 minutes
Actual Working Time:
45 minutes
Make Ahead: Partially
(see steps 2 and 4)
Can Be Frozen: No
Best Season: Spring

THIS IS AN ATTRACTIVE ASPARAGUS DISH that can be completely assembled ahead and baked just before serving. My friend Tom Johnson, an Ohio-based chef and wine specialist, shared the recipe with me. Fresh asparagus pieces are cooked with rice in chicken broth, then pureed and enriched with eggs and half-and-half. The asparagus gratin is baked and garnished with asparagus tips and a dusting of Parmesan cheese.

2 pounds asparagus, preferably medium stalks
5 cups chicken broth
1 cup long-grain rice
2 large eggs plus 4 egg whites
1⅓ cups half-and-half
½ teaspoon salt, plus more if needed
Generous grinding freshly ground black pepper
¼ teaspoon freshly grated nutmeg
2 tablespoons freshly grated imported
Parmesan cheese

1. Cut off and discard tough ends of asparagus spears. Cut off tips along with 1 inch of stalk and set aside. Cut remaining stalks into 1-inch pieces and set aside.

2. Bring broth to a simmer in a large, heavy saucepan over medium heat. When broth is simmering, add asparagus tips and cook until just tender, 2 to 3 minutes. With broth still simmering, remove asparagus tips, place in a colander and rinse under cold running water. Pat dry and set aside. (*Tips can be prepared early in the day and kept loosely covered at cool room temperature.*)

3. Add remaining asparagus pieces and rice to simmering broth and cook until rice is tender, 20 to 25 minutes. Drain well, discarding excess broth. Puree mixture in a food processor fitted with a metal blade, a food mill or a blender, then transfer to a mixing bowl. Let cool slightly. Stir in eggs, egg whites, half-and-half, ½ teaspoon salt, pepper and nutmeg. Taste and adjust seasonings, if necessary.

4. Spray a 3-quart oven-to-table baking dish with nonstick cooking spray. Turn pureed mixture into dish and smooth with a spatula. (*Dish can be prepared 2 to 3 hours ahead and kept covered and refrigerated.*)

5. When ready to bake gratin, arrange a rack at center position and preheat oven to 375°F.

6. Bake gratin until set and slightly puffed, about 35 minutes. Spread asparagus tips on top of gratin. Sprinkle with Parmesan. Serve warm.

Menu Suggestion:

This is a nice dish to serve with Salmon Fillets with Ginger and Pepper Butter (page 128) or Striped Bass with Country-Mustard Chive Butter (page 132).

New Potatoes Baked *with* Bay Leaves *and* Lemon

SERVES 8

From Start to Finish:
1 hour 5 minutes
Actual Working Time:
20 minutes, plus turning potatoes every 10 minutes
Make Ahead: No
Can Be Frozen: No
Best Seasons: All year

THIS QUICK AND EASY POTATO DISH goes equally well with roast chicken, broiled lamb chops or grilled steaks. The potatoes are tossed in lemon juice and olive oil and baked with many bay leaves nestled among them. The bay leaves are removed before serving but leave behind their enticing aroma and flavor.

2	pounds scrubbed, unpeeled small red-skin potatoes (preferably 1½-2 inches in diameter), quartered
¼	cup plus 2 tablespoons fresh lemon juice
1½	teaspoons dried oregano leaves, crumbled
1	teaspoon grated lemon zest (yellow portion of rind)
1	teaspoon salt, plus more if needed
¼	teaspoon freshly ground black pepper, plus more if needed
¼	cup chicken broth
¼	cup extra-virgin olive oil
20	small bay leaves (use bay leaves 2-2½ inches long or cut larger bay leaves in half)

1. Arrange a rack at center position and preheat oven to 375°F. Spray a large, shallow baking dish with nonstick cooking spray and add potatoes to dish.

2. Mix lemon juice, oregano, lemon zest, salt, pepper and broth in a bowl. Whisk in oil. Pour over potatoes; toss well. Tuck bay leaves around potatoes.

3. Bake, turning potatoes every 10 minutes, until potatoes are golden brown and knife pierces centers easily, about 45 minutes. Discard bay leaves. Adjust seasonings and serve.

Sugar Snap Peas
with Prosciutto *and* Mint

MANY VEGETABLES IN OUR MARKETPLACE seem to know no season today, but where I live, crunchy, bright green sugar snap peas appear on the shelves only in the spring. I look forward to their arrival and like cooking them with little bits of prosciutto and fresh mint. (*See photograph, page 45.*)

SERVES 4

From Start to Finish:
25 minutes
Actual Working Time:
25 minutes
Make Ahead: Partially
(see step 1)
Can Be Frozen: No
Best Seasons:
Spring and early summer

1 pound sugar snap peas, ends trimmed
   Salt
2½ tablespoons olive oil
2½ ounces prosciutto sliced ⅛ inch thick,
   all fat removed and slices cut into
   ¼-inch-wide strips
   Freshly ground black pepper
2 tablespoons fresh mint leaves,
   cut into ¼-inch strips, for garnish

1. Bring 3 quarts water to a boil and add peas and 4 teaspoons salt. Cook just to soften peas, 1 to 1½ minutes. Drain in a colander and rinse under cold water to cool; pat dry with a clean kitchen towel. (*Peas can be cooked 2 to 3 hours ahead. Wrap tightly in clean kitchen towels and refrigerate.*)

2. When ready to finish peas, heat oil in a large, heavy skillet over medium-low heat. When hot, add prosciutto strips and cook, stirring, for about 1 minute. Add peas and cook, stirring, until heated through, about 3 to 4 minutes.

3. Remove skillet from heat. Taste and season with salt, if needed, and pepper. Arrange peas on a warm serving platter. Garnish with mint. Serve hot.

Mashed Potatoes *with* Goat Cheese *and* Fresh Herbs

SERVES 6

From Start to Finish:
1 hour 20 minutes

Actual Working Time:
40 minutes

Make Ahead: Yes
(see step 3)

Can Be Frozen: No

Best Seasons:
All year, especially spring
and summer

O N A VISIT TO NEW YORK CITY several years ago, I strolled through the outdoor green market at Union Square. Walking by the stands laden with produce, I spied a cooking demonstration at one of the booths. A crowd was huddled around a chef making dishes with the market's fresh vegetables. An onlooker handed me a bright orange paper with recipes, but I didn't look at it until much later, on the train ride home. The dish that caught my eye was "mashed potatoes made with Yukon Golds or red-skins mixed with soft goat cheese, sautéed shallots and fresh herbs from Café Loup." I made the potatoes as soon as I got back and loved the combination of flavors. It was a bonus to discover that the dish could be made ahead and reheated when needed.

    2   teaspoons olive oil
    ¾   cup chopped shallots (about 4 large)
    2½ pounds Yukon Gold or red-skin potatoes,
          scrubbed, unpeeled
    6   ounces soft goat cheese, crumbled
          (*see Shopping Note*, page 28)
    1   cup 1% milk, heated until warm
        Salt
        Freshly ground white or black pepper
    1   tablespoon *each* chopped fresh thyme,
          chives and flat-leaf parsley or
          1 teaspoon dried thyme leaves and
          1 teaspoon crushed dried rosemary
        Sprigs of fresh herbs for garnish (*optional*)

1. Heat oil in a medium, heavy skillet over medium-high heat. When hot, add shallots and sauté, stirring, until softened and light golden, 4 to 5 minutes. Remove from heat and set aside.

2. Bring a large pot of water to a boil. Add potatoes and cook until tender, 30 to 40 minutes, depending on size of potatoes. Drain. When cool enough to handle, peel potatoes. Puree potatoes in a food mill or mash with a wooden spoon or masher. (Do not use a food processor, which will make potatoes gluey.)

3. Stir in shallots, goat cheese and milk. Add salt and pepper to taste. If serving immediately, transfer to a serving dish. (*Potatoes can be prepared 1 day ahead to this point. Place in an oven-to-table baking dish sprayed with nonstick cooking spray. Cool, cover and refrigerate. Reheat, covered, at 350°F for 15 to 25 minutes; see Time-Saver.*)

4. Stir in herbs and check seasonings again. Serve hot, garnished with a bundle of fresh herbs, if desired.

Menu Suggestion:

Serve with Cider-Roasted Chicken (page 136) or Thyme-Scented Chicken Meat Loaf (page 142).

Time-Saver:

The mashed potatoes can be reheated in a microwave-safe dish in a microwave on high power for several minutes (depending on oven) until hot. Watch carefully, as microwave ovens vary in their intensities.

Summer Corn *and* Tomato Pudding

SERVES 10

★

From Start to Finish:
1 hour 35 minutes

Actual Working Time:
45 minutes

Make Ahead: No

Can Be Frozen: No

Best Season: Summer

THIS IS SUMMER "COMFORT" FOOD AT ITS BEST. The prime summer vegetables—corn and tomatoes—and chopped fresh spinach, which adds flecks of color—are the main ingredients in this savory dish.

1¼-1½ pounds firm tomatoes, cored and
  sliced ¼ inch thick
  Salt and freshly ground black pepper
2 tablespoons olive oil
2 cups chopped onions
6-8 ears corn, scraped to make about 4 cups kernels
2 teaspoons chopped garlic
  About 6 ounces fresh spinach
  (flat-leaf if available), cleaned, dried and
  cut into thin strips (about 2½ cups packed)
1 cup half-and-half
2 large eggs plus 2 egg whites
⅛ teaspoon cayenne pepper
1¼ cups (5 ounces) shredded Gruyère cheese (*divided*)
5 tablespoons chopped fresh flat-leaf parsley
  or chives (*divided*)

1. Preheat oven to 350°F.

2. Place tomatoes on a double layer of paper towels. Sprinkle lightly with salt and pepper and cover with another double layer of paper towels.

3. In a large, heavy skillet over medium heat, heat oil until hot. Add onions and corn kernels and cook, stirring constantly, until softened, about 6 minutes. Add garlic and spinach and cook, stirring, for 1 minute more. Remove to a large bowl.

4. In a mixing bowl, whisk together half-and-half, eggs, egg whites, 1 teaspoon salt, ¾ teaspoon pepper and cayenne. Add to corn mixture and stir well. Stir in ½ cup cheese and 2 tablespoons parsley.

5. Spray a 3-quart oven-to-table baking pan with nonstick cooking spray and pour corn mixture into it. Spread evenly. Top with half of remaining cheese.

6. In an overlapping design, cover top with tomato slices. Sprinkle remaining cheese over them. Bake for 40 to 45 minutes, until pudding is set. Remove and cool for 5 minutes. Sprinkle with remaining 3 tablespoons parsley.

Healthful Variation: The half-and-half can be replaced with evaporated skim milk to lower fat, and the whole eggs can be replaced with egg substitute.

Other Variations: You might like to try other cheeses: white Cheddar, Monterey Jack or plain Havarti are possibilities.

Menu Suggestion:

This is a good dish to serve with grilled foods. Try it with Mahogany Spareribs (page 179), Mustard and Pepper Flank Steaks (page 172) or Grilled Salmon with Roasted Garlic (page 168).

Seasoned Butters
for Corn *on the* Cob

MAKES ½ CUP

From Start to Finish:
  10 minutes for each
butter

Actual Working Time:
  10 minutes for each
butter

Make Ahead: Yes

Can Be Frozen: Yes

Best Season: Summer

Cooking Technique:
  If you use sun-dried
tomatoes packed in oil,
drain them well and pat dry.
If you use dried tomatoes
(without oil), drop them in
boiling water for 2 minutes
to soften and then pat dry.

THERE IS NOTHING BETTER than freshly picked corn on the cob. These seasoned butters, each with different but distinctive flavorings, are ideal to serve with summer corn. And should you have any butter left over, you can toss it with cooked pasta or vegetables or rub it onto chicken or steaks before grilling. Each recipe makes ½ cup butter, enough for 24 ears of corn.

SUN-DRIED TOMATO AND BASIL BUTTER

8	tablespoons (1 stick) unsalted butter, softened
3	tablespoons finely chopped sun-dried tomatoes (*see Cooking Technique*)
1	teaspoon finely chopped garlic
1½	tablespoons chopped fresh basil or 1½ teaspoons dried
¼	teaspoon salt

Combine all ingredients in a mixing bowl and mix well. Place prepared butter in a small ramekin or bowl and refrigerate for up to 3 days. (*Butter can also be frozen for 2 to 3 weeks. Defrost in refrigerator. Bring to room temperature before using.*)

CUMIN-CILANTRO BUTTER

8   tablespoons (1 stick) unsalted butter, softened
2   teaspoons ground cumin
2   tablespoons chopped fresh cilantro
¼   teaspoon salt

Combine all ingredients in a mixing bowl and mix well. Place prepared butter in a small ramekin or bowl and refrigerate for up to 3 days. (*Butter can also be frozen for 2 to 3 weeks. Defrost in refrigerator. Bring to room temperature before using.*)

GARLIC-PARMESAN BUTTER

8   tablespoons (1 stick) unsalted butter, softened
4   teaspoons finely chopped garlic
2   teaspoons dried thyme leaves
½   teaspoon dried rosemary, crushed
2   tablespoons freshly grated imported
    Parmesan cheese
¼   teaspoon salt

Combine all ingredients in a mixing bowl and mix well. Place prepared butter in a small ramekin or bowl and refrigerate for up to 3 days. (*Butter can also be frozen for 2 to 3 weeks. Defrost in refrigerator. Bring to room temperature before using.*)

Green Beans *with* Roasted Onions

From Start to Finish:
1 hour 30 minutes

Actual Working Time:
25 minutes

Make Ahead: Partially
(see step 4)

Can Be Frozen: No

Best Seasons:
Summer and fall

MY STUDENTS ARE WILD about this green bean dish. Buttered onions are slowly roasted and then tossed in a subtle sweet-and-sour sauce. Cooked beans are topped with the beautiful, deep brown glazed onions.

1½-1¾	pounds medium onions (about 4 onions)
2	tablespoons unsalted butter, cut into small pieces
	Salt and freshly ground black pepper
1	cup reduced-sodium chicken broth
2	tablespoons red wine vinegar
1	tablespoon plus 2 teaspoons sugar
2	pounds tender green beans, ends trimmed on diagonal

1. Preheat oven to 450°F.

2. Peel onions without removing roots. Halve onions lengthwise, cutting though center of root. Cut each half into 8 wedges, keeping some of root with each wedge so wedge holds together.

3. Spray a large, flameproof baking pan with nonstick cooking spray. Arrange onion wedges, slightly overlapping, in pan. Dot with butter; season generously with salt and pepper. Bake until onions are browned and tender, 50 to 60 minutes, checking after 40 minutes, since ovens can vary.

4. When onions are cooked, remove from pan and set aside. Place pan over high heat and add broth, vinegar and sugar. Whisk constantly, scraping up brown drippings into sauce. Cook until sauce reduces to a thick syrup, about 4 to 5 minutes. Return onions to pan and toss in thickened sauce. Remove from heat. (*Onions can be prepared 1 day ahead. Cover and refrigerate. Reheat, stirring, over medium heat when needed.*)

5. When ready to serve, cook beans in a large pot of boiling, salted water until just tender, about 8 minutes. Drain well. Season with more salt, if needed. Mound beans on a warm serving platter and arrange warm browned onions over top.

Menu Suggestion:

These beans taste good with roasted meats and poultry. You might like them with Southern Herb-Roasted Turkey (page 144), Cider-Roasted Chicken (page 136) or Pot Roast with Rich Root Vegetable Sauce (page 148).

Roquefort-Stuffed Baked Tomatoes

SERVES 6

⋆

From Start to Finish:
1 hour

Actual Working Time:
40 minutes

Make Ahead: Partially
(see step 3)

Can Be Frozen: No

Best Seasons:
Summer and early fall

Menu Suggestion:
These colorful tomatoes are especially good with grilled steaks, lamb chops or chicken. Try them with Mustard and Pepper Flank Steaks (page 172).

ONE OF MY FRIENDS described this dish as "the king of the cheeses with the king of the vegetables." Indeed, this is a regal pairing: crumbled Roquefort combined with fresh bread cubes and herbs make a wonderful filling for ripe summer tomatoes.

3 medium-sized ripe tomatoes (each about 8 ounces)
6 ounces Roquefort cheese (*see Variation*)
2½ cups fresh bread cubes (preferably ½-inch cubes cut from good-quality French bread)
½ teaspoon freshly ground black pepper
6 teaspoons chopped fresh chives or flat-leaf parsley

1. Clean and dry tomatoes; cut out stems. Cut tomatoes in half horizontally and scoop out and discard seeds and pulp from each half.

2. Crumble Roquefort cheese into ½-inch pieces and place in a mixing bowl. Add bread cubes and pepper and mix well.

3. Fill each tomato half with some filling, pressing lightly with your hands to pack stuffing securely. Tomato halves should be slightly mounded with filling. (*If you are not baking them immediately, place on a baking sheet, cover loosely with plastic wrap and refrigerate for up to 3 to 4 hours.*)

4. When ready to bake, arrange a rack at center position and preheat oven to 350°F. Spray tops of tomatoes lightly with nonstick cooking spray. Bake until cheese is melted and tomatoes are hot, 12 to 15 minutes. Remove from oven and garnish each half with chives or parsley. Serve warm.

Variation: Try tossing 6 ounces crumbled feta cheese and 6 to 8 sliced Kalamata or Greek olives with the bread cubes. You can also replace the Roquefort cheese with the same amount of grated pepper Jack cheese to complement a Southwestern menu.

Honey *and* Brandy Carrots

ONEY AND BRANDY RAISE CARROTS to delectable new heights. For this dish, cooked sliced carrots are sautéed in butter, brown sugar and honey, then seasoned with brandy. This is a great recipe for a crowd, so the yield is larger than usual.

SERVES 8 TO 10

From Start to Finish:
45 minutes
Actual Working Time:
30 minutes
Make Ahead: Yes
(see step 2)
Can Be Frozen: No
Best Seasons:
All year, especially fall and winter

Menu Suggestion:
These carrots taste good with Roast Pork Tenderloins with Fall Fruit Stuffing (page 158) or with Cider-Roasted Chicken (page 136).

3   pounds carrots, peeled and cut on diagonal
     into ¼-inch-thick slices
2   tablespoons sugar
4   tablespoons unsalted butter (*divided*)
1   teaspoon salt, plus more if needed
3   cups water
1½ tablespoons light brown sugar
3   tablespoons honey
3   tablespoons brandy (*see Variation*)
3   tablespoons chopped fresh flat-leaf
     parsley for garnish

1. In a heavy saucepan, combine carrots, sugar, 1 tablespoon butter, 1 teaspoon salt and water and bring to a boil. Reduce heat to a simmer and cover pan. Cook until carrots are tender when pierced with a knife, 10 to 15 minutes. Drain well, taste and add more salt if needed.

2. Melt remaining 3 tablespoons butter with brown sugar and honey in a large, heavy skillet over medium-high heat. When sugar has dissolved, add carrots and sauté until they are well coated and heated through. Add brandy and cook for 3 to 4 minutes more. (*Carrots can be prepared several hours ahead. Leave loosely covered at room temperature. Reheat, stirring, over medium heat until hot.*)

3. To serve, arrange in a bowl and sprinkle with parsley.

Variation: For a pleasing orange flavor, use Grand Marnier or Cointreau in place of the brandy.

Grated Sweet Potatoes
with Honey *and* Orange

SERVES 10

From Start to Finish:
  1 hour 25 minutes
Actual Working Time:
  25 minutes
Make Ahead: Partially
  (see step 5)
Can Be Frozen: No
Best Seasons:
  Fall and winter

SWEET POTATOES prepared in this unique way—grated and tossed with orange juice, brown sugar and spices, then baked and drizzled with honey—are delicious and different. I serve them at Thanksgiving with turkey and at other times of the year as a garnish to roast pork and chicken dishes.

4½ pounds sweet potatoes
3 tablespoons unsalted butter,
   plus more for the baking dish
¾ cup fresh orange juice
¾ cup half-and-half (*see Healthful Variation*)
4½ tablespoons light brown sugar
1½ teaspoons ground coriander
¾ teaspoon ground ginger
2¼ teaspoons grated orange zest
   (orange portion of rind)
¾ teaspoon salt, plus more if needed
3 tablespoons honey
1 1-inch-wide long strip of orange,
   twisted to form a curl
   Several fresh flat-leaf parsley sprigs

1. Preheat oven to 375°F.

2. Peel sweet potatoes and coarsely grate. (Potatoes can be grated in a food processor; use a medium grating blade.) Set aside.

3. Butter a large oven-to-table baking dish; set aside.

4. Combine 3 tablespoons butter, orange juice, half-and-half, brown sugar, coriander, ginger, orange zest and ¾ teaspoon salt in a large, heavy skillet over medium-high heat. Bring to a boil, stirring constantly to blend. Remove from heat and add sweet potatoes. Mix well with a spoon. Taste, and if desired, add more salt. Spread sweet-potato mixture in baking dish. Cover with a sheet of aluminum foil.

5. Bake for 25 minutes; remove foil and stir potatoes well. Bake, uncovered, for 25 minutes more. (*Sweet potatoes can be made 1 day ahead to this point; cool, cover and refrigerate. When ready to continue, reheat in a preheated 375°F oven until hot, about 15 minutes.*)

6. Drizzle with honey and bake, uncovered, for 10 minutes more. Remove from oven and serve warm. Place orange peel in center and garnish with sprigs of parsley.

Healthful Variation: Replace the half-and-half with an equal amount of evaporated skim milk. Three-fourths of a cup of half-and-half contains 21 fat grams, whereas evaporated skim milk contains none.

Menu Suggestion:

These sweet potatoes are a great accompaniment to Southern Herb-Roasted Turkey (page 144), Roast Turkey Breast with Sage Butter (page 146) or Cider-Roasted Chicken (page 136).

Yukon Gold Mashed Potatoes
with Buttermilk

SERVES 6

★

From Start to Finish:
55 to 60 minutes

Actual Working Time:
25 minutes

Make Ahead: Yes
(see step 2)

Can Be Frozen: No

Best Seasons: All year

Shopping Note:

Developed by Canadians, Yukon Gold potatoes are yellow-fleshed potatoes of medium starch content—delicious for gratins, fries or mashed potatoes.

Menu Suggestion:

These potatoes are particularly good with Pot Roast with Rich Root Vegetable Sauce (page 148), Baked Pork Chops with Caramelized Onions and Smoked Gouda (page 152), or Thyme-Scented Chicken Meat Loaf (page 142).

DISCOVERING THIS mashed-potato dish was serendipitous. On a long trip from Ohio to Massachusetts, my husband and I, looking for a place to have dinner, made a detour off Connecticut's Interstate 84. We ended up at the Good News Café, in Woodbury, where I had roast chicken and these wonderful mashed potatoes. When I asked the waiter how they were made, Carole Peck, the chef and owner, was kind enough to come out of her kitchen and share the recipe with me. Yellow-fleshed Yukon Gold potatoes, buttermilk and seasonings of salt, pepper and butter were the simple ingredients she used to produce her special version of this American favorite.

3   pounds Yukon Gold (or baking) potatoes peeled
     and cut into 1-inch dice (*see Shopping Note*)
1   cup buttermilk, plus more if needed
2   tablespoons unsalted butter, softened
¾   teaspoon salt, plus more if needed
¾   teaspoon freshly ground black pepper,
     plus more if needed
1   tablespoon chopped fresh flat-leaf parsley
     or chives for garnish

1. Cook potatoes in a large pot of boiling water until they are very soft, 25 to 30 minutes. Drain well.

2. Transfer to a large bowl and mix on slow speed with an electric mixer. (Do not use a food processor, which will make potatoes gluey.) Add 1 cup buttermilk in a thin stream. Beat in butter, ¾ teaspoon salt and ¾ teaspoon pepper. Taste and add more salt and pepper, if needed. If potatoes seem too thick, thin with a few additional tablespoons buttermilk. (*Potatoes can be made 2 hours ahead; cool, cover with foil and leave at cool room temperature. Reheat, covered, in a preheated 350°F oven until hot, 15 to 25 minutes. Taste and add extra butter, if potatoes seem too dry.*) Serve potatoes mounded in a bowl sprinkled with parsley or chives.

Baked Butternut Squash and Apples *with* Maple Syrup

SWEET BUTTERNUT SQUASH and tart green apples are tossed in a mixture of butter, lemon juice and maple syrup and baked until soft and tender. The contrast of the sweet syrup and the tart apples is part of the appeal.

1¾-2 pounds butternut squash (about 1½ medium), peeled, quartered lengthwise, seeded, cut crosswise into ¼-inch-thick slices (about 4 cups), *see Shopping Note*

1½ pounds medium-sized tart green apples (such as Granny Smith), peeled, quartered, cored, cut crosswise into ¼-inch-thick slices (about 4 cups)

½ cup dried currants
Freshly grated nutmeg
Salt and freshly ground black pepper

½ cup pure maple syrup

3 tablespoons unsalted butter, cut into pieces

1 tablespoon fresh lemon juice

1. Arrange a rack at center position and preheat oven to 350°F.

2. Parboil squash in a large pot of boiling, salted water to soften slightly, about 3 minutes. Drain well.

3. Combine squash, apples and currants in a 13-by-9-inch glass baking dish. Season generously with nutmeg, salt and pepper. Combine maple syrup, butter and lemon juice in a small, heavy saucepan over low heat. Whisk until butter melts. Pour syrup over squash mixture and toss to coat evenly.

4. Bake, uncovered, until squash and apples are very tender, stirring occasionally, about 1 hour. Cool for 5 minutes before serving. (*Squash can be made 1 day ahead. Cover and refrigerate. Rewarm, covered, in a 350°F oven for about 30 minutes.*)

SERVES 8

From Start to Finish:
1 hour 45 minutes

Actual Working Time:
40 minutes

Make Ahead: Yes
(see step 4)

Can Be Frozen: No

Best Seasons:
Fall and winter

Shopping Note:
Some supermarkets sell peeled and seeded butternut squash. It's a real time-saver if you can find it. Count on about 1½ pounds of peeled, seeded squash for this recipe.

Menu Suggestion:
This is a terrific Thanksgiving side dish to serve with roast turkey; it also goes with Orange-Glazed Crown Roast of Pork (page 156) or Cider-Roasted Chicken (page 136).

Acorn Squash Baked *with* Rosemary *and* Toasted Bread Crumbs

SERVES 8

From Start to Finish:
2 hours if baked in a
conventional oven, 1 hour if
cooked in a microwave

Actual Working Time:
25 minutes

Make Ahead: Partially
(see steps 3 and 4)

Can Be Frozen: No

Best Seasons:
Fall and winter

B AKED ACORN SQUASH, seasoned with Parmesan cheese and rosemary and topped with toasted bread crumbs, is a pleasing departure from the traditional flavorings of butter, brown sugar and maple syrup. These squash halves can be made a day ahead and reheated just before serving.

6	acorn squash, 4 inches in diameter (about 4½ pounds total)
1	cup plus 2 tablespoons freshly grated imported Parmesan cheese
	Scant ½ teaspoon freshly ground black pepper
	Generous 1 teaspoon salt
1½	teaspoons dried rosemary, crushed
1	tablespoon unsalted butter
¾	cup fresh bread crumbs
8	small fresh rosemary sprigs for garnish (*optional*)

1. Arrange a rack at center position and preheat oven to 350°F.

2. Cut thin slices from both ends of each squash and discard slices. Cut each squash in half through stem and scoop out seeds. Place, cut side down, in a single layer in a large baking dish. Fill dish with ½ inch water and bake until soft when pierced with a knife, about 1½ hours. (*See Time-Saver.*) Let cool slightly.

3. When squash is cool enough to handle, scoop out insides, leaving a thin layer of flesh in each shell so that halves will retain their shapes. Discard 4 shells. Combine scooped-out flesh with cheese, pepper, salt and rosemary. Stir well to mix. Refill remaining 8 squash shells, mounding filling in each. Arrange squash in a baking dish that will hold them comfortably. (*Squash can be prepared 1 day ahead to this point; cover and refrigerate.*)

4. Heat butter in a medium, heavy skillet over medium-high heat. When hot, add bread crumbs and toss until crumbs are a deep golden brown, 3 to 4 minutes. Remove crumbs to a bowl. (*Bread crumbs can be made 1 to 2 days ahead. Cover loosely and leave at cool room temperature.*)

5. Before serving, reheat squash in a preheated 350°F oven for 15 to 20 minutes. Or reheat in a microwave until hot, about 5 minutes. Sprinkle generously with golden bread crumbs and garnish with a rosemary sprig, if desired. Arrange on a platter to serve.

Menu Suggestion:

This squash can be served with the same dishes as Baked Butternut Squash and Apples with Maple Syrup (see page 213).

Time-Saver:

Arrange squash halves, hollowed side down, in a single layer in a large, microwave-safe baking dish. Fill dish with ½ inch water. Cover with plastic wrap and cook in microwave on high power until squash is very tender when pierced with a knife, about 18 or more minutes. Check after 18 minutes, since microwaves vary in power.

Spicy Cabbage *and* Leeks

SERVES 6

★

From Start to Finish:
55 minutes

Actual Working Time:
55 minutes

Make Ahead: Partially
(see step 2)

Can Be Frozen: No

Best Season: Winter

Menu Suggestion:

This is great with store-bought roast chicken. I cut a 3-to-3½-pound chicken into 8 pieces, heat it and arrange on top of the cabbage.

FOR YEARS, the only way I ever ate cabbage was as a side dish with corned beef, but now, this is my favorite winter cabbage dish. Sliced cabbage and leeks are sautéed in butter and simmered in chicken broth, then seasoned with crushed red pepper flakes and Parmesan cheese.

2 medium cabbages (each about 2½ pounds),
    with pretty outer leaves

2 tablespoons unsalted butter

4 cups cleaned, chopped leeks, white parts only
    (4-5 medium; *see Cooking Technique*, page 296)

2 cups chicken broth

1½ teaspoons salt, plus more if needed

¼ teaspoon crushed red pepper flakes,
    plus more if needed

⅓ cup freshly grated imported Parmesan cheese

1. Remove pretty outer leaves from cabbages and set aside. Cut each cabbage in half through stem end. Cut out and discard center cores. Cut cabbage into ¼-to-½-inch-wide strips.

2. Heat butter in a large, heavy skillet (or 2 medium) over medium heat. Add leeks and sauté, stirring constantly, until softened, 3 to 4 minutes. Add cabbage and cook, stirring, until softened, 6 to 8 minutes. Add broth, 1½ teaspoons salt and ¼ teaspoon red pepper flakes and cook, stirring often, until cabbage is tender, about 15 minutes. (*Cabbage can be prepared 2 hours ahead to this point. Cool, cover loosely with foil and leave at cool room temperature. Reheat over medium heat, stirring constantly.*)

3. About 1 minute before cabbage is done, place reserved cabbage leaves over mixture in skillet(s) for about 1 minute, or until they turn bright green; watch carefully. Remove leaves and set aside. Stir in cheese. Taste and add more salt and red pepper flakes, if needed.

4. To serve, arrange blanched cabbage leaves on a serving platter. Mound cooked cabbage on top.

[handwritten: DINNER 12.24.19]

✗ Mustard-Scented Scalloped Potatoes

[handwritten: NICE, EASY]

[handwritten, right margin: RSTED SOME CHIX W/ THIS + MADE 1/2 THE RECIPE]

FOR THIS DELICIOUS DISH, layers of potatoes are sprinkled liberally with grated Gruyère cheese and seasoned with dill. A mixture of half-and-half, Dijon mustard and broth is poured over the potatoes just before baking. When cooked, the potatoes are crusty and brown on top and creamy and rich underneath. This is a dish in which indulgence reigns, and cheese and half-and-half are used liberally.

3½ pounds russet potatoes, peeled, cut into ⅛-inch-thick slices (*divided*) *[handwritten: — USE MANDOLINE]*
   Salt and freshly ground black pepper
1½ teaspoons dried dill (*divided*), *see Variation*
3 cups (about 10 ounces) grated Gruyère cheese (*divided*)
1⅓ cups half-and-half
1⅓ cups chicken broth, *[handwritten: LOW OR NO SODIUM]*
¼ cup Dijon mustard

SERVES 8

★

From Start to Finish:
   1 hour 55 minutes
Actual Working Time:
   45 minutes
Make Ahead: No
Can Be Frozen: No
Best Seasons:
   All year, but especially winter

Menu Suggestion:
   These potatoes go well with all types of roasted chicken, beef or lamb. They also make an excellent side dish to Grilled Salmon with Roasted Garlic (page 168).

1. Preheat oven to 400°F. Coat a 13-by-9-inch baking pan with non-stick cooking spray.

2. Overlap one-third of potatoes in prepared pan. Season generously with salt and pepper. Sprinkle with ½ teaspoon dill and 1 cup cheese. Repeat layering twice, using one-third of potatoes, ½ teaspoon dill and 1 cup cheese for each layer. *[handwritten: WATCH SALT AMOUNT IF BROTH HAS SOME IN IT.]*

3. Whisk half-and-half, broth and mustard in a bowl. Pour over potatoes. Bake until potatoes are tender and top is crusty and brown, about 1 hour. Cool for 10 minutes and serve.

[handwritten: DILL + MUSTARD DID NOT OVER WHELM DISH]

Variation: In place of dried dill, use an equal amount of crushed dried thyme leaves or crushed dried rosemary.

217

Wintertime Corn Pudding

SERVES 6 TO 8

★

From Start to Finish:
1 hour 30 minutes

Actual Working Time:
45 minutes

Make Ahead: Yes
(see step 6)

Can Be Frozen: No

Best Season: Winter

IN THE MIDST OF WINTER, when no fresh corn is in sight, corn pudding satisfies cravings for that summer vegetable. It is made with frozen corn and canned creamed corn, sautéed onions, sweet pepper and garlic, all combined with milk, eggs and Cheddar cheese. A small addition of cornmeal to the pudding and crushed tortilla chips as a topping add a little crunch.

1½ teaspoons olive oil
1 cup chopped onions
½ cup chopped red bell pepper
1 teaspoon minced garlic
2 cups (16 ounces) frozen corn,
   defrosted and patted dry
1 15-ounce can creamed corn
½ teaspoon salt
⅛ teaspoon cayenne pepper
⅛ teaspoon freshly ground black pepper
1 cup whole milk
¼ cup cornmeal, preferably yellow
1 large egg plus 2 egg whites
1½ cups (about 6 ounces) grated sharp
   Cheddar cheese (*divided*)
2 tablespoons chopped fresh flat-leaf parsley
½ cup tortilla chips, crushed
   (*see Cooking Technique,* page 236)

1. Preheat oven to 375°F.

2. In a heavy skillet over medium-high heat, heat oil. When hot, sauté onions and red pepper for 3 to 4 minutes, until softened. Add garlic and cook, stirring, for 1 to 2 minutes more. Remove from heat.

3. In a mixing bowl, mix defrosted corn, creamed corn, salt, cayenne and pepper. Add sautéed onion mixture.

4. In a heavy saucepan over medium-high heat, bring milk to a simmer. Slowly stir in cornmeal and simmer, stirring constantly, until thickened, 2 to 3 minutes. Remove from heat and set aside.

5. In a separate bowl, whisk egg and egg whites together and slowly add thickened cornmeal. Pour into corn mixture. Stir in 1 cup cheese and parsley. Pour into a 3½-quart oven-to-table baking dish sprayed lightly with nonstick cooking spray. Top with tortilla chips and remaining ½ cup cheese.

6. Bake until firm, 40 to 45 minutes. (*Pudding can be baked 2 hours ahead; cool and cover loosely with aluminum foil. Reheat, uncovered, in a preheated 350°F oven until hot, 15 to 20 minutes or more.*) Serve hot.

Menu Suggestion:

This corn pudding is a nice accompaniment to Mahogany Spareribs (page 179) or Chilied Ribs (page 180).

Potato *and* Sweet Red Pepper Gratin

SERVES 6

From Start to Finish:
1 hour 25 minutes

Actual Working Time:
25 minutes

Make Ahead: Yes
(see step 4)

Can Be Frozen: No

Best Seasons: All year

THIS RICH AND SATISFYING potato gratin is lower in fat and calories than most. Layers of thinly sliced potatoes and red pepper strips are seasoned with thyme and Parmesan cheese, then baked in a mixture of chicken broth and white wine. The gratin is cooked until the potatoes are crisp and golden brown on top and soft and tender inside.

2   pounds baking potatoes, peeled and
    cut into ⅛-inch-thick slices (*divided*)

2   medium-sized red bell peppers,
    seeds and membranes discarded,
    cut into ¼-inch-thick strips (*divided*)

2½   teaspoons dried thyme leaves

1   teaspoon salt

½   teaspoon freshly ground black pepper

½   cup imported Parmesan cheese,
    preferably Parmigiano-Reggiano (*divided*)

2   tablespoons olive oil (*divided*)

⅓   cup dry white wine

⅓   cup chicken broth

3-4   fresh thyme sprigs for garnish (*optional*)

1. Arrange a rack at center position and preheat oven to 375°F.

2. Coat a large oven-to-table baking dish with nonstick cooking spray. Place one-third of potatoes in overlapping rows in dish. Sprinkle half of red peppers over potatoes. Mix thyme, salt and pepper in a small bowl and sprinkle one-third of mixture over potatoes and peppers. Sprinkle one-third of cheese over vegetables and drizzle with one-third of oil.

3. Repeat, making a second layer, using one-third of potatoes and remaining peppers, plus one-third of seasonings, cheese and oil. With remaining potatoes, make final layer. Combine wine and broth and pour over potatoes. Sprinkle with remaining seasonings, cheese and oil.

4. Bake until potatoes are tender when pierced with a knife and top layer is golden brown, about 1 hour. Remove from oven; cool for 5 minutes. (*Dish can be baked several hours ahead. Leave at room temperature and reheat, loosely covered with foil, at 350°F until hot, 15 to 20 minutes.*) Garnish center of the gratin with a cluster of thyme sprigs, if desired, and serve.

Menu Suggestion:

These potatoes are perfect with roast chicken or beef or with grilled steaks or baked ribs. Try them with Michael's Grilled Rosemary Steaks (page 176).

Chapter 9

Special Side Dishes
Rice, Grains, Beans, Pasta, Dressings *and* Stuffings

Rosemary Bacon Rice

RED BELL PEPPERS AND YELLOW SQUASH, diced and sautéed, with seasonings of rosemary and bacon, can turn ordinary white rice into something special. Vivid and flavorful, this is a good dish to serve with roasted or grilled chicken, sautéed shrimp or broiled lamb chops.

1 tablespoon unsalted butter

¾ cup diced red bell pepper (¼-inch dice)

¾ cup diced yellow squash (¼-inch dice)

2 cups long-grain white rice, preferably converted white rice (*see Shopping Note*, page 230)

1 teaspoon dried rosemary

¼ teaspoon salt, plus more if needed
Several sprinklings cayenne pepper

4 cups chicken broth

4-5 slices lean bacon, cooked until crisp, crumbled (*see Shopping Note*, page 335)

1. Place butter in a large, deep-sided pot over medium heat. When butter melts, add red pepper and squash and sauté for 2 minutes, stirring. Add rice and toss well. Add rosemary, ¼ teaspoon salt, cayenne and broth. Bring to a simmer. Cover pan and lower heat.

2. Simmer until all liquid is absorbed, 25 to 30 minutes. Stir in bacon. (*Rice can be made 2 to 3 hours ahead; cool, cover and refrigerate. When ready to heat, preheat oven to 350°F. Reheat, covered, until warm, 15 to 20 minutes.*)

3. Taste for seasoning, add more salt, if desired, and serve.

SERVES 6

From Start to Finish:
50 minutes

Actual Working Time:
20 minutes

Make Ahead: Yes
(see step 2)

Can Be Frozen: No

Best Seasons: All year

Menu Suggestion:
This recipe goes with Cajun-Style Cornish Hens (page 140); the flavors of the rice work perfectly with the spicy seasonings of the hens.

Cumin Corn Rice

SERVES 6

From Start to Finish:
35 minutes

Actual Working Time:
20 minutes

Make Ahead: Yes
(see step 2)

Can Be Frozen: No

Best Seasons:
Summer and early fall

Menu Suggestion:
You can serve mounds of this rice in shallow soup bowls and ladle Black Bean Soup with Fresh Orange Relish (page 78) over it. This rice is also perfect with Swordfish with Tomato-Lime Salsa (page 127).

MY FRIEND Carolyn Claycomb from Columbus, Ohio, thought of cooking white rice with fresh corn kernels and onions along with a generous seasoning of cumin. The result is a delicious side dish with an assertive yet light flavor.

> 2 tablespoons vegetable oil
> 2 teaspoons minced garlic
> 1¼ cups chopped onions
> 1½ cups long-grain white rice, preferably converted white rice (*see Shopping Note, page 230*)
> 3 cups chicken broth, plus more if needed for reheating
> 1 cup corn kernels, cooked (about 2 ears)
> 2 tablespoons ground cumin
> Salt and freshly ground black pepper
> ¼ cup chopped fresh cilantro

1. Heat oil in a medium saucepan over medium heat. Add garlic and onions and sauté until onions are translucent, about 5 minutes. Add rice and stir well to coat. Add 3 cups broth and bring to a boil.

2. Reduce heat to a simmer and cook, covered, for 10 minutes. Stir in corn, cumin, salt and pepper. Continue cooking until rice is tender and all liquid has been absorbed, about 5 minutes more or longer. (*Rice can be prepared 1 day ahead. Coat a large baking dish with nonstick cooking spray. Spread rice in dish; cool, cover and refrigerate. When ready to reheat, arrange a rack at center position and preheat oven to 350°F. Bake rice, sprinkled with a little extra broth, covered, until hot, about 20 minutes.*)

3. To serve, transfer to a serving bowl and stir in cilantro. Serve warm.

Simple Saffron Rice

PLAIN WHITE RICE, cooked in boiling water until fluffy, was a staple at our table when I was growing up. However, when rice is sautéed in a little butter and simmered in broth enhanced with a hint of saffron, the result is sublime—and requires only a few minutes' extra time. Rice cooked this way is richly flavored and has a golden yellow tint.

2 tablespoons unsalted butter

2 cups long-grain white rice, preferably converted white rice (*see Shopping Note*, page 230)

½ teaspoon salt

4 cups chicken broth
   Scant ⅛ teaspoon powdered saffron
   (*see Shopping Note*, page 98)

⅓ cup chopped fresh chives or flat-leaf parsley

1. Heat butter in a large, heavy casserole over medium heat. When it has melted, add rice and cook, stirring, until grains are coated with butter. Add salt and broth and mix well. Add saffron and stir to mix.

2. Bring to a simmer, reduce heat to low and cover. Cook until all liquid has been absorbed, 20 to 25 minutes. (*Rice can be used immediately or kept covered for 45 minutes.*)

3. Just before serving, stir in chives or parsley.

SERVES 6

From Start to Finish:
35 minutes

Actual Working Time:
10 minutes

Make Ahead: Yes
(see step 2)

Can Be Frozen: No

Best Seasons: All year

Menu Suggestion:
I serve this rice with California Lamb Chops (page 177). Grilled shrimp brushed with garlic butter are also delectable served over a mound of this rice.

Southwestern Brown Rice *with* Confetti Vegetables

SERVES 6

From Start to Finish:
1 hour 15 minutes

Actual Working Time:
1 hour 15 minutes

Make Ahead: Yes
(see step 3)

Can Be Frozen: No

Best Seasons:
Summer and early fall

Shopping Notes:
Chicken bouillon granules add a distinct dose of chicken flavor to this dish. They are sold in jars in the soup section of most supermarkets. Wyler's is a good brand.

Quick-cooking brown rice is precooked long-grain brown rice. It cooks in about 10 minutes rather than the 30 needed for regular brown rice.

SEVERAL YEARS AGO, when quick-cooking brown rice first appeared on market shelves, I began to use it, because it cooks more quickly than ordinary brown rice. June McCarthy, the current chef of the Governor of Ohio, gave me the idea for flavoring brown rice with bold spices like cumin and chili powder and brightly colored vegetables like corn, zucchini and red bell pepper.

1½	tablespoons vegetable oil (*divided*)
1	cup finely chopped onions
2	teaspoons finely chopped garlic
1½	cups quick-cooking brown rice (*see Shopping Notes*)
3¾	cups chicken broth
1-1½	tablespoons chili powder
	(use larger amount for spicier flavor)
½	teaspoon chicken bouillon granules
	(*see Shopping Notes*)
1	teaspoon ground cumin
2	cups diced unpeeled zucchini (about 2 small)
2	cups fresh corn kernels (scraped from 3 to 4 ears)
1	cup diced red bell pepper
	(about 1 large, seeded and stemmed)
3	slices turkey bacon or regular bacon, fried or microwaved until crisp, crumbled (*see Shopping Note*, page 335)
¼	cup chopped fresh cilantro
	Salt and freshly ground black pepper

1. Heat ¾ tablespoon oil in a large, heavy skillet over medium heat until hot. Add onions and garlic and sauté, stirring, until onions are translucent, 3 to 4 minutes.

2. Stir in rice and cook for 1 minute. Add broth, chili powder, bouillon and cumin. Bring to a boil and reduce heat to low so liquid simmers. Cover pan and cook until liquid is absorbed and rice is tender, about 10 minutes. Remove from heat and set aside.

3. Meanwhile, place remaining ¾ tablespoon oil in a large, heavy skillet over medium-high heat. When hot, add zucchini, corn and red pepper. Cook, stirring, until softened, 5 to 6 minutes. Stir vegetables, bacon and cilantro into cooked rice. Season to taste with salt and pepper. (*Rice can be prepared 2 hours ahead and left at cool room temperature. If planning to reheat rice, do not stir in cilantro with vegetables and bacon, since it would lose its color during reheating. Reheat rice, covered, in an ovenproof dish or pan in a 350°F oven for 15 to 20 minutes. Then stir in cilantro.*)

Menu Suggestion:

This is a great dish to serve with Chilied Ribs (page 180).

Wild Rice *with* Red *and* Green Grapes

SERVES 8

From Start to Finish:
1 hour 20 minutes

Actual Working Time:
45 minutes

Make Ahead: Partially
(see step 4)

Can Be Frozen: No

Best Seasons:
Fall and winter

Cooking Technique:
To toast almonds, spread on a rimmed baking sheet and place on center rack of a preheated 350°F oven. Bake until golden, 8 to 10 minutes. Watch carefully and stir once or twice. Remove baking sheet from oven and allow almonds to cool.

RED AND GREEN SEEDLESS GRAPES are a wonderful addition to wild rice, giving color and moistness to the dish. The grapes are stirred into wild and white rice at the end so that they will hold their shape.

1¼	cups wild rice (*see Shopping Note*, page 282)
4	tablespoons (½ stick) unsalted butter, plus 2 optional extra tablespoons
¾	cup finely chopped onions
¾	cup finely chopped celery
1¼	cups long-grain white rice, preferably converted white rice (*see Shopping Note*, page 230)
3	cups chicken broth
1	teaspoon dried thyme leaves
½	teaspoon salt, plus more if needed
1	cup *each* seedless red and green grapes, cleaned and halved lengthwise
½	cup sliced almonds, toasted (*see Cooking Technique*)
4	tablespoons chopped fresh flat-leaf parsley

1. Arrange a rack at center position and preheat oven to 350°F.

2. Cook wild rice in boiling water to cover for 8 to 10 minutes; drain well and reserve.

3. Melt 4 tablespoons butter in a large, heavy casserole over medium heat. Add onions and celery and sauté, stirring constantly, 4 to 5 minutes. Add wild rice and white rice, and stir until grains are lightly coated with butter. Add broth, thyme and ½ teaspoon salt and bring to a simmer on top of stove, then cover and transfer to oven.

4. Bake until all liquid has been absorbed and rice is tender, about 25 minutes. Taste and season with more salt, if needed. (*Rice can be made ahead to this point. Cool, cover and refrigerate; reheat, covered, in a 350°F oven until hot, 15 to 20 minutes.*)

5. To finish rice, stir in grapes and bake for 5 minutes more. Remove from oven and stir in almonds and parsley. Taste and add more salt, if needed. If you want a richer flavor, stir in 2 tablespoons more butter. Serve in a warm bowl or on a warm platter.

Menu Suggestion:

This rice is a fine holiday accompaniment. You can serve it with Southern Herb-Roasted Turkey (page 144) or as a stuffing for Orange-Glazed Crown Roast of Pork (page 156).

Wild *and* White Rice *with* Sausage, Apples *and* Prunes

SERVES 10

From Start to Finish:
1 hour 40 minutes

Actual Working Time:
45 minutes

Make Ahead: Yes
(see step 3)

Can Be Frozen: No

Best Seasons:
Fall and winter

Shopping Note:

White rice has the husk, bran and germ removed. For converted white rice, the unhulled grain is soaked, pressure-steamed and dried before it is milled. This process produces rice that is fluffier when cooked and infuses some of the nutrients of the bran and germ into the kernel. I prefer converted rice because it separates easily when cooked and has extra nutritional value. Plain long-grain white rice, however, can be used in its place.

I ADORE THE COMBINATION OF FLAVORS IN THIS DISH. Slightly salty sausage, sweet prunes and tart, refreshing apples are used as strong accents to the wild and white rice. Since this rice makes a wonderful holiday dish, I have made the yield large enough to serve a crowd.

1½	cups wild rice (*see Shopping Note*, page 282)
3	tablespoons unsalted butter
1½	cups chopped onions
6	ounces andouille or other smoked sausage (such as kielbasa), cut into ½-inch cubes (*see Shopping Note*, page 116)
1¼	cups long-grain white rice, preferably converted white rice (*see Shopping Note*)
5	cups canned reduced-sodium chicken broth, plus up to 1 cup more if needed
9	ounces pitted prunes, chopped (about 1½ cups)
¾	teaspoon dried thyme leaves, crumbled
¾	teaspoon salt, plus more if needed
2	medium-sized tart green apples, peeled, cored, cut into ½-inch pieces
	Freshly ground black pepper
2-3	tablespoons chopped fresh flat-leaf parsley for garnish

1. Cook wild rice in a large pot of boiling water for 10 minutes; drain and reserve.

2. Melt butter in a large, heavy saucepan over medium-high heat. Add onions and sauté until they begin to soften, about 5 minutes. Add sausage, wild rice and white rice and cook, stirring, for 1 minute. Mix in 5 cups broth, prunes, thyme and ¾ teaspoon salt. Bring to a boil, stirring occasionally. Reduce heat to medium-low, cover and cook for 30 minutes.

3. Stir in apples with a fork. Cover and cook until all broth is absorbed and rice is tender, adding enough remaining broth to moisten if mixture is dry, about 20 minutes longer. Season with additional salt and pepper to taste. (*Rice can be made 1 day ahead. Cool, cover and refrigerate. Before serving, reheat, covered, in a 350°F oven until hot, about 40 minutes.*)

4. Sprinkle with parsley and serve.

Menu Suggestion:

This rice is very good with Southern Herb-Roasted Turkey (page 144).

Summer Vegetable Couscous

SERVES 8

★

From Start to Finish:
45 minutes

Actual Working Time:
45 minutes

Make Ahead: Yes
(see step 4)

Can Be Frozen: No

Best Seasons:
Summer and early fall

Shopping Note:

Quick-cooking couscous
is made with precooked
semolina grains. It takes
only about 5 minutes to
cook. It is available in most
supermarkets, usually in the
section where rice is sold.
Sometimes the label may
not say "quick-cooking,"
but if the directions on
the package say it cooks
in 5 minutes, it is the
right product.

SUMMER'S BOUNTY—zucchini, yellow squash and tomatoes—finds a perfect home in this dish. The vegetables are tossed with quick-cooking couscous along with some garbanzo beans and almonds, both added for texture. A little cumin and cayenne pepper add extra zest to the dish.

3	cups chicken broth
2	cups quick-cooking couscous (*see Shopping Note*)
2	small zucchini (6-8 ounces total)
2	small yellow squash (6-8 ounces total)
3	tablespoons olive oil
1	cup chopped onions
1½	tablespoons finely chopped garlic
2	cups seeded, diced (¼-inch) plum tomatoes (¾-1 pound)
1	19-ounce can garbanzo beans (2 cups), drained, rinsed and patted dry
2	teaspoons ground cumin
¾	teaspoon salt, plus more if needed
¼	teaspoon cayenne pepper, plus more if needed
½	cup sliced almonds, toasted (*see Cooking Technique*, page 228), *optional*
	Several fresh mint sprigs for garnish (*optional*)

1. Bring broth to a simmer in a medium, heavy saucepan over medium-high heat. Add couscous. Reduce heat to a simmer and cook until most of the liquid has been absorbed, 2 to 3 minutes. Remove from heat. Cover and let rest for 5 minutes.

2. Cut zucchini and yellow squash in half lengthwise, then cut each half into very thin half-circles.

3. Heat oil in a large, heavy skillet over medium heat. When hot, add onions and sauté, stirring, until softened, about 3 minutes. Add garlic and sauté for 1 minute more. Add zucchini and squash; stir and cook for 3 to 4 minutes more.

4. Remove pan from heat and stir in couscous, tomatoes and gar-banzo beans. Add cumin, ¾ teaspoon salt and ¼ teaspoon cayenne. Mix well. Add more salt and cayenne as needed. (*Couscous can be made ahead. Coat a large baking dish with nonstick cooking spray. Spread couscous and vegetables in dish. Cool completely, cover with plastic wrap and refrigerate for up to 1 day. When ready to reheat, preheat oven to 350°F. Bake couscous, uncovered, on center shelf until hot, about 30 minutes.*)

5. Place in a serving dish and garnish with toasted almonds and mint sprigs, if desired.

Menu Suggestion:

Grilled lamb chops, shrimp or chicken are good with this couscous.

Winter Fruits Couscous

SERVES 6

★

From Start to Finish:
25 minutes

Actual Working Time:
25 minutes

Make Ahead: Yes
(see step 2)

Can Be Frozen: No

Best Seasons:
All year, especially winter

Menu Suggestion:
This couscous can be served with simple roast chicken or broiled lamb chops. It can also be used as a filling for Orange-Glazed Crown Roast of Pork (page 156).

THIS COUSCOUS DISH draws from winter's larder. Dried apricots, golden raisins and currants enhance quickly cooked couscous, along with flavorings of lemon juice and sesame oil.

3 cups chicken broth
2 cups quick-cooking couscous
   (*see Shopping Note*, page 232)
½ cup finely diced dried apricots
2 tablespoons golden raisins, soaked in
   hot water for 5 minutes to soften, drained
2 tablespoons dried currants, soaked in
   hot water for 5 minutes to soften, drained
2 tablespoons dark Asian sesame oil
1½ teaspoons grated lemon zest
   (yellow portion of rind)
4 teaspoons fresh lemon juice
3 tablespoons chopped fresh flat-leaf parsley,
   plus several sprigs for garnish
⅓ cup finely chopped green onion,
   including 2 inches of green tops
   Salt

1. Bring broth to a simmer in a medium, heavy lidded saucepan over medium-high heat. Stir in couscous, apricots, raisins and currants. Cover and remove from heat. Let rest for 5 minutes.

2. Uncover pan and stir in sesame oil, lemon zest and juice, chopped parsley and green onion. Taste and season with salt. (*Couscous can be made 20 to 30 minutes ahead. Keep covered in pan.*)

3. To serve, mound couscous in a serving bowl and garnish center with several parsley sprigs. Serve warm.

Orzo *with* Parmesan Cheese *and* Basil

ORZO, THE TINY RICE-SHAPED PASTA that is slightly smaller than a pine nut, is great in soups and stews. I also like to use it as a side dish. In this simple recipe, it is quickly cooked and tossed with grated Parmesan cheese and fresh basil.

3 tablespoons unsalted butter

1½ cups orzo (*see Shopping Note*)

3 cups chicken broth

½ cup freshly grated imported Parmesan cheese

6 tablespoons fresh basil leaves, cut into thin strips, or 1½ teaspoons dried, plus optional sprigs for garnish

Salt and freshly ground black pepper

1. Melt butter in a large, heavy skillet over medium-high heat. Add orzo and sauté for 2 minutes. Add broth and bring to a boil. Reduce heat, cover and simmer until orzo is tender and liquid is absorbed, about 20 minutes.

2. Remove from heat and mix in cheese and basil leaves or dried basil. Season with salt and pepper. Transfer to a shallow serving bowl. Garnish with basil sprigs, if desired.

SERVES 6

From Start to Finish:
30 minutes

Actual Working Time:
10 minutes

Make Ahead: No

Can Be Frozen: No

Best Seasons: All year

Menu Suggestion:
This dish is good with Grilled Salmon with Roasted Garlic (page 168).

Shopping Note:
Orzo can be found in most supermarkets in the section where pasta is sold.

Pinto Beans
with Tortilla Cheese Crust

SERVES 6 TO 8

★

From Start to Finish:
1 hour 10 minutes

Actual Working Time:
40 minutes

Make Ahead: Yes
(see step 3)

Can Be Frozen: No

Best Seasons: All year

Cooking Technique:
You can grind the tortilla chips in a food processor fitted with a metal blade or you can place chips in a plastic bag and crush with a rolling pin.

THESE BAKED BEANS can be put together in about an hour's time. There are no beans to soak overnight or cook for several hours. Rather, canned pinto beans are combined with sautéed red and yellow peppers, chopped canned tomatoes and spicy seasonings, then baked with a topping of crushed tortillas and grated pepper Jack cheese. Served hot from the oven, the beans are an easy side dish to offer (when time is in short supply) with grilled hamburgers, barbecued chicken or spareribs.

4 15-ounce cans pinto beans
2 tablespoons vegetable oil
2 cups chopped onions
1 cup diced red bell pepper
1 cup diced yellow bell pepper
2 tablespoons chopped garlic
2 tablespoons chili powder
2 teaspoons ground cumin
1 28-ounce can Italian-style plum tomatoes, drained, juice reserved, chopped
1 cup chicken broth
1 teaspoon red pepper sauce, preferably Tabasco
1 teaspoon salt, plus more if needed
½ cup chopped fresh cilantro (*divided*)
¾ cup very finely ground tortilla chips (*see Cooking Technique*)
1 cup (4 ounces) grated pepper Jack cheese

1. Drain beans in a colander and rinse well. Puree one-fourth of beans in a food processor fitted with a metal blade or a blender, or mash well with a wooden spoon in a bowl. Set aside.

2. Heat oil over medium-high heat. When hot, add onions and peppers and sauté until softened, about 4 minutes. Add garlic and sauté for about 1 minute. Add chili powder and cumin and cook, stirring, for 2 minutes more.

3. Add tomatoes and ½ cup reserved tomato juice, broth, pureed beans and whole beans, red pepper sauce and 1 teaspoon salt. Cook, stirring, for 3 to 5 minutes. Taste and season with more salt, if needed. Stir in 6 tablespoons cilantro and pour mixture into a 13-by-9-inch oven-to-table baking dish. (*Casserole can be prepared 1 day ahead; cool, cover and refrigerate.*)

4. To bake beans, preheat oven to 375°F. Sprinkle with tortilla crumbs. Bake until beans are hot, 20 to 25 minutes. Sprinkle cheese over casserole and return to oven until cheese melts, about 5 minutes. Remove and sprinkle with remaining 2 tablespoons cilantro.

Menu Suggestion:
Serve these with Mahogany Spareribs (page 179) or Chilied Ribs (page 180).

Caraway Noodles

SERVES 6

★

From Start to Finish:
  20 minutes
Actual Working Time:
  10 minutes
Make Ahead: No
Can Be Frozen: No
Best Seasons: All year

Menu Suggestion:
  These noodles are especially good with Wintertime Sausage and Beef Stew (page 102).

Cooking Technique:
  To crush caraway seeds, place in a small plastic bag and pound with a meat pounder or rolling pin, just to crush lightly.

CRUSHED CARAWAY SEEDS ADD AN UNUSUAL TOUCH to wide egg noodles, which are cooked until tender and tossed with butter and grated Parmesan cheese. Noodles prepared this way make a fine companion to hearty meat stews.

1 pound ½-inch-wide egg noodles (dried or fresh)
  Salt
1 tablespoon caraway seeds, plus more if needed, crushed (*see Cooking Technique*)
¼ cup freshly grated imported Parmesan needed
4 tablespoons (½ stick) unsalted butter
  Freshly ground black pepper
2 tablespoons chopped fresh flat-leaf parsley for garnish

1. Bring 4 quarts water to a boil in a large, heavy pot. Add noodles and 2 to 3 teaspoons salt and cook until tender, about 12 minutes for dried, 4 to 5 for fresh. Drain well and place in a bowl.

2. Toss noodles with 1 tablespoon caraway seeds, cheese and butter. Season with more salt and extra caraway seeds, if desired, and pepper to taste.

3. Place noodles on a warm serving tray and sprinkle with parsley.

Corn Bread Crumbs

Homemade corn bread is the basis for all good corn-bread stuffings. I make crumbs from this recipe, which my family has handed down for generations. It is prepared without sugar and with less oil than most corn breads, and the crumbs are perfect for making the stuffings on the following pages. I also serve this corn bread warm from the skillet.

4 teaspoons vegetable oil
2 large eggs (*see Healthful Variation*)
¾ cup buttermilk
¾ teaspoon baking powder
¾ teaspoon salt
¼ teaspoon baking soda
1 cup yellow cornmeal

MAKES 1 LOAF,
ABOUT 4 CUPS
CRUMBS

From Start to Finish:
30 minutes
Actual Working Time:
10 minutes
Make Ahead: Yes
(see step 3)
Can Be Frozen: Yes
(see step 3)
Best Seasons: All year

1. Preheat oven to 450°F. Pour oil into a 9-inch cast-iron skillet or round cake pan. Place pan in oven to heat.

2. Combine eggs and buttermilk in a large bowl. Mix in baking powder, salt and baking soda. Mix in cornmeal.

3. Pour batter into prepared pan. Bake until a tester inserted into center comes out clean, 15 to 20 minutes. Turn out bread onto a rack and cool. (*Corn bread can be prepared 1 day ahead; wrap tightly and let stand at a cool room temperature. It can also be frozen. Double-bag loaf in resealable plastic food-storage bags. Defrost before continuing.*)

4. To use for stuffing, tear loaf into pieces and process into fine crumbs in batches in a food processor fitted with a metal blade or crumble by hand.

Healthful Variation: The eggs can be replaced with egg substitute.

Corn Bread *and* Sweet Pepper Dressing

SERVES 10

★

From Start to Finish:
1 hour 50 minutes

Actual Working Time:
50 minutes

Make Ahead: Partially
(see step 1)

Can Be Frozen: No

Best Seasons:
Fall and winter

Shopping Note:
Pepperidge Farm and
Arnold's make good white
bread that works well in
this recipe.

MY FAMILY WOULD NOT COME to the table on Thanksgiving if corn bread dressing were not part of the menu. In this variation on a traditional Southern favorite, I add sautéed red and yellow bell peppers and use leeks in place of onions. The colorful dressing, which is baked separately rather than in the bird, is crusty on top and rich and moist underneath.

2 recipes Corn Bread Crumbs (page 239)

1 16-ounce loaf best-quality white bread, processed to coarse crumbs (about 8 cups), *see Shopping Note*

3 tablespoons dried sage leaves, crumbled

2 teaspoons salt

1 teaspoon freshly ground black pepper

10 tablespoons (1¼ sticks) unsalted butter

2 cups chopped leeks, white parts only, (about 3 medium), *see Cooking Technique,* page 296

1½ cups chopped celery

2 red bell peppers, seeds and membranes removed, chopped

2 yellow bell peppers, seeds and membranes removed, chopped

4 cups reduced-sodium chicken broth

4 large eggs, beaten to blend (*see Healthful Variation*)

FOR GARNISH

Fresh sage sprigs (*optional*)

6 red bell pepper strips (about ½ pepper, seeds and membranes removed)

6 yellow bell pepper strips (about ½ pepper, seeds and membranes removed)

1. Mix corn bread crumbs and white bread crumbs, dried sage leaves, salt and pepper in a large bowl. Melt butter in a large, heavy skillet over high heat. Add leeks, celery and peppers. Sauté until vegetables begin to soften, about 10 minutes. Pour contents of skillet over bread crumbs and mix well. (*Mixture can be prepared 1 day ahead; cover and refrigerate.*)

2. Preheat oven to 350°F. Butter a 13-by-9-inch glass baking dish. Mix broth and eggs into dressing. Transfer dressing to prepared dish. Bake until cooked through and top is brown and crusty, covering lightly with aluminum foil if top browns too quickly, about 1 hour.

3. Arrange sage sprigs, if desired, and pepper strips over dressing in a decorative pattern. Serve hot.

Healthful Variation: The eggs can be replaced with egg substitute.

Menu Suggestion:
This dressing can accompany any roasted turkey or chicken, but I especially like it with Southern Herb-Roasted Turkey (page 144).

Corn Bread Dressing Loaf
with Bacon *and* Sage

SERVES 6 TO 8

★

From Start to Finish:
2 hours
Actual Working Time:
1 hour 10 minutes
Make Ahead: Yes
(see step 3)
Can Be Frozen: No
Best Seasons:
Fall and winter

THIS IS AN UNUSUAL WAY TO SERVE CORN BREAD dressing. It is baked in a bread loaf pan and, when done, removed and cut into attractive slices for serving.

6   tablespoons (¾ stick) unsalted butter,
      plus ½-1 tablespoon for greasing pan
1   cup chopped onions
¾   cup chopped celery
1   recipe Corn Bread Crumbs (page 239)
4   cups fine fresh bread crumbs
6   bacon slices, cooked until crisp and crumbled,
      plus 4 optional extra slices, cooked and crumbled
      for garnish (*see Healthful Variation*)
1½   teaspoons dried sage leaves, crumbled,
      plus more if needed
¾   teaspoon salt, plus more if needed
½   teaspoon freshly ground black pepper,
      plus more if needed
6   large eggs, beaten (*see Healthful Variation*)
1   cup chicken broth
      Fresh sage leaves (*optional*)

1. Arrange a rack at center position and preheat oven to 350°F. Butter an 8½-by-4½-by-2½-inch loaf pan (*see Variation*), and line bottom and sides with parchment or a triple thickness of wax paper, extending 2 inches over long sides. Butter parchment or wax paper.

2. Melt 6 tablespoons butter in a large, heavy skillet over medium-high heat. Add onions and celery and sauté until soft, about 8 minutes. Mix corn bread crumbs and bread crumbs in a large bowl. Add onion mixture, 6 crumbled bacon slices, 1½ teaspoons dried sage, ¾ teaspoon salt and ½ teaspoon pepper. Mix in eggs and broth. Taste and adjust seasoning, adding more salt, pepper or sage, if desired.

3. Transfer mixture to pan; smooth top. Bake until top forms a golden brown crust, about 50 minutes. Run a small, sharp knife around pan sides to loosen. Unmold onto a platter. Peel off parchment or wax paper. (*Loaf can be made several hours ahead. Cool and wrap tightly in foil and leave at cool room temperature. To reheat, preheat oven to 350°F and place loaf, still wrapped in foil, on center rack. Bake until completely heated through, 20 to 30 minutes or more.*)

4. To finish dish, sprinkle loaf with 4 crumbled bacon slices, if desired, and garnish with fresh sage leaves, if using. Serve warm.

Variation: For a more unusual presentation, bake this dressing in an 11½-by-3½-by-2½-inch deep terrine. The loaf, longer and narrower, looks sleek this way. The baking time will be slightly less; bake about 40 minutes until completely cooked in center.

Healthful Variation: The eggs can be replaced with egg substitutes. Instead of regular bacon, try a good brand of turkey bacon, such as Louis Rich.

Menu Suggestion:

This dressing loaf can be served with roast turkey or chicken and is also good with Orange-Glazed Crown Roast of Pork (page 156).

Sourdough Bread Stuffing *with* Mushrooms *and* Leeks

SERVES 12

★

From Start to Finish:
1 hour 40 minutes

Actual Working Time:
1 hour 10 minutes

Make Ahead: Partially
(see steps 2 and 5)

Can Be Frozen: No

Best Seasons:
Fall and winter

THIS DELICIOUS STUFFING is made with sourdough bread crumbs, sautéed leeks and mushrooms, crisp crumbled bacon and generous seasonings of sage and thyme. It can be completely readied several hours ahead and is baked outside rather than inside the bird.

12 cups (18 ounces) good-quality sourdough bread, cut or torn into ½-inch pieces

¾ pound sliced hickory-smoked bacon, cut into ½-inch pieces (*see Healthful Variation*)

3 cups chopped leeks, white parts only, green tops saved for optional garnish (about 4-5), *see Cooking Technique*, page 57

3 cups chopped celery

¾ pound sliced mushrooms

2-3 cups chicken or turkey broth (*divided*)

2 large eggs (*see Healthful Variation*)

1½ teaspoons baking powder

1½ teaspoons salt

¾ teaspoon freshly ground black pepper

1½ tablespoons dried sage leaves, crumbled

1½ teaspoons dried thyme leaves

1. Preheat oven to 325°F.

2. Spread bread pieces on 2 rimmed baking sheets and bake until dry and lightly brown, tossing every 5 minutes, 20 to 25 minutes. Remove from oven and cool. (*Bread can be toasted 1 to 2 days ahead. Keep covered at room temperature.*)

3. In a large, heavy skillet, sauté bacon until golden and crisp. Remove with a slotted spoon and set aside to drain on paper towels. In bacon drippings remaining in pan, sauté 3 cups leeks and celery, stirring constantly, for 5 minutes, until softened. Add mushrooms and sauté, stirring, for 4 to 5 minutes more, until lightly browned. Add 2 cups broth and stir well. Remove from heat.

4. Place toasted bread in a large mixing bowl. Add leek mixture and bacon. In a bowl, beat eggs lightly with baking powder and toss with bread mixture. Add salt, pepper, sage and thyme and mix well. If mixture seems too dry, add ½ to 1 cup more broth.

5. Spray 1 large or 2 medium oven-to-table baking dishes with non-stick cooking spray and spread stuffing evenly in pan(s). (*Stuffing can be assembled 2 to 3 hours ahead. Cover and refrigerate.*)

6. When ready to bake stuffing, preheat oven to 350°F. Bake until golden brown on top, 25 to 30 minutes.

7. If you like, while stuffing is baking, blanch 5 to 6 leek greens for 10 to 20 seconds in a skillet of simmering water. Remove, pat dry and cut off ends on diagonal. Arrange greens in a spoke pattern on top of stuffing after it has been baked.

Healthful Variation: The eggs can be replaced with egg substitute, and instead of regular bacon, try a good brand of turkey bacon, such as Louis Rich.

Menu Suggestion:
Although this dressing is good with any roast turkey or chicken, it makes an especially fitting accompaniment to Roast Turkey Breast with Sage Butter (page 146).

Chapter 10

Tried-and-True Salads with New Touches

COLE SLAWS, GREEN SALADS, VEGETABLE SALADS AND POTATO SALADS

CHICKEN SALADS AND MORE

SEAFOOD SALADS

BEAN AND GRAIN SALADS

Mixed Greens *in* Orange Balsamic Dressing

I LIKE THE LIGHT, REFRESHING FLAVOR of the orange juice and zest in this dressing. It takes only a few minutes to assemble, can be made a day ahead and is good over all manner of mixed greens.

FOR DRESSING

2   tablespoons balsamic vinegar
1   tablespoon fresh orange juice
2   teaspoons finely grated orange zest
    (orange portion of rind)
½   teaspoon salt
6   tablespoons olive oil, preferably extra-virgin
2   tablespoons chicken broth

FOR SALAD

12-14   cups mixed greens (red-leaf, Boston and spinach
        work well), cleaned and torn into bite-sized pieces
        Salt and freshly ground black pepper

1. **To prepare dressing:** Combine vinegar, orange juice, orange zest and salt in a bowl. Whisk in oil and broth. (*Dressing can be made 1 day in advance; cover and refrigerate. Whisk well before using.*)

2. **To assemble salad:** Place cleaned salad greens in a bowl. Toss with half of dressing. Add only enough remaining dressing to coat leaves lightly. Season to taste with salt and pepper and serve. (*Extra dressing can be covered, refrigerated, and saved for another use.*)

SERVES 8

From Start to Finish:
15 minutes
Actual Working Time:
15 minutes
Make Ahead: Partially
(see step 1)
Can Be Frozen: No
Best Seasons: All year

Menu Suggestion:
This salad can be used wherever a simple green salad is appropriate.

Fresh Cole Slaw
with Fennel Seed Dressing

SERVES 6

From Start to Finish:
4 hours 30 minutes
(includes 4 hours of
refrigeration)
Actual Working Time:
30 minutes
Make Ahead: Yes
(see step 2)
Can Be Frozen: No
Best Seasons: All year

Cooking Technique:
To crush fennel seeds,
simply place them in a small
plastic bag and, using a
meat pounder or a rolling
pin, crush them until they
resemble a very coarse
powder.

COLE SLAW IS INDEED an American classic, but more often than not, I have been served bland, predictable renditions. In this version, I add crushed fennel seeds to the dressing to boost flavor, and I combine thinly sliced (rather than grated) cabbage with thin slices of fresh fennel. Bits of sweet red and green peppers add color and texture.

1   large head green cabbage, with attractive
       outer leaves
⅔   cup chopped red bell pepper
⅔   cup chopped green bell pepper
1   large fennel bulb, halved, cored and cut
       into very thin slices
       (*see Shopping Note*, page 93)
⅔   cup tarragon vinegar
⅓   cup olive oil
⅓   cup sugar
2¼   teaspoons fennel seeds, crushed
       (*see Cooking Technique*)
¼   cup reduced-fat mayonnaise
       (*see Shopping Notes*, page 272)
¼   cup reduced-fat sour cream
       Salt and freshly ground pepper

1. Remove 6 outer leaves from cabbage for garnish and place in a plastic bag. Shut tightly and refrigerate. Core cabbage, then quarter it. Thinly slice cabbage to make 9 cups (reserve any remainder for another use). Combine sliced cabbage, red and green peppers and sliced fennel in a large bowl.

2. Combine vinegar, oil, sugar and fennel seeds in a small saucepan. Cook, stirring, over medium heat until sugar dissolves and mixture is heated through, about 3 minutes. Pour over sliced cabbage mixture. Mix together mayonnaise and sour cream and add to salad. Toss well. Season to taste with salt and pepper. Cover and refrigerate for at least 4 hours or overnight, tossing occasionally.

3. Place 1 cabbage leaf on each of 6 salad plates. Using a slotted spoon, fill with coleslaw and serve.

Healthful Variation: For a less fattening version of this slaw, omit the mayonnaise and sour cream.

Menu Suggestion:

This cole slaw goes well with grilled or barbecued foods. Try it with Mahogany Spareribs (page 179), Mustard and Pepper Flank Steaks (page 172) or Grilled Salmon with Roasted Garlic (page 168).

Spinach Salad
with Brown Mushrooms *in*
Lemon-Garlic Dressing

SERVES 4 TO 6

★

From Start to Finish:
35 minutes

Actual Working Time:
20 minutes

Make Ahead: Partially
(see step 1)

Can Be Frozen: No

Best Seasons: All year

Shopping Note:

Crimini, or brown, mushrooms are available in many supermarkets. They are a variation of cultivated white mushrooms. Their texture and flavor are slightly better than the domestic white variety. I like to use brown mushrooms because of their earthy color, but if they are not available, white mushrooms work fine.

THIS IS AN UPDATED VERSION of another American favorite, the classic spinach salad served with sliced boiled eggs, white mushrooms and crumbled bacon. In this new version, created by Ohio cooking teacher Shirley Kindrick, the bacon is replaced with crunchy slices of water chestnut. Brown mushrooms are used instead of white, and the eggs are omitted. The lemon-garlic dressing is delicious and can be used with other greens as well.

FOR LEMON DRESSING

1   tablespoon chopped garlic
1   tablespoon grated lemon zest
    (yellow portion of rind)
3   tablespoons fresh lemon juice
3   tablespoons white wine vinegar
2   tablespoons Dijon mustard
½   cup vegetable oil
⅓   cup olive oil

FOR SALAD

1   pound spinach, preferably flat-leaf,
    cleaned and dried (*see Time-Saver*)
½   pound brown mushrooms, sliced (*see Shopping Note*)
1   8-ounce can sliced water chestnuts,
    drained and patted dry (*optional*)
    Salt and freshly ground black pepper

1. **To prepare dressing:** Place all ingredients in a food processor fitted with a metal blade or a blender and process for 30 seconds until mixture is thick and opaque. To prepare by hand, mince garlic and place in a nonreactive mixing bowl with lemon zest and juice, vinegar and mustard. Whisk well. Gradually whisk in oils. (*Dressing can be prepared 1 day ahead. Cover and refrigerate. Whisk well before using.*)

2. **To assemble salad:** Remove stems from spinach leaves. Pat leaves dry and tear into large pieces.

3. Place mushrooms and water chestnuts, if desired, in a mixing bowl. Add ⅓ cup dressing and toss to coat. Marinate for 15 minutes. Add spinach leaves. Add enough of remaining dressing to coat leaves; you will not need to add all of it. (*Extra dressing can be covered and refrigerated for 2 days.*)

4. Taste and season salad with salt and pepper as needed. Serve immediately.

Menu Suggestion:

This salad goes with all manner of dishes. It is good with soups or with simple grilled steaks or roast chicken.

Time-Saver:

Some markets sell good-quality spinach prewashed. Buying spinach prepared this way will save time, even though it is a little more expensive. When I am really in a rush, I pick up spinach greens at the salad bar in the supermarket.

Mexican Layered Salad
with Cumin-Honey Dressing

SERVES 10

★

From Start to Finish:
1 hour

Actual Working Time:
1 hour

Make Ahead: Partially
(see step 1)

Can Be Frozen: No

Best Seasons: All year

Cooking Technique:

To toast cumin seeds,
place them in a small dry
skillet over medium-high
heat, shaking pan back and
forth, for 2 to 3 minutes.
Watch carefully so seeds do
not burn. Remove seeds
from pan and grind in an
electric spice grinder or
place in a plastic bag and
crush with a rolling pin.

THIS LAYERED SALAD owes its distinction to a special dressing flavored with toasted cumin seeds, honey and lime. The salad is composed of a layer of greens, a colorful layer of red bell pepper, cucumber, grapefruit and red onion and a final layer of greens, all tossed in the dressing.

FOR DRESSING

2 teaspoons seeded and minced jalapeño pepper
(*see Cooking Technique,* page 274)

4 teaspoons cumin seeds, toasted and ground
(*see Cooking Technique*)

4 teaspoons chopped fresh cilantro

4 teaspoons chopped fresh flat-leaf parsley

4 teaspoons honey

4 tablespoons plus 2 teaspoons fresh lime juice

1½ teaspoons salt
Freshly ground black pepper

½ cup olive oil

½ cup chicken broth

FOR SALAD

1 large red onion, peeled and chopped (1½ cups)

1 large grapefruit, peeled, seeded and cut between membranes into segments

1 large red bell pepper, stem and membranes removed, seeded and chopped

1 large cucumber, peeled, seeded and chopped

12 lightly packed cups cleaned and torn mixed greens
(spinach, curly endive and romaine are a good combination)
Salt and freshly ground black pepper

1. **To prepare dressing**: Place jalapeño pepper, cumin seeds, cilantro, parsley, honey, lime juice, salt and pepper in a nonreactive bowl. Whisk in oil and broth. Set aside. (*Dressing can be made 3 to 4 hours ahead; cover and refrigerate. Bring to room temperature 30 minutes before using and whisk well.*)

2. **To prepare salad**: Place onion, grapefruit, red pepper and cucumber in a medium nonreactive mixing bowl and toss with half of dressing. Taste, and if desired, add more salt and pepper. Marinate for 15 minutes.

3. When ready to serve salad, toss greens in a mixing bowl with enough remaining dressing to coat lightly. Be careful not to saturate greens; you may have some dressing left over. (*Extra dressing can be covered, refrigerated, and saved for another use.*) Salt and pepper greens lightly.

4. **To assemble salad:** Place half of greens in a clear-glass salad bowl and top with half of marinated vegetables. Repeat with remaining greens and vegetables.

Variation: One large ripe avocado can replace the grapefruit, if you prefer the texture. It will, however, add extra calories to the dish.

Menu Suggestion:
This salad is especially good with Chilied Ribs (page 180).

"Waldorf of Sorts" Salad

SERVES 6

★

From Start to Finish:
1 hour

Actual Working Time:
50 minutes

Make Ahead: Partially
(see steps 1 and 2)

Can Be Frozen: No

Best Seasons: All year

WALDORF SALAD, that crunchy blend of diced apples, celery and nuts held together with mayonnaise dressing, was a ubiquitous salad during my youth. My mother made it routinely, it was always on school lunch menus, and restaurants never tired of serving it. I loved the crisp flavor of the apples and the crunchy texture of the nuts but found little else to merit the dish's popularity. This 1990s version includes paper-thin slices of tart apples, tender green beans and mixed greens all tossed in a light lemon dressing. Chopped walnuts and a sprinkling of cheese top the salad.

FOR SALAD DRESSING

2 tablespoons fresh lemon juice
2 tablespoons white wine vinegar
1 teaspoon salt
½ teaspoon freshly ground black pepper
¼ cup chicken broth
¼ cup olive oil

FOR SALAD

Salt
1 pound tender green beans, ends trimmed
2 tart apples (Granny Smith or McIntosh work well), washed, unpeeled
6 cups mixed salad greens (red-leaf, Boston and spinach are a good combination), cleaned and torn into bite-sized pieces
Freshly ground black pepper
¼ pound grated sharp Cheddar cheese or crumbled blue cheese for topping
¼ cup coarsely chopped walnuts for topping

1. **To prepare dressing:** Place lemon juice, vinegar, salt, pepper and broth in a nonreactive mixing bowl. Whisk well to blend, then whisk in oil. (*Dressing can be made 1 day ahead. Cover and refrigerate. Whisk well before using.*)

2. **To prepare beans:** Bring 3 quarts water to a boil and add 1 table-spoon salt and beans. Cook until beans are tender, about 8 minutes. Place beans in a colander and rinse under cold running water. Pat dry. (*Beans can be prepared 1 day ahead; wrap in a kitchen towel and plastic wrap and refrigerate.*)

3. **To assemble salad:** Halve and core but do not peel apples. Slice into thin wedges. Place apples in a salad bowl and toss with dressing. Marinate for 10 minutes. Add beans and salad greens and toss well. Taste and season with more salt and pepper, if needed. Divide and arrange salad on 6 salad plates. Sprinkle each serving with a little cheese and walnuts.

Menu Suggestion:

This is a good salad to serve with roast chicken or roast pork.

Fall Apple *and* Greens Salad *in* Warm Cider Dressing

**SERVES 6 AS
SALAD COURSE,
4 AS MAIN COURSE**

★

From Start to Finish:
50 minutes

Actual Working Time:
50 minutes

Make Ahead: Partially
(see step 1)

Can Be Frozen: No

Best Season: Fall

SALADS TOSSED WITH WARM DRESSINGS are part of America's culinary tradition. For this apple and greens salad, I have created a warm cider dressing flavored with lemon, vinegar and a surprising accent of crushed fennel seeds. The sweet and slightly tart seasonings of the dressing mix deliciously with tart apples, brown mushrooms, red onions, crumbled blue cheese and lettuce greens.

FOR CIDER DRESSING

1 cup apple cider

1 teaspoon grated lemon zest
(yellow portion of rind)

3 tablespoons fresh lemon juice

2 teaspoons red wine vinegar

2 teaspoons fennel seeds, crushed
(*see Cooking Technique*, page 248)

1 tablespoon olive oil

½ teaspoon salt
Freshly ground black pepper

FOR SALAD

½ pound brown or white mushrooms, cleaned
and thinly sliced through stems
(*see Shopping Note*, page 250)

1 medium-sized red onion, peeled,
halved lengthwise, thinly sliced

2 medium-sized tart apples (Macoun, Jonathan
or Granny Smith), cleaned but unpeeled
Salt and freshly ground black pepper

1-2 heads red oak leaf or red-leaf lettuce,
cleaned and torn into bite-sized pieces
(enough to make 8 cups, packed)

⅓ pound Saga blue cheese, thinly sliced, or another
good-quality blue cheese, crumbled

1. **To prepare dressing**: Heat cider in a small, heavy saucepan for
several minutes until it has reduced by half. Transfer to a nonreactive
mixing bowl. Add lemon zest and juice, vinegar, fennel seeds, oil, salt
and pepper and whisk well. (*Dressing can be made 1 day ahead. Cover and
refrigerate.*) When ready to serve, heat just to warm.

2. **To assemble salad**: Place mushrooms and onion in a mixing bowl.
Halve apples lengthwise and core. Slice very thinly. Add to bowl and
toss with half of warm dressing. Season with salt and pepper, if
needed.

3. Place greens in another bowl and toss with just enough of remaining dressing to coat lightly. Season with salt and pepper, if needed.

4. Use 4 dinner plates (if serving salad as a main course) or 6 salad
plates (if serving as a first course or a side dish) and divide greens
evenly among plates. Divide and mound apple mixture over greens.
Sprinkle blue cheese over salads. Drizzle each serving with a little remaining dressing.

Menu Suggestion:

This salad is good as a
first course to precede roast
chicken or pork. Or serve it
as a main course along with
a bowl of soup, such as
Butternut Squash and
Sausage Soup (page 66).

Roasted New Potato *and* Watercress Salad

SERVES 6

From Start to Finish:
2 hours 30 minutes
(includes 45 minutes for
roasting potatoes and 1
hour for cooling salad)
Actual Working Time:
35 minutes
Make Ahead: Partially
(see steps 2 and 3)
Can Be Frozen: No
Best Seasons:
Spring and summer

POTATOES USED IN SALAD traditionally are boiled, but in this preparation, I roast them with chopped garlic, herbs and olive oil. I use red-skins, which are sliced and left unpeeled, and, after roasting, toss them with mustard, vinegar and shallots. Just before serving, I stir peppery watercress sprigs into the salad.

2½	pounds red-skin new potatoes, cleaned, unpeeled
1½	tablespoons finely minced garlic (about 6 large cloves)
1	teaspoon salt, plus more if needed
½	teaspoon freshly ground black pepper, plus more if needed
½	teaspoon dried thyme leaves
½	teaspoon dried rosemary leaves
½	cup extra-virgin olive oil, plus more if needed
2	tablespoons white wine vinegar, plus more if needed
1	teaspoon Dijon mustard
¼	cup finely chopped shallots
1	cup watercress sprigs, cleaned and patted dry

1. Arrange a rack at the center position and preheat oven to 375°F.

2. Spray a large, heavy baking pan or a large, ovenproof cast-iron skillet with nonstick cooking spray. Cut each potato in half lengthwise and slice potatoes into ½-inch-thick wedges; place in pan. Combine garlic, 1 teaspoon salt, ½ teaspoon pepper, thyme, rosemary and ½ cup oil in a small mixing bowl and whisk well to blend. Pour mixture evenly over potatoes and toss well. Bake potatoes until they are tender when pierced with a knife and lightly golden, 45 to 55 minutes or more, stirring every 10 to 12 minutes to be sure they don't stick.

When done, remove and cool to room temperature. (*Potatoes can be baked 4 to 5 hours ahead and left loosely covered with foil at cool room temperature.*)

3. **To assemble salad:** Transfer potatoes with a slotted spoon to a mixing bowl. Pour all liquid and pan drippings from pan into a measuring cup. If you do not have ⅓ cup, add enough oil to make this amount. Add 2 tablespoons vinegar, mustard and shallots. Whisk well to blend. Pour mixture over potatoes and taste and season as needed with vinegar, salt and pepper. Let potatoes stand for at least 1 hour or up to 2 hours, uncovered, at a cool room temperature.

4. Just before serving, toss salad with watercress sprigs and taste once more for seasoning. Serve salad at room temperature, mounded on a serving platter or in an earthenware bowl.

Menu Suggestion:

Serve with main courses of grilled chicken, meat or fish. It goes well with Grilled Plum Chicken (page 164), Grilled Swordfish with Tomato-Orange Sauce (page 170) or Mustard and Pepper Flank Steaks (page 172).

Red-Skin Potato *and* Asparagus Salad *with* Warm Mustard Dressing

SERVES 8

★

From Start to Finish:
1 hour 5 minutes

Actual Working Time:
45 minutes

Make Ahead: Partially
(see steps 1 and 4)

Can Be Frozen: No

Best Seasons:
Spring and summer

THIS POTATO SALAD IS DIFFERENT from typical ones in two ways. First, in addition to boiled potatoes, it contains an equal amount of cooked sliced asparagus. Second, the dressing is warm and made with balsamic vinegar, Dijon mustard and olive oil rather than with mayonnaise. The finished dish, garnished with herbs and mounded on Boston lettuce and radicchio leaves, bursts with color and flavor. (*See photograph, page 36.*)

1½ teaspoons minced garlic
2¼ teaspoons Dijon mustard
6 tablespoons balsamic vinegar
Salt
¾ cup plus 3 tablespoons extra-virgin olive oil
  (*see Healthful Variation*)
2 pounds small red-skin potatoes (about 2 inches
  in diameter), cleaned but not peeled
2 pounds large asparagus (*see Other Variations*)
½ cup chopped green onion, including
  2 inches of green tops
  Freshly ground black pepper
1 head Boston lettuce, cleaned and dried
1 head radicchio, cleaned and dried
¼ cup chopped fresh flat-leaf parsley
  or chives or a combination for garnish

1. Place garlic, mustard, vinegar and ¾ teaspoon salt in a nonreactive bowl and whisk well. Gradually whisk in oil. (*Dressing can be made 1 day ahead, covered and refrigerated.*)

2. Bring 4 quarts water to a boil and add potatoes and 1 tablespoon salt. Cook until potatoes are tender when pierced with a knife, 15 to 20 minutes. Drain well. Cut potatoes into quarters, then halve quarters. Set aside.

3. Cut off and discard tough ends from asparagus stalks. With a vegetable peeler, peel stalks, starting just below tips. Cut stalks on diagonal into 2-inch pieces.

4. Bring 4 quarts water to a boil and add 2 teaspoons salt and asparagus. Boil until tender, 3 to 4 minutes. Drain in a colander and refresh under cold running water. Pat dry. (*Potatoes and asparagus can be prepared up to 2 hours ahead, covered loosely with plastic wrap and left at room temperature.*)

5. When ready to serve, toss potatoes, asparagus and green onion in a large bowl. Heat dressing in a small, heavy saucepan over medium heat until hot. Pour over vegetables and toss well to coat. Season to taste with salt and pepper.

6. Arrange a border of alternating lettuce and radicchio leaves on a serving plate or in a shallow bowl. Mound salad on leaves and sprinkle with fresh herbs.

Healthful Variation: The extra-virgin olive oil plays an important role in the overall flavor of this dish. However, if you want to lower the fat, you can replace up to 7 tablespoons of the oil with chicken broth.

Other Variations: Fresh, tender green beans can be substituted for the asparagus. This salad makes a good side dish, or you can add cooked shrimp and serve it as a main course. Or grill boneless chicken breasts, slice and place on top of salad and serve as a main course.

Menu Suggestion:

I like this salad with grilled chicken or fish dishes. It is ideal, for example, with Grilled Salmon with Roasted Garlic (page 168).

Southwestern Chicken
and Tomato Salad

SERVES 6

From Start to Finish:
1 hour 20 minutes

Actual Working Time:
40 minutes

Make Ahead: Yes
(see step 2)

Can Be Frozen: No

Best Seasons:
Summer and early fall

Shopping Note:
Baked tortilla chips are delicious and have less fat than fried ones. Guiltless Gourmet and Frito Lay's Baked Tostitos are brands I use.

T HIS DISH IS SO POPULAR WITH MY FAMILY that it has replaced all my traditional chicken-salad recipes. Made with chunks of poached white-meat chicken, pepper Jack cheese, fresh chopped tomatoes and light mayonnaise, it is overflowing with flavor. I mound the salad on beds of romaine lettuce, add crunchy tortilla chips and offer it as a main course.

About 6 cups chicken broth

3 pounds boneless, skinless chicken breasts,
  excess fat removed and discarded

1½ cups (about 6 ounces) shredded pepper Jack cheese

¾ cup finely chopped shallots

3 cups seeded and diced, unpeeled ripe tomatoes

1½ cups reduced-fat mayonnaise
  (*see Shopping Notes*, page 272)

2 tablespoons fresh lemon juice

2 tablespoons chopped fresh cilantro,
  plus 6 sprigs for garnish
  Salt and freshly ground black pepper

1 large head romaine lettuce, cleaned and dried
  Tortilla chips, preferably baked, not fried
  (*see Shopping Note*)

1. Bring 6 cups broth to a simmer in a large, heavy pan. Add chicken. If it is not covered with broth, add more broth or water just to cover. Simmer, covered, until chicken is cooked through, 6 to 10 minutes, depending on thickness.

2. Remove chicken from broth and cool completely. Save broth for another use. Cut chicken into ¾-inch cubes and place in a large non-reactive bowl. Add cheese, shallots, tomatoes, mayonnaise, lemon juice and chopped cilantro. Toss well and season with salt and pepper, if needed. (*Salad can be prepared 2 to 3 hours ahead; cover and refrigerate.*)

3. To serve, arrange 3 or 4 romaine leaves on 6 individual dinner plates. Divide salad evenly and mound on lettuce. Top each serving with a cilantro sprig and surround with tortilla chips.

Menu Suggestion:

Offer this salad as a main course for a light lunch or supper and serve Margarita Cheesecake (page 378) for dessert.

Roasted Chicken *and* Basil Salad

SERVES 10

★

From Start to Finish:

1 hour

Actual Working Time:

45 minutes

Make Ahead:

Partially (see step 3)

Can Be Frozen: No

Best Seasons:

Summer and early fall

Shopping Note:

Many supermarkets offer a variety of roast chickens, with seasonings ranging from honey mustard to Cajun spices. For this recipe, a plain roast chicken or one that is flavored with lemon is best.

EVEN WHEN I AM ON THE OTHER SIDE of the Atlantic, thousands of miles from home, I find myself making American favorites. During one stay in southern France, after buying roast chickens, tender green beans, plump, juicy tomatoes and a huge bunch of basil in a local market, I returned to the kitchen of our rented house to prepare this salad. I cut the chicken into strips, cooked the beans and combined both with thin slices of Gruyère cheese. I tossed everything in a light basil dressing and served the salad garnished with tomato wedges on a bed of lettuce. It was a superb summer dish and took only minutes to prepare because the chickens were purchased already roasted. Much to my delight, I can make this salad just as easily at home, for supermarkets across America are now selling chickens roasted on the premises.

¼ cup red wine vinegar

1 teaspoon Dijon mustard

Salt

6 tablespoons extra-virgin olive oil

6 tablespoons chicken broth

½ cup chopped fresh basil leaves

1 pound tender green beans, ends cut off on diagonal

½ pound Gruyère cheese, cut into strips
¼ by 2 inches

2 3-pound roast chickens, skin removed, meat cut
into strips ½ by 2 inches (*see Shopping Note*)
Freshly ground black pepper

6 medium tomatoes, cut into ½-inch-thick wedges

1 large head Boston lettuce, cleaned and dried

1. Combine vinegar, mustard and 1 teaspoon salt in a mixing bowl. Whisk in oil and broth, then stir in basil. Set aside.

2. Bring 2 quarts water to a boil and add 1 tablespoon salt and beans. Cook until beans are just tender, 4 to 5 minutes for tiny young beans and 8 to 10 minutes or more for large beans. Place in a colander and refresh under cold running water to stop cooking and set color. Pat beans dry.

3. Combine beans, cheese and chicken in a large bowl and mix with ⅔ cup dressing. Taste and season with salt and pepper, if needed. (*Salad can be prepared 1 hour ahead; cover and refrigerate. Bring to room temperature 30 minutes before continuing.*)

4. Toss tomatoes with remaining dressing. Taste and season with salt and pepper, if needed.

5. Arrange lettuce leaves on a large serving plate. Mound chicken mixture in center. Arrange tomatoes around salad. Serve immediately.

Menu Suggestion:

This salad makes an excellent main course for warm summer lunches or suppers. Serve it with a basket of warm Last-Minute Rosemary Corn Bread (page 285) or hot crusty French bread. Fresh fruit and White Chocolate- and Pecan-Studded Brownies (page 380) are a great dessert.

Harvest Turkey, Cranberry *and* Rice Salad

SERVES 6 TO 8

★

From Start to Finish:
1 hour 15 minutes

Actual Working Time:
40 minutes

Make Ahead: Yes
(see step 4)

Can Be Frozen: No

Best Season: Fall

Shopping Notes:

Rice vinegar, which is slightly sweet, is made from fermented rice. It is available in the Asian-foods section of most large supermarkets.

Uncle Ben's Rice Trio, a combination of white, brown and wild rice, works beautifully in this recipe.

THIS SALAD MAKES PERFECT USE of leftover roast turkey and is ideal to serve as a light post-Thanksgiving main course. It is a combination of diced roast turkey, dried cranberries, grapes, toasted pecans and rice, all tossed in an orange and tarragon dressing. This salad, with its light citrus dressing, is satisfying yet refreshing.

FOR ORANGE DRESSING

4 tablespoons orange juice concentrate, defrosted

2 tablespoons rice wine vinegar (*see Shopping Notes*)

1 tablespoon fresh tarragon, chopped,
   or 1-1½ teaspoons dried

½ teaspoon minced garlic

1 teaspoon salt, plus more if needed

1 teaspoon freshly ground black pepper

½ cup vegetable oil

FOR SALAD

1 cup dried cranberries (*see Shopping Note*, page 183)

2 teaspoons unsalted butter

2 cups mixed-rice blend, including white,
   brown and wild rices (*see Shopping Notes*)

4 cups chicken broth

1 pound roasted skinless turkey breast,
   cut into ½-inch dice

1¼ cups pecans, toasted and coarsely chopped
   (*see Cooking Technique*, page 278)

½ cup sliced green onion
   (including 2 inches of green tops)

¾ cup seedless green grapes, halved

1½ tablespoons chopped fresh tarragon
   or 1½ teaspoons dried, plus more if needed

2   tablespoons grated orange zest
     (orange portion of rind)
    Salt and freshly ground black pepper
    Spinach or Boston lettuce leaves, cleaned and dried
    Chopped fresh tarragon or flat-leaf parsley
     for garnish (*optional*)
1   orange, thinly sliced, for garnish (*optional*)

1. **To prepare dressing**: Combine orange juice concentrate, vinegar and tarragon in a nonreactive bowl. Whisk in garlic, salt, pepper and oil until blended. Set aside.

2. **To prepare salad**: Soak cranberries in hot water to cover for 10 minutes; drain and pat dry.

3. Melt butter in a medium, heavy saucepan over medium heat. Add rice and stir until all grains are well coated. Add broth, bring to a boil, cover, reduce heat to low and simmer until tender, about 25 minutes. Remove from heat and cool.

4. Toss rice with dressing. Add turkey, cranberries, pecans, green onion, grapes, tarragon and orange zest. Toss well; taste and season with salt, pepper and additional tarragon, if desired. (*Salad can be made 1 day ahead. Cover and refrigerate. Bring to room temperature 30 minutes before serving.*)

5. To serve, arrange a border of spinach or lettuce leaves on a serving platter or in a shallow bowl. Mound rice salad on top. Garnish with tarragon or parsley and a border of orange slices, if desired.

Healthful Variation: Although the pecans add an important flavor to this dish, they are high in fat. You could reduce the amount by half and sprinkle them over each serving rather than incorporating them into the salad.

Menu Suggestion:
A bowl of warm soup with this salad makes a complete main course. Curried Carrot and Parsnip Soup (page 57) is a good choice. Prince Albert Pumpkin Brownies (page 382), served with a scoop of vanilla ice cream or frozen yogurt and warmed store-bought caramel sauce, can end the meal.

Lobster Salad *with* Warm Sherry Dressing

SERVES 4

★

From Start to Finish:
50 minutes

Actual Working Time:
50 minutes

Make Ahead: Partially
(see step 1)

Can Be Frozen: No

Best Seasons:
All year, especially
summer

Shopping Note:

You can buy cooked
lobster meat at good fish
markets. Or, if you have the
time, you can purchase live
lobsters, cook them yourself
and remove the meat. A
pound of uncooked lobster
will yield about ¼ pound
cooked meat. For this
recipe, two 2-pound
lobsters or three 1¼-pound
lobsters will yield 1 pound
of cooked meat.

THIS IS DEFINITELY A SALAD FOR A SPECIAL OCCASION, one you might use to begin an important meal. It is expensive but distinctive. Cooked lobster meat, along with sautéed red bell pepper and green onions, is tossed in a warm sherry vinegar dressing and served on a bed of mixed greens. A sprinkling of fresh basil provides a simple garnish. (*See photograph on the cover.*)

FOR SALAD DRESSING

7 tablespoons olive oil (*divided*)
½ cup finely chopped shallots
7 tablespoons sherry wine vinegar (*divided*),
  see *Shopping Note, page 270*
1 teaspoon Dijon mustard
¾ teaspoon salt
  Freshly ground black pepper
6 tablespoons chicken broth

FOR SALAD

2 tablespoons olive oil
1 large red bell pepper, seeds and membranes
  removed, cut into ¼-inch-wide strips
4 green onions, including 2 inches of
  green tops, chopped
1 pound cooked lobster meat
  (*see Shopping Note and Variation*)
6 cups mixed greens (Boston, Bibb and red-leaf
  lettuces), cleaned, dried and torn into
  bite-sized pieces
  Salt and freshly ground black pepper
½ cup fresh basil leaves, cut into ¼-inch-wide strips
  (*divided*)

1. **To prepare dressing**: Heat 1 tablespoon oil in a medium, heavy skillet over medium-high heat. Add shallots and cook until softened, stirring frequently, about 3 minutes. Add 2 tablespoons vinegar and cook, stirring, for 30 seconds. Remove from heat and add remaining 5 tablespoons vinegar, mustard, salt and pepper to taste. Whisk in broth. Gradually whisk in the remaining 6 tablespoons oil. Set aside. (*Dressing can be made up to 4 hours ahead. Cover and store at cool room temperature.*)

2. **To prepare salad**: Heat oil in a large, heavy skillet over medium-high heat. Add red pepper and sauté until just tender, about 3 minutes. Add green onions and cook for 1 minute more. Add lobster and cook, stirring, just until heated through. Remove from heat.

3. Place greens in a large bowl. Heat dressing in a small, heavy saucepan over low heat, stirring constantly. Pour about half of dressing into bowl with greens and mix to coat lightly. Taste and season with salt and pepper. Divide greens among 4 salad plates. Stir ¼ cup basil into lobster mixture. Toss lobster mixture with enough remaining dressing to coat lightly. Spoon lobster mixture over greens. Sprinkle with remaining ¼ cup basil. Serve warm.

Variation: You can substitute good-quality cooked lump crabmeat for the lobster with good results.

Menu Suggestion:

This is an ideal first-course salad, or you can pair it with soup for a light main dish.

269

Honey *and* Ginger Scallop Salad

SERVES 6

★

From Start to Finish:
55 minutes

Actual Working Time:
55 minutes

Make Ahead: Partially
(see step 1)

Can Be Frozen: No

Best Seasons:
Spring and summer

Shopping Note:
Many large supermarkets sell sherry wine vinegar, a subtle yet flavorful vinegar that complements seafood nicely. It can also be found in specialty-food shops.

IN THIS LIGHT MAIN-COURSE SALAD, tender sea scallops, crunchy sugar snap peas and tiny green peas are sautéed and then tossed in a delectable honey and fresh ginger dressing.

FOR HONEY-GINGER DRESSING

4½ tablespoons honey

3 tablespoons sherry wine vinegar (*see Shopping Note*)

1 tablespoon finely chopped peeled gingerroot

¾ teaspoon dried rosemary leaves, crushed

6 tablespoons vegetable oil

FOR SALAD

Salt

¾ pound sugar snap peas, ends cut off on diagonal

2¼ pounds sea scallops

5 tablespoons vegetable oil (*divided*),
   plus more if needed

¾ cup frozen small peas, defrosted

2 teaspoons grated lemon zest
   (yellow portion of rind)
   Freshly ground black pepper

1 head Boston lettuce, leaves removed,
   cleaned and dried

1. **To prepare dressing**: Combine honey, vinegar, gingerroot, rosemary and oil in a food processor fitted with a metal blade or a blender. Process for several seconds, until mixture is well blended. Alternatively, whisk ingredients in a mixing bowl. (*Dressing can be made 2 days ahead. Store in a nonreactive container; cover and refrigerate. Bring to room temperature when needed.*)

2. **To prepare salad**: Bring 2 quarts water to a boil and add 2 teaspoons salt and sugar snap peas. Cook just to set color, 1 to 2 minutes. Drain and pat dry.

3. Remove connective tissue from sides of scallops (*see Cooking Technique, page 90*) and discard. Pat scallops dry.

4. Heat 2½ tablespoons oil in a large, heavy skillet over medium-high heat. When oil is hot, add enough scallops to fit comfortably in a single layer. Sauté, turning, until scallops are light golden and cooked through, 4 to 5 minutes. Remove scallops with a slotted spoon and drain on paper towels. Discard any liquid that has collected in pan. Add remaining 2½ tablespoons oil and cook remaining scallops in same way, adding more oil, if needed; drain.

5. Pour out any liquid that has collected in skillet in which scallops were cooked and add sugar snap and defrosted peas to pan. Stir and cook, tossing, just to heat through, 2 to 3 minutes. Place peas, scallops and lemon zest in a mixing bowl. Toss well with dressing. Season generously with salt and pepper.

6. To serve, arrange 2 or 3 lettuce leaves on each of 6 dinner plates. Divide and mound salad on top. Serve warm.

Menu Suggestion:
Serve a light soup and warm crusty French bread with this salad for a spring or summer meal.

Shrimp Salad *with* Mango Chutney Dressing

SERVES 8

★

From Start to Finish:
35 minutes

Actual Working Time:
35 minutes

Make Ahead: Partially
(see step 1)

Can Be Frozen: No

Best Seasons: All year

Shopping Notes:

Hellman's makes a good
reduced-fat mayonnaise.

If you prefer, you can buy
3 pounds shrimp in the
shell and peel, devein and
cook them yourself in
4 quarts boiling, salted
water until pink and curled,
2 to 3 minutes or more.

I
F YOU USE SHELLED, COOKED SHRIMP, you can assemble this
salad in only a few minutes. The dressing is made with store-
bought reduced-fat mayonnaise that is flavored with mango
chutney and curry powder. A little dressing is tossed with lettuce greens, then shrimp are placed on the greens and more dressing
is spooned over. A sprinkling of toasted almonds and currants are last-
minute touches.

FOR MANGO CHUTNEY DRESSING

1 cup reduced-fat mayonnaise
 (*see Shopping Notes*)

¼ cup mango chutney, chutney pieces chopped

2 teaspoons curry powder

½ teaspoon ground cumin

1 teaspoon ground coriander

¼ teaspoon cayenne pepper

¼ teaspoon salt

FOR SALAD

¼ cup chicken broth, plus 2-3 tablespoons more
 if needed (*divided*)

4-5 large heads Bibb lettuce, cleaned, dried
 and torn into bite-sized pieces
 (enough to make 8 cups)
 Salt

2½ pounds large (21-30 per pound) shelled,
 deveined and cooked shrimp (*see Shopping Notes*)

¼ cup dried currants for topping

½ cup toasted almonds for topping
 (*see Cooking Technique, page 228*)

1. **To prepare dressing**: Combine all ingredients in a mixing bowl and stir well to blend. (*Dressing can be made 1 day ahead; cover and refrigerate. Bring to room temperature 30 minutes before using.*)

2. **To prepare salad**: Transfer ⅓ cup dressing to a large mixing bowl and whisk in ¼ cup broth to thin it. Add lettuce and toss well so that greens are lightly coated with dressing. Salt lightly.

3. Divide greens among 8 individual salad plates. Divide shrimp evenly and arrange on top of greens. Whisk remaining dressing; if it appears to be too thick, thin it with 2 to 3 tablespoons more broth. Drizzle dressing over shrimp and sprinkle each serving with currants and toasted almonds. Serve immediately.

Menu Suggestion:

Offer this light main-course salad with a basket of warm French bread and, for dessert, Fresh Fruit in Red Wine and Ginger Sauce (page 347).

Black Bean *and* Cinnamon Rice Salad

SERVES 10

★

From Start to Finish:
1 hour 15 minutes

Actual Working Time:
1 hour

Make Ahead: Yes
(see steps 2, 3 and 4)

Can Be Frozen: No

Best Seasons:
Summer and fall

Cooking Technique:
Be careful when working with peppers! The tissues around your mouth, nose, eyes and ears are sensitive to the oils and fumes of hot peppers, and if you touch any of these areas with pepper-coated fingers, you will feel unpleasant burning sensations. I use rubber gloves to protect my hands, taking care to remove and wash them as soon as I am finished.

THIS BIG, COLORFUL SALAD is perfect for a crowd. The base of the salad is a combination of black beans and white rice cooked with a hint of cinnamon, then tossed in a dressing. A spicy fresh tomato salsa covers the dish. The salsa and the rice and beans can be made a day ahead and assembled on a large platter before serving. (*See photograph, page 38.*)

FOR SALAD

2 cups long-grain white rice, preferably converted white rice (*see Shopping Note,* page 230)
  Salt
6 whole cloves
2 cinnamon sticks, broken in half
4 14-ounce cans black beans, rinsed and drained (about 7 cups)
  Freshly ground black pepper
4½ tablespoons red wine vinegar
¾ cup olive oil

FOR FRESH TOMATO SALSA

3¾-4 cups coarsely chopped, stemmed, unpeeled tomatoes (about 1½ pounds)
3 tablespoons seeded and minced jalapeño peppers (5 to 6 medium peppers), *see Cooking Technique*
1 cup finely chopped onions
1 garlic clove, minced
6 tablespoons chopped fresh cilantro
2-2½ tablespoons fresh lime juice
  Salt and freshly ground black pepper
  Spinach leaves, cleaned and dried

1. **To prepare salad:** Bring 3 quarts water to a boil. Add rice, 1½ teaspoons salt, cloves and cinnamon sticks and cook until rice is fluffy and tender, 12 to 15 minutes or more. Drain well and cool. Remove cloves and cinnamon sticks.

2. Mix rice and beans together in a large bowl and add 1 teaspoon pepper. Combine vinegar and 1 teaspoon salt in a nonreactive mixing bowl. Whisk in oil. Toss rice and beans with dressing. Taste and season with more salt and pepper, if desired. (*Rice and beans can be prepared 1 day ahead; cover and refrigerate. Bring to room temperature before using.*)

3. **To prepare salsa:** Place tomatoes in a colander to drain for 10 minutes. Place tomatoes, jalapeños, onions, garlic and cilantro in a large nonreactive mixing bowl and mix well. Add lime juice, a little at a time, to taste. Season as needed with salt and pepper. (*Salsa can be made 1 day ahead. Keep covered and refrigerated.*)

4. To serve, arrange a bed of spinach leaves on a serving platter. Mound rice and bean mixture on spinach. Spoon salsa with a slotted spoon over beans and rice. (*Salad can be made 3 to 4 hours ahead and refrigerated. Bring to room temperature 20 to 30 minutes before serving.*) Serve at room temperature.

Menu Suggestion:

This salad hits the spot with corn on the cob and Chilied Ribs (page 180). Margarita Cheesecake (page 378) is a fine dessert.

Tomato, Basil *and* Couscous Salad

SERVES 6

★

From Start to Finish:
30 minutes

Actual Working Time:
30 minutes

Make Ahead: Yes
(see step 2)

Can Be Frozen: No

Best Seasons:
Summer and early fall

THIS SUMMER SALAD takes only 30 minutes to prepare from start to finish. Quick-cooking couscous is ready in 5 minutes and is tossed with a balsamic dressing. Bright red diced tomatoes, green onions and fresh basil complete this uncomplicated dish.

2½ cups chicken broth (*divided*)
1½ cups quick-cooking couscous
     (a 10-ounce box; *see Shopping Note,* page 232)
¼   cup balsamic vinegar
¼   teaspoon crushed red pepper flakes
     Freshly ground black pepper
¼   cup extra-virgin olive oil
½-¾ cup chopped green onions
     (including 2 inches of green tops)
1   cup diced plum or cherry tomatoes
     (stems, seeds and pulp removed),
     plus halved plum or cherry tomatoes
     for garnish
¼   cup fresh basil, cut into ¼-inch-wide strips,
     plus sprigs for garnish
     Salt

1. Heat 2¼ cups broth in a medium, heavy saucepan with a lid until it comes to a boil. Stir in couscous; cover and remove from heat. Let stand for 5 minutes. Fluff with a fork and let cool for 5 to 10 minutes.

2. Combine vinegar, red pepper flakes, a generous grinding of pepper, oil and remaining ¼ cup broth; mix well. Pour over couscous and mix well. Stir in green onions, diced tomatoes and basil strips. Taste and season with salt and pepper, if needed. (*Salad can be prepared 3 or 4 hours ahead to this point; cover and refrigerate. Bring to room temperature 30 minutes before serving.*)

3. To serve, mound salad in a shallow bowl and surround with a border of basil sprigs and halved tomatoes.

Menu Suggestion:

Serve this summer salad with grilled chicken, lamb chops or shrimp.

Wild Rice, Asparagus *and* Pecan Salad

SERVES 6 TO 8

★

From Start to Finish:
1 hour 45 minutes

Actual Working Time:
1 hour

Make Ahead: Yes
(see steps 2 and 4)

Can Be Frozen: No

Best Seasons:
Spring and summer

Cooking Technique:
To toast pecans, spread
on a rimmed baking sheet
and place on center rack of
a preheated 350°F oven.
Bake until golden, 5 to 8
minutes, stirring once or
twice. Watch carefully.
Remove from oven and
let cool.

WHEN I TASTED THIS SALAD at a summer cookout a few years ago, I was intrigued after the very first bite. The flavors and textures were so well blended that I hardly touched anything else on my plate. Wild and brown rice, sliced asparagus and toasted pecans were tossed in a lemon-yogurt dressing seasoned with fresh mint and cilantro. The host, sensing my interest in his creation, shared with me the guidelines for the dish. Since he hadn't cooked with exact measurements, I subsequently developed the following recipe.

¾-1	pound slim to medium asparagus, tough ends trimmed and discarded
1	tablespoon unsalted butter
1	cup brown rice
½	cup wild rice (*see Shopping Note*, page 282)
3½	cups chicken broth
1	cup (5 ounces) tiny frozen peas, defrosted
4	green onions, including 2 inches of green tops, chopped
3	tablespoons chopped fresh cilantro
2	tablespoons chopped fresh mint
1	cup coarsely chopped pecans, toasted (*see Cooking Technique*)
1-2	teaspoons salt
½	cup nonfat plain yogurt
1½	tablespoons fresh lemon juice, plus more if needed
2	teaspoons grated lemon zest (yellow portion of rind)
3	tablespoons olive oil
	Freshly ground black pepper
	Boston or other lettuce leaves, cleaned and dried, for garnish

1. Cut asparagus diagonally into ¾-inch pieces. Bring 3 cups water to a boil in a saucepan or skillet and cook asparagus until just tender, about 3 minutes. Drain, reserving cooking liquid. Rinse asparagus under cold running water to set color. Pat dry and set aside.

2. Heat butter in a large, heavy saucepan or pot over medium-high heat. When hot, add brown and wild rice and cook, stirring, to coat well for 1 minute. Add broth and 1½ cups reserved asparagus cooking liquid. Bring mixture to a simmer, reduce heat to low and cover. Cook for 35 to 45 minutes, or until rice is tender but still has a little bite when tasted. Do not overcook or rice will become too soft. Drain and discard any liquid from rice. Blot rice dry with paper towels. (*Rice can be cooked 1 day ahead. Cover and refrigerate.*)

3. Place rice, asparagus, peas, green onions, cilantro, mint and pecans in a mixing bowl and toss well to mix.

4. Whisk 1 teaspoon salt, yogurt, 1½ tablespoons lemon juice, lemon zest and oil in a small bowl, then add to rice mixture. Toss well to mix. Taste and add more lemon juice and salt, if needed, and season with pepper. (*Salad can be made 3 to 4 hours ahead; cover and refrigerate.*)

5. To serve, arrange a border of lettuce leaves on a platter or in a shallow bowl. Mound salad on lettuce leaves.

Menu Suggestion:

This salad is a great choice for summer menus. Serve it with grilled salmon or lamb chops as a side dish, or top it with skewers of grilled shrimp and turn it into a main course. You can also scoop out large tomato halves and fill them with this salad.

Fresh Corn *and* Rice Salad *with* Lime

SERVES 6

From Start to Finish:
1 hour 30 minutes

Actual Working Time:
35 minutes

Make Ahead: Yes
(see step 3)

Can Be Frozen: No

Best Seasons:
Summer and early fall

Shopping Note:
Packages of long-grain
white rice mixed with
smaller amounts of
wild rice and brown rice
are available in most
supermarkets. Be sure not
to buy a blend that includes
a seasoning mix, since you
will not need the mix for
this recipe. Uncle Ben's
Rice Trio, a combination
of white, brown and wild
rice, works beautifully in
this recipe.

THIS IS A GOOD SUMMER SALAD to serve with grilled chicken and meats. A mixture of white, brown and wild rice, combined with fresh cooked corn and chopped jalapeño peppers, is tossed with lime juice and olive oil and then seasoned with cilantro. I like the assertive flavor combinations in this light dish.

4¼	cups chicken broth (*divided*)
2	cups mixed long-grain white, brown and wild rice (*see Shopping Note*)
2½	cups cooked fresh corn kernels (about 6 ears, cooked, then scraped)
1½	tablespoons chopped jalapeño peppers, seeds and membranes removed (about 1½ medium peppers), *see Cooking Technique*, page 274
2	teaspoons grated lime zest (green portion of rind)
2	tablespoons chopped fresh cilantro, plus several sprigs for garnish
¼	cup fresh lime juice
2	tablespoons olive oil
	Generous dash cayenne pepper
	Salt

1. Bring 4 cups broth to a boil over medium heat and add rice. Lower heat and simmer, covered, until all liquid has been absorbed, 30 minutes or more. Check several times to make certain rice is cooking at a simmer and liquid is not being absorbed too quickly.

2. When done, transfer cooked rice to a large nonreactive bowl and let cool to room temperature. Add corn, jalapeño peppers, lime zest and chopped cilantro and mix well.

3. Combine lime juice, remaining ¼ cup broth and oil in a small bowl. Whisk well to combine and add to rice mixture. Stir and toss rice well. Add cayenne and taste. Add more cayenne for a spicier flavor, then season to taste with salt. If you use salted broth, you may not need additional salt. (*Salad can be made 1 day ahead and brought to room temperature before serving.*)

4. To serve, arrange salad in a bowl and garnish with cilantro sprigs. Serve at room temperature.

Menu Suggestion:
Serve this salad with Grilled Chicken with Pineapple Salsa (page 166).

Tomato *and* Wild Rice Salad

SERVES 8 TO 10

★

From Start to Finish:
3 hours 30 minutes
(includes 2 hours
refrigeration)

Actual Working Time:
40 minutes

Make Ahead: Yes
(see steps 2 and 3)

Can Be Frozen: No

Best Seasons:
Summer and early fall

Shopping Note:
Wild rice is not a true rice but, rather, a marsh grass that grows in wet areas, especially in the northern Great Lakes region. It is expensive, particularly when purchased boxed. Some supermarkets and specialty stores sell it in lower-priced bulk. There are varying qualities of wild rice; the best varieties include long, slender dark brown grains.

TENDER, JUICY PLUM TOMATOES, green onions and fresh basil are the summer accents that make this salad so delicious. These ingredients are combined with wild and brown rice and tossed in a slightly spicy dressing made with balsamic vinegar, olive oil and crushed red pepper flakes.

1 cup wild rice (*see Shopping Note*)
3 cups chicken broth (*divided*)
2 cups quick-cooking brown rice
   (*see Shopping Note,* page 104)
⅓ cup balsamic or red wine vinegar
   Salt and freshly ground black pepper
½ teaspoon crushed red pepper flakes,
   plus more if needed
½ cup olive oil
1 cup (2 bunches) chopped green onions,
   including 2 inches of green tops
1½ cups tomatoes, stems and seeds removed,
   cut into ½-inch dice
½ cup fresh basil leaves, cut into ¼-inch-wide strips
1 large head red leaf lettuce for garnish
½ cup (2-3 ounces) feta cheese, crumbled,
   for garnish (*optional*)

1. Cook wild rice in boiling, salted water to cover until just tender, 30 to 45 minutes. Drain well.

2. Bring 2½ cups broth to a boil over medium-high heat, reduce heat to a simmer and stir in brown rice. Cover and simmer until all liquid is absorbed, about 10 minutes. Combine wild and brown rice in a large nonreactive mixing bowl. (*Rice can be prepared 1 day ahead; cover and refrigerate.*)

3. To prepare dressing, combine vinegar, ½ teaspoon salt, several grindings of pepper and ½ teaspoon red pepper flakes in a bowl. Mix well and whisk in oil and remaining ½ cup broth. Pour over rice and stir well to mix. Cool to room temperature. Add green onions, tomatoes and basil and stir to mix well. Taste and add more salt and red pepper flakes, if desired. Add red pepper flakes sparingly, as they are quite hot. (*Cover and refrigerate for at least 2 hours or for as long as 5 hours.*)

4. To serve, arrange overlapping lettuce leaves as a border on a large serving tray or in a large shallow bowl. Mound salad over leaves and sprinkle, if desired, with crumbled feta.

Menu Suggestion:

This is an excellent side dish with grilled chicken or lamb. Prepared without the feta cheese, it makes a beautiful accompaniment to serve with a platter of sliced Fillet of Beef Stuffed with Red Peppers, Spinach and Goat Cheese (page 150) for a special summer dinner.

Chapter 11

American Classics
Quick Breads

Last-Minute Rosemary Corn Bread

S O QUICK, SO GOOD, SO DELICIOUS" is the way one of my cooking students described this corn bread. Hints of brown sugar and rosemary add flavor. This bread is best served warm from the oven.

¾ cup sifted all-purpose flour
1 tablespoon light brown sugar
2½ teaspoons baking powder
1 teaspoon salt
1¼ cups yellow cornmeal, preferably stone-ground
2 large eggs (*see Healthful Variation*)
4 tablespoons (½ stick) unsalted butter, melted
1 cup 1% milk
1¼ teaspoons crumbled dried rosemary leaves
Fresh rosemary sprigs for garnish (*optional*)

1. Arrange a rack at center position and preheat oven to 425°F. Spray a heavy, ovenproof 9-inch skillet (preferably a cast-iron one; *see Cooking Technique*) or a 9-by-9-inch baking pan with nonstick cooking spray. Place in preheated oven for 5 minutes while you assemble batter.

2. Sift flour, brown sugar, baking powder and salt together into a large mixing bowl. Add cornmeal. In a separate bowl, whisk together eggs, butter and milk. Whisk liquid into dry ingredients. Add dried rosemary and whisk just to combine. Remove hot skillet or pan from oven and pour batter into it. Bake until loaf is golden on top and firm to the touch, about 25 minutes.

3. Cut into 8 portions. Serve hot in a napkin-lined basket garnished with fresh rosemary sprigs, if desired.

Healthful Variation: You can replace eggs with egg substitute in this recipe.

SERVES 8

★

From Start to Finish:
35 minutes
Actual Working Time:
10 minutes
Make Ahead: No
Can Be Frozen: No
Best Seasons: All year

Cooking Technique:
Black cast-iron skillets are my favorite type of pan to use for corn bread. Other heavy, ovenproof skillets can also be used. However, I would avoid nonstick skillets, since their surfaces can be harmed by high oven heat.

Menu Suggestion:
This corn bread is delicious with a warm bowl of soup. Serve it with Orange and Basil Tomato Soup (page 58) or Roasted Garlic and White Cheddar Soup (page 74).

Apple-Cheddar Corn Bread

SERVES 8 TO 10

★

From Start to Finish:
1 hour
Actual Working Time:
30 minutes
Make Ahead: No
Can Be Frozen: No
Best Seasons:
Fall and winter

ALTHOUGH THERE IS NO SUGAR in this corn bread, it has a slightly sweet taste from the little bits of dried apples in it. The fruit, grated white Cheddar cheese and spices all contribute to the subtle flavor. This bread is especially good served warm with breakfast or brunch dishes.

1½	cups yellow cornmeal
½	cup all-purpose flour
2½	teaspoons baking powder
¾	teaspoon salt
½	teaspoon dried sage leaves, crumbled
½	teaspoon dried thyme leaves
¼	teaspoon ground coriander
⅛	teaspoon cayenne pepper
1½	cups (6 ounces) shredded sharp white Cheddar cheese (*divided*)
1	cup (3-4 ounces) very finely chopped dried apples
1¼	cups buttermilk
1	large egg
5	tablespoons unsalted butter
¼	teaspoon baking soda
¼	cup warm water

1. Arrange a rack at center position and preheat oven to 400°F.

2. Place cornmeal, flour, baking powder, salt, sage, thyme, coriander and cayenne in a large mixing bowl and stir well to blend. Add 1 cup cheese and apples and toss well to coat with dry ingredients. Set aside.

3. In another bowl, whisk together buttermilk and egg. Pour into dry ingredients and stir to mix.

4. Melt butter in a heavy, ovenproof 10-inch (preferably cast-iron) skillet over medium-high heat. When melted, pour all but 1 tablespoon into batter and stir gently until blended.

5. Dissolve baking soda in water and stir to mix. Add to batter.

6. Pour batter into remaining melted butter in hot skillet. Sprinkle remaining ½ cup cheese over batter.

7. Bake until a tester inserted in center comes out clean and bread is a rich golden brown, about 25 minutes. Remove from oven, invert onto a serving plate and turn again so cheese-crusted side is on top; cool for 5 minutes. Cut into wedges and serve hot.

Fresh Basil-Parmesan Corn Bread

SERVES 6 TO 8

★

From Start to Finish:
35 minutes

Actual Working Time:
10 minutes

Make Ahead: No

Can Be Frozen: No

Best Seasons:
Summer and early fall

Cooking Technique:
Do not use a nonstick pan; most cannot go into an oven over 400°F because the high heat can damage the coating.

Menu Suggestion:
This corn bread is a perfect accompaniment to Meal-in-Itself Vegetable Soup (page 72).

TWO SIMPLE INGREDIENTS—fresh basil and Parmesan cheese—turn ordinary corn bread into a distinctive loaf. When cut, this crusty bread, flavored mildly with cheese, reveals golden slices speckled with basil.

2	large eggs
¾	cup buttermilk
¼	cup light sour cream
¾	teaspoon baking powder
¼	teaspoon baking soda
¾	teaspoon salt
	Freshly ground black pepper
⅓	cup freshly grated imported Parmesan cheese
1	cup yellow cornmeal
⅓	cup finely chopped fresh basil leaves
1½	teaspoons olive oil

1. Arrange a rack at center position and preheat oven to 450°F.

2. Place eggs, buttermilk and sour cream in a mixing bowl and mix lightly. Add baking powder, baking soda, salt, several grindings of pepper and Parmesan cheese and mix well. Stir in cornmeal and basil; batter will be loose.

3. Heat oil in an 8-inch heavy, ovenproof skillet (preferably cast-iron) or an 8-inch round or square baking pan (*see Cooking Technique*) over medium heat, or place in preheated oven for 5 minutes. When hot, swirl oil in pan to coat bottom and sides. Pour batter into pan.

4. Bake until firm to the touch, 15 to 20 minutes. Remove from oven and cool for 3 to 5 minutes. Run a knife around edges of pan to loosen bread. Unmold and cut into wedges or squares. Serve hot on a plate or in a napkin-lined basket.

Mustard Biscuits

LIKE ALL GOOD BISCUITS, these are light and flaky. They have a zesty flavor from the generous amounts of stone-ground Dijon mustard and freshly ground black pepper in the dough. The biscuits are small, only about two inches in diameter, making them ideal to stuff and use for appetizers (see page 11).

MAKES 18 TO
20 BISCUITS,
EACH 2 INCHES

★

From Start to Finish:
30 minutes
Actual Working Time:
15 minutes
Make Ahead: No
Can Be Frozen: No
Best Seasons: All year

2   cups all-purpose flour
1   tablespoon baking powder
½   teaspoon salt
1   teaspoon freshly ground black pepper
6   tablespoons (¾ stick) unsalted butter,
      well chilled and cut into small chunks
½   cup plus 2 tablespoons whole milk,
      plus extra to brush tops of biscuits
2   tablespoons country (whole-grain)
      Dijon mustard

1. Arrange a rack at center position and preheat oven to 400°F. Spray a baking sheet with nonstick cooking spray.

2. In a food processor fitted with a metal blade, place flour, baking powder, salt and pepper. Pulse several times to blend. Add butter and pulse for several seconds until mixture has a crumbly texture. Alternatively, to mix by hand, place dry ingredients in a mixing bowl and cut in butter with a pastry blender or 2 table knives until crumbly.

3. In a large mixing bowl, whisk together ½ cup plus 2 tablespoons milk and mustard. Add dry mixture and stir just to blend.

4. Shape dough into a ball, and on a floured work surface, roll dough out to a ⅜-to-½-inch thickness. Use a 2-inch round cutter to cut 18 or more biscuits. Transfer biscuits to baking sheet and brush tops with extra milk. Bake biscuits until golden, 12 to 14 minutes. Serve piping hot in a napkin-lined bowl or basket.

Cranberry-Orange Biscuits

MAKES 20
BISCUITS,
EACH 2 INCHES

★

From Start to Finish:
50 minutes
Actual Working Time:
35 minutes
Make Ahead: No
Can Be Frozen: No
Best Seasons:
Fall and winter

AN ASSISTANT WHO HELPED CREATE THIS RECIPE laughingly suggested that we call these little morsels "biscones," since they seem to be a cross between a savory biscuit and a sweet scone. The sweetness in the biscuits comes from dried cranberries. Toasted pecans and orange zest complement the dried fruit. A honey-butter glaze, added during the last minutes of baking, gives them a special sheen.

FOR BISCUITS

½ cup orange juice
6 tablespoons chopped dried cranberries
  (*see Shopping Note*, page 183)
2 cups all-purpose or pastry flour
3 tablespoons sugar
2 teaspoons baking powder
½ teaspoon salt
2 teaspoons grated orange zest
  (orange portion of rind)
4 tablespoons (½ stick) unsalted butter,
  chilled and cut into small pieces
¼ cup toasted pecans, chopped
  (*see Cooking Technique*, page 278)
⅔ cup 1% or 2% milk

FOR HONEY-BUTTER GLAZE

2 tablespoons honey
1 tablespoon unsalted butter

1. **To prepare biscuits:** Arrange a rack at center position and preheat oven to 400°F. Line a baking sheet with aluminum foil and spray with nonstick cooking spray.

2. Heat orange juice in a small saucepan until hot. Remove from heat and add cranberries. Let sit for 5 to 10 minutes until softened. Drain, discarding juice. Set aside.

3. In a food processor fitted with a metal blade, place flour, sugar, baking powder, salt, orange zest and butter. Process for 5 to 10 seconds to incorporate ingredients. Add cranberries and pecans and pulse several times just to mix. Pour in milk and process for about 30 seconds more to incorporate. (Alternatively, to mix by hand, place dry ingredients and butter in a large mixing bowl and cut butter into mixture with a pastry blender or 2 table knives. Add cranberries and pecans and mix well. Add milk and stir just to mix.)

4. Remove dough to a lightly floured surface and knead for several seconds. Roll out dough to ¾ inch thickness and cut out biscuits with a 2-inch round cutter. Place on baking sheet and bake for 8 minutes.

5. **Meanwhile, make glaze**: Heat honey and butter until butter is melted. Mix well to blend.

6. Remove biscuits from oven after 8 minutes and brush tops with glaze. Return biscuits to oven and bake until golden, about 7 minutes more.

7. Remove from oven. Let cool for a few minutes, then arrange on a serving plate and serve hot.

Blue Cheese-Walnut Muffins

MAKES 12 MUFFINS

★

From Start to Finish:
50 minutes

Actual Working Time:
30 minutes

Make Ahead: No

Can Be Frozen: No

Best Seasons:
Fall and winter

Cooking Technique:
To toast walnuts, place on
a rimmed baking sheet in a
preheated 350°F oven and
bake on center rack until
nuts are lightly browned,
5 to 8 minutes. Remove
and cool.

BLUE CHEESE IS AN UNEXPECTED yet marvelous flavor in these savory muffins. Toasted walnuts and a generous seasoning of thyme complete the trio of bold flavors. My friend Roger Mandle, who suggested the idea for these muffins, serves them at breakfast to accompany egg dishes and with salads and hearty soups for other meals.

2	cups all-purpose flour
2	teaspoons baking powder
¾	teaspoon salt
1½	teaspoons dried thyme leaves
1	teaspoon light brown sugar
½	cup finely chopped toasted walnuts
	(*see Cooking Technique*)
⅔	cup packed (about 4 ounces) Danish blue cheese,
	at room temperature, crumbled
2	large eggs
¾	cup 1% or 2% milk
4	tablespoons (½ stick) unsalted butter,
	melted and cooled slightly

1. Arrange a rack at center position and preheat oven to 400°F. Spray a standard-sized 12-mold muffin tin with nonstick cooking spray and set aside.

2. Combine flour, baking powder, salt, thyme, brown sugar and walnuts in a large mixing bowl and stir well to blend. Sprinkle blue cheese over dry ingredients. Using your fingertips, rub cheese into dry ingredients until mixture resembles coarse meal.

3. In a separate bowl, combine eggs, milk and butter and mix well. Add to dry ingredients and stir just to combine. Do not overmix.

4. Spoon batter evenly into prepared muffin molds. Bake until golden and a toothpick inserted in center of muffin comes out clean, 15 to 17 minutes. Do not overbake, or muffins will be dry. Remove from oven and invert to release muffins. Serve in a napkin-lined basket or bowl.

Cheddar-Rosemary Pear Loaf

MAKES 16 SLICES,
EACH ½ INCH
THICK

From Start to Finish:

1 hour 40 minutes

Actual Working Time:

30 minutes

Make Ahead: Yes

(see step 5)

Can Be Frozen: Yes

(see step 5)

Best Seasons:

Fall and winter

Shopping Notes:

Fresh rosemary is an important yet subtle flavor in this bread. You can substitute a scant 1 teaspoon crushed dried rosemary for the fresh, but the flavor will not be quite as distinctive.

Del Monte or Libby's pears in light syrup work well in this recipe.

THIS BREAD CAN BE ASSEMBLED in a short time and, in that respect resembles other quick breads like banana, date nut or zucchini loaves. The similarity ends there, however. The inspiration of my talented assistant, Emily Bell, this special loaf is laced with cheese and scented with fresh rosemary. Pureed pears, made from a can of pears packed in light syrup, add a barely discernible flavor but a wonderful moistness. Enjoy this bread warm, cold or even toasted.

2 cups all-purpose flour, plus
    1 tablespoon for coating pan

2 teaspoons baking powder

1 teaspoon baking soda

1 teaspoon salt

2 teaspoons finely chopped fresh rosemary
    (*see Shopping Notes*)

1 15-to-16-ounce can pears packed in light syrup
    (*see Shopping Notes*)

½ cup buttermilk

3 tablespoons unsalted butter, softened

1 large egg

1¾ cups (about 7 ounces) packed grated
    sharp white Cheddar cheese (*divided*)

1. Arrange a rack at center position and preheat oven to 350°F. Spray an 8½-by-4½-inch loaf pan with nonstick cooking spray. Use 1 tablespoon flour to coat bottom and sides of pan and shake out excess.

2. Combine remaining 2 cups flour, baking powder, baking soda, salt and rosemary in a mixing bowl and stir well to mix. Set aside.

3. Drain pears well and puree in a food processor fitted with a metal blade, a blender or a food mill. Transfer puree to a mixing bowl and whisk in buttermilk. Set aside.

4. In a large bowl, with an electric mixer on medium speed or by hand, cream butter until smooth. Add egg and beat just to blend. Add dry ingredients, alternating with buttermilk mixture, beginning and ending with dry ingredients. Add 1½ cups cheese and mix well.

5. Pour batter into pan and smooth top evenly with a spatula. Sprinkle remaining ¼ cup cheese over top. Bake until a tester comes out clean, 55 to 60 minutes. Remove and cool for at least 10 minutes before slicing. (*Bread can be made 2 days ahead; cool, cover tightly with foil and leave at cool room temperature. It can also be frozen; wrap in plastic wrap, then tightly in foil, and seal in a plastic bag. Defrost before using.*)

6. To serve, cut into 16 slices, each ½ inch thick. Serve warm or at room temperature.

Menu Suggestion:

Serve this bread warm with "Waldorf of Sorts" Salad (page 254) or toast it for breakfast or for sandwiches. Try smoked turkey with cranberry chutney (or sauce) between two toasted slices of this bread for a special sandwich.

Hot Leek *and* Basil Bread

SERVES 6 TO 8

★

From Start to Finish:
30 minutes

Actual Working Time:
20 minutes

Make Ahead: Partially
(see step 5)

Can Be Frozen: No

Best Seasons: All year

Cooking Technique:
To clean and prepare a leek for cooking, cut off and discard root ends and dark green portion of leaves (unless the recipe calls for including the dark green parts). What remains—a section that is white near the root end and pale green at the other—is considered the "white part" of the leek. Make a lengthwise slit down the leek and hold under cold running water to wash out any sand or grit that may be trapped in between the layers. Pat dry and use as directed.

I FIRST SAMPLED THIS BREAD at the Fog City Diner, in San Francisco. It was my favorite of all the outstanding dishes I tried on my visit. A loaf of French bread was partially sliced and filled with a mixture of sautéed leeks seasoned with basil. The loaf, brushed with melted butter and olive oil, arrived piping hot at the table. This bread has so much personality that I would suggest serving it with fairly simple foods, like roast chicken or plain grilled steaks.

1   loaf French bread, about 20 inches long
       and 3 inches in diameter
5   tablespoons unsalted butter (*divided*)
5   tablespoons olive oil (*divided*)
2   cups cleaned, chopped leeks, white parts only
       (about 3; *see Cooking Technique*)
1   teaspoon dried basil leaves
     Salt
     Generous pinch cayenne pepper
     Fresh basil sprigs for garnish (*optional*)

1. Slice bread on diagonal at 1-inch intervals, almost but not quite all the way through loaf.

2. Heat 4 tablespoons butter and 4 tablespoons oil together in a medium, heavy saucepan over medium heat until butter is melted. Stir to mix well.

3. Generously brush mixture over top and sides of loaf and between each slice.

4. Heat remaining 1 tablespoon butter and remaining 1 tablespoon oil in a skillet over medium heat until hot. Add leeks and cook, stirring constantly, until leeks are softened, about 4 minutes. Add dried basil and cook for 1 minute more. Remove and season with salt and cayenne. Stir to mix.

5. Place loaf on a baking sheet lined with aluminum foil. Spread leek mixture between each slice. (*Bread can be prepared 1 hour ahead to this point. Cover loosely with foil and keep at room temperature.*)

6. When ready to bake, arrange a rack at center position and preheat oven to 350°F. Bake, uncovered, until warm and crispy, 5 to 8 minutes. For ease in serving, place on a chopping board; cut through slices, and if desired, garnish with basil sprigs.

Sinfully Good Garlic and Blue Cheese Bread

MAKES ABOUT 16
SLICES

★

From Start to Finish:
30 minutes
Actual Working Time:
15 minutes
Make Ahead: Partially
(see step 3)
Can Be Frozen: No
Best Seasons: All year

THIS BREAD IS MADE BY EMBELLISHING a store-bought loaf. Nonni Casino, a chef from Columbus, Ohio, created it. She brushed split loaves of Italian bread with garlic-scented butter, then topped the halves with crumbled blue cheese, red onion slices, black olives and rosemary. Baked until the cheese has melted, it is best served straight from the oven.

4   large garlic cloves, finely chopped
8   tablespoons (1 stick) unsalted butter, melted
1   loaf Italian bread, about 13 inches long
     and 4-6 inches wide
8   ounces blue cheese, crumbled
1   medium-sized red onion, peeled and halved
     lengthwise through stem end and
     cut into paper-thin slices
     Freshly ground black pepper
12 Kalamata or other black olives, pitted and halved
¾-1 teaspoon finely chopped fresh rosemary
     or ¼-½ teaspoon dried, crushed well

1. Combine garlic and butter in a small bowl and set aside.

2. Slice bread in half lengthwise. Top half will have a slightly rounded top. Cut a lengthwise strip from crust of top half and turn bread over so it lies flat. (Strip of crust can be used for bread crumbs.) Place bread halves, cut sides up, on a foil-lined baking sheet.

3. Brush cut side of each half with garlic-butter mixture. Sprinkle each half with blue cheese, then top with onion slices. Season to taste with pepper. Arrange olive pieces over both halves and sprinkle with rosemary. (*Bread can be prepared 2 to 3 hours ahead to this point. Cover loosely with plastic wrap and leave at cool room temperature or refrigerate.*)

4. When ready to bake bread, preheat oven to 400°F. Bake until cheese melts and bread is hot, 8 to 10 minutes. Remove and let cool for 2 minutes. Cut into slices 1½ inches wide. Serve warm, arranged on a serving platter.

Menu Suggestion:

This is a wonderful bread with simple grilled chicken or meats, or serve it as an appetizer. Just cut the loaves into slightly smaller 1-inch slices, arrange on a tray, then garnish with fresh rosemary sprigs.

Chapter 12

A Fresh Start

Breakfast Treats

Sausages, Ham *or* Canadian Bacon Glazed *with* Sweet-Hot Mustard

S O SIMPLE, SO STRAIGHTFORWARD and such good results" is the way one of my students described this dish. My friend June McCarthy suggested heating sweet-hot mustard and apple jelly together to use as a glaze for sautéed breakfast meats. The sharp taste of mustard combined with the sweet jelly makes a noteworthy glaze for sausages, ham or Canadian bacon.

1 pound turkey kielbasa, ¼-inch-thick lean
  ham slices or ¼-inch-thick Canadian bacon slices
  (*see Shopping Notes*)
¼ cup apple jelly
3 tablespoons sweet-hot mustard (*see Shopping Notes*)
  Fresh thyme or sage sprigs for garnish (*optional*)

1. If using kielbasa, cut on diagonal into 4-inch-long pieces.

2. Place a large, heavy skillet over medium heat and spray with nonstick cooking spray. When hot, add kielbasa, ham or Canadian bacon. Sauté, turning once or twice, until meat is hot and lightly browned, 3 to 5 minutes. Remove to a side dish.

3. Reduce heat to low and whisk apple jelly into pan. Add mustard and whisk constantly until jelly has melted and blends with mustard, about 1 minute. Return meat to pan and stir and turn until each piece is coated with glaze. Arrange meat on a warm serving plate and garnish with thyme or sage sprigs, if desired.

SERVES 4 TO 6

From Start to Finish:
  15 minutes
Actual Working Time:
  15 minutes
Make Ahead: No
Can Be Frozen: No
Best Seasons: All year

Shopping Notes:
  Turkey kielbasa is lower in fat than pork sausages but is moist and has a robust flavor. Hillshire Farms is a good brand.
  Aidells Sausage Company from California produces a superb chicken and apple sausage that would also be delicious in this recipe.
  Sweet Hot Mister Mustard is available in most markets and works well here.

Menu Suggestion:
  These glazed breakfast meats are attractive served on a platter alongside scrambled eggs. You can also add some sautéed apple rings to the tray.

Double Banana Pancakes

MAKES ABOUT
16 TO 18
PANCAKES,
EACH 3½ TO
4 INCHES

★

From Start to Finish:
30 minutes
Actual Working Time:
30 minutes
Make Ahead: No
Can Be Frozen: No
Best Seasons: All year

THESE GOLDEN BROWN PANCAKES get a double shot of banana flavoring. Pureed bananas are incorporated into the batter, and warm, sautéed banana slices top the griddle cakes.

FOR PANCAKES

1	cup all-purpose flour
1¾	teaspoons baking powder
¾	teaspoon salt
1	tablespoon plus 1 teaspoon sugar
2	large very ripe bananas
⅔	cup 1% or 2% milk
2	large eggs (*see Healthful Variation*)
2	teaspoons vegetable oil
	Unsalted butter and vegetable oil for cooking pancakes (*see Healthful Variation*)

FOR TOPPING

1	tablespoon unsalted butter
2	large ripe bananas, sliced
	Freshly grated nutmeg
¾	cup pure maple syrup, warmed

1. **To prepare pancakes:** In a large mixing bowl, sift together flour, baking powder, salt and sugar. Mix to blend and set aside.

2. Puree bananas in a food processor fitted with a metal blade to a smooth, liquid consistency. Or mash bananas with a fork and beat to a liquid consistency. Transfer puree to a mixing bowl and add milk, eggs and oil. Whisk just enough to blend well. Add dry ingredients and whisk to incorporate well.

3. Preheat oven to 250°F. Heat a griddle or a large, heavy skillet over medium-high heat. Add just enough butter and oil in equal amounts to film bottom of griddle or skillet. When butter and oil are hot, ladle 2 tablespoons of batter per pancake onto griddle or skillet and cook until tops of pancakes bubble and undersides are golden brown, 2 to 3 minutes. Turn and cook until golden brown on other side, about 2 minutes more.

4. Transfer to a baking sheet and keep warm in oven (don't stack, because they will steam and become flabby). Continue until all batter has been used, adding more butter and oil to pan as necessary.

5. **To prepare topping**: Heat butter in a large, heavy skillet over medium-high heat. When hot, add sliced bananas and sauté, stirring constantly, until bananas are warm, about 1 minute.

6. To serve, arrange 4 pancakes on each of 4 dinner plates and top with sautéed bananas. Grate some nutmeg over bananas and drizzle with maple syrup.

Healthful Variation: The eggs can be replaced with egg substitute. You can also use nonstick spray for cooking pancakes, but they will be less rich in flavor.

Pecan Griddle Cakes
with Orange Butter

MAKES ABOUT
12 PANCAKES,
EACH 5 TO 6
INCHES

From Start to Finish:
40 minutes

Actual Working Time:
40 minutes

Make Ahead: Partially
(see step 1)

Can Be Frozen: No

Best Seasons: All year

THESE PANCAKES ARE MADE WITH BOTH white and whole wheat flours, and the pecans in the batter give them a slightly crunchy texture. What makes them so irresistible is the delectable butter garnish flavored simply with orange marmalade and honey. Because the topping gives the pancakes a rich butter taste, I use nonstick cooking spray in place of butter and oil to cook the griddle cakes. (*See photograph, page 35.*)

FOR ORANGE BUTTER

6 tablespoons (¾ stick) unsalted butter, softened

3 tablespoons sweet orange marmalade

1½ teaspoons honey

FOR PANCAKES

¾ cup all-purpose flour

¾ cup whole wheat flour

2 tablespoons light brown sugar

1¾ teaspoons baking powder

½ teaspoon salt

2-2¼ cups 1% or 2% milk

1 large egg plus 1 large egg white

2 tablespoons unsalted butter, melted

⅔ cup toasted pecans, chopped
(*see Cooking Technique*, page 278)
Pure maple syrup, warmed (*optional*)

1. **To prepare butter:** Place all ingredients in a mixing bowl and mix well. Transfer to a small serving bowl or ramekin. Cover and refrigerate if not using immediately. (*Butter can be made up to 2 days ahead; cover and refrigerate. Bring to room temperature 30 minutes before using.*)

2. **To prepare pancakes**: Sift flours, brown sugar, baking powder and salt into a mixing bowl. In a large bowl, whisk together 2 cups milk, egg, egg white and butter. Whisk dry ingredients into liquid ones. If batter seems too thick, thin with remaining milk. Mix in pecans.

3. Preheat oven to 250°F. Spray a nonstick griddle or skillet with nonstick cooking spray. Place griddle or skillet over medium heat. Working in batches, pour batter onto hot griddle or skillet by scant ¼ cupfuls. Cook until bubbles appear and bottoms of pancakes are golden, about 3 minutes. Turn and cook until golden on other side, about 2 minutes. Transfer to a baking sheet and keep warm in oven (don't stack because they will steam and become flabby). Continue until all batter has been used. Serve with orange butter and, if desired, maple syrup.

Pumpkin Waffles

SERVES 8

★

From Start to Finish:
  40 minutes

Actual Working Time:
  40 minutes

Make Ahead: No

Can Be Frozen: No

Best Seasons:
  Fall and winter

Shopping Note:
  Buy plain, unsweetened pumpkin puree without added seasonings. It can be found in the canned-vegetable section of most supermarkets.

Cooking Technique:
  Most electric waffle irons, once seasoned according to manufacturers' instructions, do not need to be greased. Check the instructions with your own appliance.

FLAVORED WITH PUMPKIN PUREE and spices, these golden waffles are perfect for a special breakfast or brunch. I have suggested a variety of interesting toppings that complement them. Choose one or two garnishes, or offer the full array.

1½ cups cooked, pureed pumpkin (*see Shopping Note*)
  4 large eggs, separated (*see Healthful Variation*)
1¼ cups 1% or 2% milk
  4 tablespoons (½ stick) unsalted butter, melted
2½ cups sifted all-purpose flour
  4 teaspoons baking powder
  ½ teaspoon salt
  1 teaspoon ground cinnamon
  ¼ teaspoon ground ginger
    Pinch freshly grated nutmeg
    Pinch ground cloves
  ¼ cup firmly packed light brown sugar

SUGGESTED TOPPINGS

Chopped walnuts
Minced candied ginger
Raisins
Diced dried apricots
Plain yogurt, sprinkled with cinnamon
Pure maple syrup, warmed
Honey, warmed
Butter, melted

1. Preheat waffle iron but do not grease (*see Cooking Technique*). Preheat oven to 250°F.

2. Combine pumpkin, egg yolks, milk and butter in a large bowl.

3. Sift together flour, baking powder, salt, cinnamon, ginger, nutmeg and cloves and add to pumpkin mixture. Stir in brown sugar. Stir well to mix.

4. Beat egg whites until soft peaks form and gently fold into pumpkin batter. Cook waffles in waffle iron until golden and crisp. Place cooked waffles on a baking sheet, loosely covered with aluminum foil, in oven to keep warm.

5. When ready to serve, place waffles on a heated platter and serve with toppings of choice.

Healthful Variation: The eggs can be replaced with egg substitute.

Spiced French Toasts
with Orange Maple Syrup

SERVES 4

★

From Start to Finish:
30 minutes

Actual Working Time:
30 minutes

Make Ahead: No

Can Be Frozen: No

Best Seasons: All year

T HESE FRENCH TOASTS are twice flavored with orange. Orange zest, along with cinnamon and nutmeg, is added to the egg and milk mixture for soaking the bread slices, and maple syrup, steeped with orange zest and a cinnamon stick, is poured over the cooked toasts.

FOR ORANGE MAPLE SYRUP

½ cup pure maple syrup

1½ teaspoons grated orange zest
   (orange portion of rind)

1 3-inch-long cinnamon stick

FOR TOASTS

2 large eggs (*see Healthful Variation*)

½ cup 1% or 2% milk

½ teaspoon grated orange zest

¼ teaspoon freshly grated nutmeg

¼ teaspoon ground cinnamon

8 slices good-quality day-old white bread
   Unsalted butter
   Vegetable oil

1. **To prepare orange maple syrup:** Place all ingredients in a small, heavy saucepan over medium-high heat and bring to a boil. Immediately remove from heat and let syrup steep for 10 to 15 minutes to infuse flavors. Remove cinnamon stick.

2. **To prepare toasts:** Preheat oven to 250°F. Place eggs, milk, orange zest, nutmeg and cinnamon in a mixing bowl and whisk until well combined. Pour into a large, shallow glass or ceramic dish and add enough bread slices to fit comfortably. Soak bread, turning once, for 1 minute or less. Remove and continue until all bread slices have been evenly soaked.

3. Place ½ tablespoon each butter and oil in a large, heavy skillet over medium-low heat. When butter and oil are hot, add enough slices to fit comfortably in a single layer and cook until golden brown on bottoms, 2 minutes or more. Turn toasts and cook until golden brown on other side, 2 minutes or more. Remove cooked toasts to a baking sheet and place in oven to keep warm. Continue to cook toasts in this manner, adding more butter and oil in equal amounts as needed, and placing cooked batches in oven to keep warm.

4. To serve, arrange 2 toasts on each of 4 dinner plates and drizzle with warm orange maple syrup.

Healthful Variation: The eggs can be replaced with egg substitute.

Eggnog French Toasts

SERVES 4

★

From Start to Finish:
  35 minutes
Actual Working Time:
  35 minutes
Make Ahead: No
Can Be Frozen: No
Best Seasons:
  Fall and winter, especially
between Thanksgiving and
New Year's Day

Shopping Notes:
  Light eggnog is a good
lower-fat alternative to
traditional eggnog. Look
for it in the dairy section,
especially around the
holidays, between
Thanksgiving and
New Year's Day.
  Look for a round loaf of
sourdough bread, about 8
to 10 inches in diameter.

M Y FRIEND BRENDA McDOWELL, a food publicist in Chicago, told me that French toasts could be made with eggnog. I tried it, with splendid results. The toasts are delicious and take only minutes to prepare because the eggs and milk are already combined in the eggnog. Light eggnog, lower in fat than the traditional kind, works beautifully in this recipe.

1½ cups light eggnog (*see Shopping Notes*)
  8 ½-inch-thick slices crusty sourdough bread
      (*see Shopping Notes*) or 8 slices good-quality
      day-old white bread
  2 tablespoons unsalted butter, plus more if needed
  2 tablespoons vegetable oil, plus more if needed
      Freshly grated nutmeg
      Ground cinnamon
      Pure maple syrup, warmed

1. Preheat oven to 250°F.

2. Pour eggnog into a large, shallow dish or pan. (A 13-by-9-inch Pyrex dish works well.) Add bread slices and turn to coat on all sides, stacking slices, if necessary.

3. Heat 1 tablespoon each butter and oil in a large, heavy skillet over medium to medium-low heat. When butter and oil are hot, add enough bread slices to fit in a single layer. Cook until golden brown on bottoms, 2 to 3 minutes, then turn and cook until golden brown on other sides, 2 to 3 minutes more. Transfer cooked toasts to a baking sheet and place in oven to keep warm.

4. Continue to cook French toasts, adding more butter and oil in equal amounts as needed and keeping each batch warm in oven.

5. To serve, arrange 2 toasts on each of 4 dinner plates and sprinkle generously with nutmeg and cinnamon. Pour maple syrup over top.

Scrambled Eggs *with* Sausage *and* Pepper Cheese

Y SON MICHAEL, home for a weekend visit, surprised his father and me one Sunday morning with these wonderful scrambled eggs. He sautéed diced kielbasa sausage and onions together, then stirred those ingredients, along with grated pepper Jack cheese and some crushed rosemary, into lightly beaten eggs before scrambling them. The assertive flavors of the sausage, onions and cheese splendidly complement the creamy eggs.

SERVES 4

From Start to Finish:
  20 minutes
Actual Working Time:
  20 minutes
Make Ahead: No
Can Be Frozen: No
Best Seasons: All year

8 eggs (*see Healthful Variation*)
3 tablespoons unsalted butter (*divided*)
1 cup chopped onions
4 ounces turkey kielbasa, finely diced (about 1 cup);
   see Shopping Notes, page 301
1 teaspoon crushed dried rosemary
   Salt and freshly ground black pepper
1 cup (4 ounces) grated pepper Jack cheese
   Fresh rosemary sprigs for garnish (*optional*)

1. Beat eggs lightly in a mixing bowl and set aside.

2. Heat 1 tablespoon butter in a large, heavy skillet over medium heat. When hot, add onions and kielbasa and cook, stirring, until onions are just softened and sausage is hot, about 4 minutes.

3. Remove with a slotted spoon and add to beaten eggs. Stir in dried rosemary and season generously with salt and pepper.

4. Heat remaining 2 tablespoons butter in same skillet, and when hot, add egg mixture. Sprinkle with cheese. Cook, stirring constantly, until eggs are scrambled to a soft consistency. Remove and arrange on a warm serving platter. Garnish with fresh rosemary sprigs, if desired.

Healthful Variation: The eggs can be replaced with egg substitute.

Eastern Market Scrambled Eggs *with* Salmon, Green Onions *and* Potatoes

SERVES 4

From Start to Finish:
35 minutes

Actual Working Time:
35 minutes

Make Ahead: Partially
(see step 1)

Can Be Frozen: No

Best Seasons:
All year, especially spring

I GOT THE IDEA FOR THIS DISH while eating breakfast in a small, unpretentious cafe in the corner of the Eastern Market, a wonderful covered market on Washington's Capitol Hill. I was already enjoying a stack of pancakes when I spotted a blackboard with the day's specials scribbled on it. One of them was eggs scrambled with salmon, green onions and potatoes. It was too late for me to order that dish, but all the way home on the plane, I could think of nothing else. A few days later in my own kitchen, I interpreted the dish in the following way.

2 small new potatoes or 1 medium (6 ounces total),
   scrubbed but not peeled
3 tablespoons unsalted butter (*divided*)
½ cup (1 bunch) chopped green onion,
   including 2 inches of green tops
   Salt and freshly ground black pepper
8 large eggs (*see Healthful Variation*)
3-4 ounces thinly sliced smoked salmon,
   cut into ½-inch-wide strips
3 ounces reduced-fat cream cheese,
   broken into small chunks
2 tablespoons chopped fresh flat-leaf parsley
   for garnish

1. Cut potatoes into ¼-inch dice. Melt 1 tablespoon butter in a large, heavy skillet over medium heat. When hot, add potatoes and cook, stirring, until just lightly browned, about 3 minutes. Turn heat to low and cover with a lid. Let potatoes cook until just tender, 3 to 5 minutes. Remove lid and stir in green onion. Stir and cook for 1 minute more. Season with salt and pepper. Remove from heat. (*Potatoes and green onion can be cooked ahead and held, uncovered, in the skillet for 30 minutes before continuing.*)

2. In a mixing bowl, beat eggs lightly just to blend. Add salmon and cream cheese and stir to mix. Salt and pepper mixture lightly.

3. To finish, place skillet with potatoes over medium heat. Add remaining 2 tablespoons butter and cook, stirring constantly, until butter is melted and hot. Pour in egg mixture and cook, stirring constantly, until eggs are scrambled to a soft consistency. Taste and season with more salt and pepper, if needed. Remove and arrange on a warm platter. Sprinkle with parsley.

Healthful Variation: The eggs can be replaced with egg substitute.

Potato *and* Pepper Jack Cheese Omelet

SERVES 4

From Start to Finish:
50 minutes

Actual Working Time:
50 minutes

Make Ahead: No

Can Be Frozen: No

Best Seasons: All year

THE INGREDIENTS FOR THIS OMELET are reminiscent of Tex-Mex cooking, but it is made like an Italian frittata. To prepare it, thin potato slices are browned and then topped with a mixture of beaten eggs, grated pepper Jack cheese and bits of cream cheese. The omelet, in true frittata-style, is cooked slowly on top of the stove until set and is put under the broiler to finish. Served unmolded, it is garnished with chopped tomatoes and fresh cilantro.

6 eggs (*see Healthful Variation*)
4 ounces low-fat cream cheese, broken into chunks
1 cup (about 4 ounces) grated pepper Jack cheese
1 tablespoon unsalted butter (*divided*)
½ cup finely chopped onion
1 tablespoon finely chopped garlic
1 baking potato (about 8 ounces), peeled and cut into ⅛-inch-thick slices
Salt and freshly ground black pepper
½ cup diced, seeded tomatoes
2-3 tablespoons chopped fresh cilantro

1. Arrange a rack 5 to 6 inches from heat source and preheat broiler.

2. Place eggs, cream cheese and pepper Jack cheese in a mixing bowl and whisk until well blended. Set aside.

3. Generously spray a 9- or 10-inch heavy, ovenproof skillet with non-stick cooking spray. Add ½ tablespoon butter and set over medium-high heat. When butter is hot, add onion and sauté until softened, about 3 minutes. Add garlic and cook for 1 minute more. Transfer to a side dish.

4. Spray skillet again and add remaining ½ tablespoon butter. When hot, add potato slices and cook over medium heat, stirring and turning, until they are golden on each side, about 5 minutes.

5. Spread potatoes over entire bottom of skillet. Season to taste with salt and pepper. Spread garlic-onion mixture evenly over top. Pour in egg mixture and cook over medium heat, loosening edges with a spatula, about 10 minutes.

6. When eggs are set but still not completely firm on top, place skillet under broiler to finish cooking for 2 to 3 minutes or more. Watch carefully. When done, remove from oven and run a spatula around edges and under omelet to loosen. Invert onto a serving plate. Garnish with tomatoes and cilantro. Cut omelet into wedges. Serve warm or at room temperature.

Healthful Variation: The eggs can be replaced with egg substitute.

Menu Suggestion:

Serve as a light lunch or supper main course, offering warm corn bread and a green salad as accompaniments and peeled, sliced oranges topped with Honey-Cream Sauce (page 345) for dessert.

Sunday Morning Asparagus *and* Potato Omelets

SERVES 4

⋆

From Start to Finish:
50 minutes

Actual Working Time:
50 minutes

Make Ahead: Partially
(see step 2)

Can Be Frozen: No

Best Seasons:
Spring and summer

THESE OMELETS are quickly cooked, then filled and rolled into oval shapes. The filling is a mixture of red-skin potato, asparagus and leeks, plus a little prosciutto and lemon zest for extra flavor. I like to make the omelets in spring and summer when asparagus is at its best.

Salt

1 red-skin potato (5-6 ounces), scrubbed
but not peeled

½ pound medium asparagus spears, tough ends
trimmed and discarded, stalks cut into
½-inch pieces

5½ teaspoons unsalted butter (*divided*)

3-4 thin slices prosciutto or Black Forest ham
(about 2 ounces), coarsely chopped

1 cup cleaned, chopped leeks, white parts only
(about 1 large), *see Cooking Technique*, page 296

2 teaspoons grated lemon zest
(yellow portion of rind)
Freshly ground black pepper

8 large eggs (*see Healthful Variation*)

6 tablespoons freshly grated imported
Parmesan cheese (*divided*)

4 teaspoons chopped fresh chives, flat-leaf
parsley or tarragon

1. To make filling, bring 2 quarts water to a boil in a large saucepan. Add 1 teaspoon salt. Cut potato into ½-inch cubes and add to pan. Cook until tender, 4 to 5 minutes. Remove with a slotted spoon, drain, pat dry and set aside. Add asparagus to boiling water and cook until just tender, 3 to 4 minutes. Remove to a colander and rinse under cold water. Pat dry and set aside.

2. Place 1½ teaspoons butter in a medium, heavy skillet over medium-high heat. When hot, add prosciutto or ham and sauté, stirring constantly, until browned, about 2 minutes. Add leeks and potato cubes and cook, stirring, for about 4 minutes more. Remove from heat and stir in lemon zest and ¼ teaspoon pepper. If making omelets immediately, stir in asparagus. (*Filling can be assembled 2 to 3 hours ahead. Cool mixture; then stir in asparagus. Taste and season with salt, if desired. Cover and refrigerate until needed.*)

3. To make omelets, beat eggs in a mixing bowl and season generously with salt and pepper. Heat 1 teaspoon butter in a 7- or 8-inch omelet pan over medium heat. Swirl butter to cover bottom of pan. Add one-fourth of eggs to pan, and using a fork, gently and quickly stir eggs with a circular motion until set but moist. Spread one-fourth of filling over eggs and sprinkle 1½ tablespoons cheese over filling. Using a spatula, flip one-third of omelet (starting at end nearest pan handle) over onto center. Then, placing both hands on handle, lift pan and slide omelet to far side of pan opposite handle. Gently slide omelet onto center of a dinner plate and fold over again to form an oval. Sprinkle with fresh herbs. Repeat, making 3 more omelets. Finished omelets can be kept warm, loosely covered with aluminum foil, but it is best to serve each one as soon as it is made.

Healthful Variation: The eggs can be replaced with egg substitute.

Menu Suggestion:

These omelets make a good light lunch or supper main course. A watercress salad tossed with Orange Balsamic Dressing (page 247) is a good side dish, and a bowl of fresh strawberries sprinkled with confectioners' sugar and garnished with mint is a simple dessert.

Mulled Hot Chocolate

SERVES 6

From Start to Finish:
15 minutes

Actual Working Time:
15 minutes

Make Ahead: Yes
(see step 2)

Can Be Frozen: No

Best Seasons:
All year, especially winter

Shopping Note:
Dutch-process cocoa powder is treated with an alkali, which helps to neutralize cocoa's natural acidity. Dröste is a brand I use often.

HERE's A SLIGHTLY DIFFERENT TWIST on one of America's favorite warm breakfast drinks. Milk is simmered with cinnamon and freshly grated nutmeg to infuse it with a spicy flavor. In addition to the usual cocoa powder, some chopped semisweet chocolate is added for extra smoothness and richness. Served in mugs with cinnamon-stick stirrers, this hot chocolate is hard to resist, especially on a cold-weather morning. Whole milk tastes better than 1% or 2% in this recipe, but they can be substituted.

6	cups whole milk
1½	teaspoons ground cinnamon
1	teaspoon freshly grated nutmeg
3	ounces good-quality semisweet chocolate, cut into chunks (do not use chocolate chips)
¼	cup unsweetened cocoa powder, preferably Dutch-process cocoa (*see Shopping Note*)
½	cup sugar
½	cup boiling water
2	teaspoons vanilla extract
	Long cinnamon sticks for stirring

1. In a medium, heavy saucepan over medium heat, heat milk, ground cinnamon, nutmeg and chocolate, stirring constantly, until chocolate is melted. Set aside.

2. In a large saucepan, combine cocoa powder, sugar and boiling water and stir to make a thick paste. Whisk in milk mixture, and stir over medium heat until well blended and hot. Stir in vanilla extract. (*Hot chocolate can be made several hours ahead; cool, cover and refrigerate. Reheat, stirring, when needed.*)

3. To serve, pour hot chocolate into cups or mugs and put a cinnamon stick in each cup.

Cranberry Citrus Coolers

THESE REFRESHING COOLERS are a nice change from the usual juices served at breakfast and brunch. To make them, a light sugar syrup is infused with fresh mint leaves and combined with orange and cranberry juices. Sparkling water is added at the last minute. I serve these coolers well chilled and garnish them with an orange slice and a sprig of mint.

MAKES A LITTLE MORE THAN 2 QUARTS OR 8 SERVINGS

From Start to Finish: 40 minutes

Actual Working Time: 10 minutes

Make Ahead: Partially (see step 2)

Can Be Frozen: No

Best Seasons: All year

2　large thick-skinned lemons

1⅓　cups water

½　cup sugar

⅔　cup fresh mint leaves, packed, plus 8 sprigs for garnish

3　cups freshly squeezed or good-quality store-bought orange juice

1　cup cranberry juice cocktail

3　cups well-chilled sparkling water from an unopened bottle

8　very thin orange slices for garnish

1. With a vegetable peeler, peel 5 strips about 3 inches long by 1 inch wide from lemons. Juice lemons to get 5 tablespoons juice. Set aside.

2. Place lemon strips, water, sugar and mint leaves in a small saucepan over medium heat. Stir constantly and bring to a boil. Remove from heat. Strain, discarding lemon strips and mint leaves, and cool completely in a large nonreactive pitcher or bowl. Stir in reserved lemon juice, orange juice and cranberry juice cocktail. (*Drink can be prepared 1 day ahead; cover and refrigerate.*)

3. When ready to serve, fill a large 3-quart pitcher with ice and add orange and cranberry juice mixture. Add sparkling water. Stir mixture to blend well.

4. To serve, pour into juice or wine glasses and garnish each with an orange slice and a mint sprig.

Chapter 13

Sandwich Specials

South-of-the-Border Grilled Cheese and Salsa Sandwiches

I LOVE ANY KIND OF GRILLED CHEESE SANDWICH, but these are particularly appealing because the spicy tomato salsa makes such a good accompaniment to the melted cheese. Crusty sourdough bread slices are the best for these sandwiches, which are perfect fare for lunch or a light supper.

8 ¼-inch-thick slices cut from a crusty loaf of sourdough bread (*see Shopping Notes*)

7-8 ounces plain Havarti cheese, Monterey Jack or mild white Cheddar cheese, thinly sliced (*see Shopping Notes*)

½-¾ cup best-quality store-bought fresh tomato salsa, drained, at room temperature (*see Shopping Notes*)

¼ cup fresh cilantro sprigs
Tortilla chips for garnish (*optional*)

1. Spray a large, heavy (preferably cast-iron) skillet or a griddle generously with nonstick cooking spray (preferably olive-oil cooking spray) and place over medium-high heat. When hot, add 4 bread slices and toast just until lightly browned, then turn. Arrange half of cheese on 2 bread slices and watch carefully until cheese starts to melt, about 1 minute or more. Top with 2 tablespoons salsa and several cilantro sprigs and then with 2 bread slices remaining in pan. Cook sandwiches only about 1 minute more, until cheese melts and salsa is heated through. Remove and keep warm while preparing remaining 2 sandwiches.

2. Slice sandwiches on diagonal and serve, if desired, with tortilla chips.

SERVES 4

From Start to Finish:
15 minutes
Actual Working Time:
15 minutes
Make Ahead: No
Can Be Frozen: No
Best Seasons: All year

Shopping Notes:
An 8- or 10-inch round crusty loaf of sourdough works well for this recipe.

My favorite cheese for these sandwiches is Havarti, because it melts to a smooth, creamy consistency.

Try to buy fresh salsa, the kind stored in the refrigerator section of the supermarket, and drain it well before using. Mild salsa is my first choice, but if you like, a hot version can be used.

Grilled Apple *and* Cheddar Sandwiches

SERVES 4

★

From Start to Finish:
20 minutes

Actual Working Time:
20 minutes

Make Ahead: No

Can Be Frozen: No

Best Seasons:
All year, especially fall and winter

Menu Suggestion:
Bowls of Butternut Squash and Sausage Soup (page 66) make a hearty accompaniment to these sandwiches. Since both the soup and the sandwich are robust fare, end this menu with a plate of fresh fruit.

IT'S AMAZING WHAT paper-thin, crisp, tart apple slices can do for a grilled cheese sandwich! Granny Smiths pair splendidly with Cheddar, while honey mustard adds a little extra bite.

4   tablespoons (½ stick) unsalted butter or
     2 tablespoons butter and 2 tablespoons
     vegetable oil (*divided*)
8   slices good-quality whole wheat or
     white sandwich bread
4   ounces medium-sharp white Cheddar cheese,
     thinly sliced (*see Variation*)
1   Granny Smith apple, unpeeled, halved, cored,
     and cut into paper-thin slices
     Honey mustard

1. Arrange a rack at center position and preheat oven to 300°F.

2. Heat 1 tablespoon butter (or ½ tablespoon each butter and oil) in a medium, heavy skillet over medium heat. When hot, add 2 slices bread and cook just until lightly browned on bottom. Turn bread and top 1 slice with one-quarter of cheese. Top with 6 or 7 apple slices. Lift remaining bread slice from pan and spread toasted side with honey mustard. Place, mustard side down, over other slice. Cook, turning sandwich several times, until cheese is melted and bread is toasted, about 1 minute. Remove and place on a baking sheet in oven to keep warm. Repeat to make 3 more sandwiches, adding 1 tablespoon butter (or ½ tablespoon each butter and oil) to pan each time and placing finished sandwiches in oven to keep warm.

3. Slice sandwiches in half diagonally and serve hot.

Variation: Other cheeses can be substituted for the Cheddar. Havarti, Monterey Jack and Fontina all melt readily and work well in this recipe.

Jarlsberg Cheeseburgers *with* Grilled Red Onions

A LITTLE THYME ADDS FLAVOR to these beef burgers. Grilled red onion rings, Jarlsberg cheese and Mustard-Maple Mayonnaise are other embellishments.

½ recipe Mustard-Maple Mayonnaise (page 192)
1 pound lean ground beef
1 teaspoon dried thyme leaves
½ teaspoon salt
¼ teaspoon freshly ground black pepper
Vegetable oil for grill and for brushing onion slices
4 ¼-inch-thick slices red onion, cut from 1 large onion
4 ounces thinly sliced Jarlsberg cheese (*see Shopping Note*)
4 good-quality hamburger buns, split

1. Prepare Mustard-Maple Mayonnaise, and if not using immediately, cover and refrigerate. (*Mayonnaise can be prepared 1 day ahead.*)

2. Place ground beef, thyme, salt and pepper in a mixing bowl and mix well to blend. Shape into 4 patties. (*Burgers can be prepared 1 day ahead; cover and refrigerate.*)

3. When ready to cook, arrange a rack 5 inches from heat source, oil lightly and preheat grill. Brush onion slices lightly with oil and grill, turning once, until softened slightly (but not limp) and dark brown grill marks appear, 3 to 4 minutes. Remove and set aside. Grill burgers until pink inside, 3 to 4 minutes per side. Watch carefully, since type of grill and intensity of heat vary. Grill buns just to toast lightly. When burgers are almost done, cover each with some cheese and an onion slice, and cook just until cheese melts.

4. To serve, arrange burgers on buns spread with mayonnaise.

SERVES 4

From Start to Finish:
30 minutes
Actual Working Time:
30 minutes
Make Ahead: Partially
(see steps 1 and 2)
Can Be Frozen: No
Best Seasons: All year

Shopping Note:
Jarlsberg is a mild Swiss-style cheese that is imported from Norway. It has a pale yellow rind and pale yellow interior with large holes. Jarlsberg is available in the cheese department of most large supermarkets or in specialty-cheese shops. You can substitute other Swiss-style cheeses, but the rich yet subtle flavor of Jarlsberg makes it my first choice.

Portobello Burgers

SERVES 4

★

From Start to Finish:
20 minutes

Actual Working Time:
20 minutes

Make Ahead: No

Can Be Frozen: No

Best Seasons:
All year, especially
summer

MY HUSBAND, A TRUE MEAT-AND-POTATOES FAN, is always dieting but routinely sneaks out for hamburgers and fries at the local take-out. When he first tasted these new "burgers" made with giant grilled portobello mushrooms spread with melted Boursin cheese and topped with sliced tomatoes and lettuce, he could not believe how good they were. The cooked mushrooms have the texture of a tender steak and a robust beefy flavor. He now calls portobellos the "miracle mushroom" for fat-conscious meat lovers!

4   large portobello mushrooms, about 4 inches
     in diameter and 4 ounces each

6   tablespoons extra-virgin olive oil,
     plus extra for grill

¼   cup chopped fresh flat-leaf parsley
     Salt and freshly ground black pepper

4-6   ounces reduced-fat Boursin cheese,
     at room temperature

4   good-quality hamburger buns, split

4   large tomato slices

4   small Boston lettuce leaves, cleaned and dried

1. Wipe portobellos clean with a damp paper towel and twist off and discard stems. Place 6 tablespoons oil in a small bowl and add parsley. Brush mushrooms on all surfaces with oil and generously season with salt and pepper on both sides. Set aside.

2. Mushrooms can be cooked on an outdoor grill or in a pan on stovetop. If using an outdoor grill, arrange a rack 5 inches from heat source and rub rack with extra oil; preheat grill. If using a stovetop pan, oil it lightly with extra oil. To grill mushrooms, cook rounded sides up for 2 to 3 minutes and then turn and cook for about 2 minutes more. Mushrooms are done when they are very soft and tender when pierced with a knife. Continue to cook longer until tender, if necessary. If mushroom cavities have collected liquid in them, carefully remove from grill and pour out liquid.

3. Return mushrooms to grill, cavity side up, and spread evenly with Boursin cheese. Place split buns on grill to toast lightly, then remove. When cheese melts, remove mushrooms and place on bottom halves of buns. Season mushrooms with salt and pepper. Top each mushroom with a tomato slice and lettuce and with tops of buns.

4. To serve, cut burgers in half and arrange on plates.

Menu Suggestion:

Corn on the cob and Roasted New Potato and Watercress Salad (page 258) are fine side dishes to offer with these burgers for a summer meal. Slices of store-bought pound cake, mounded with fresh blueberries or strawberries and topped with Honey-Cream Sauce (page 345), make an easy dessert.

Spicy Turkey Burgers
with Fresh Tomato Salsa

SERVES 8

From Start to Finish:
40 minutes

Actual Working Time:
40 minutes

Make Ahead: Partially
(see steps 1 and 2)

Can Be Frozen: No

Best Seasons:
All year, especially
summer and early fall

Shopping Note:
Be certain to buy ground
turkey that does not include
the skin (which contains a
high amount of fat). Check
the package label or ask the
butcher.

T HESE BURGERS ARE MADE WITH GROUND TURKEY in place of ground beef and are assertively seasoned with cumin, chili powder and lemon juice. When grilled, they are moist and infused with strong flavors. Served on toasted buns, they are garnished with a colorful fresh tomato salsa.

FOR SALSA

6 ounces (about 2) plum tomatoes, unpeeled, seeded and chopped
½ medium cucumber, peeled, seeded and coarsely chopped
1½ teaspoons fresh lime juice
   Scant teaspoon salt
½ teaspoon finely chopped garlic

FOR BURGERS

1¼ pounds fresh ground turkey (*see Shopping Note*)
2 tablespoons fresh bread crumbs
1 tablespoon fresh lemon juice
2¼ teaspoons chili powder
2 teaspoons ground cumin
½ teaspoon salt
¼ teaspoon freshly ground black pepper
2 tablespoons chopped fresh cilantro
4 good-quality hamburger buns or rolls, split

1. **To prepare salsa:** Combine ingredients in a nonreactive mixing bowl and stir to mix. Transfer to a serving bowl. Cover and refrigerate. (*Salsa can be made 1 day ahead. If too much liquid has accumulated in the bowl, drain before using.*)

2. **To prepare burgers**: Combine turkey, bread crumbs, lemon juice, chili powder, cumin, salt, pepper and cilantro in a bowl and mix well to blend. Shape into 4 patties. (*Burgers can be made 1 day ahead; cover and refrigerate until ready to cook.*)

3. Arrange a rack 5 inches from heat source and preheat grill. Cook patties until they are completely done all the way through, about 5 minutes per side. Watch carefully; cooking time will vary depending on intensity of heat and type of grill. While burgers are cooking, grill buns so they are lightly toasted. To serve, arrange burgers on buns and pass salsa separately.

Menu Suggestion:

Corn on the cob with Cumin-Cilantro Butter (page 205) and Pinto Beans with Tortilla Cheese Crust (page 236) are good side dishes for the burgers. White Chocolate- and Pecan-Studded Brownies (page 380) complete the meal.

Turkey Burgers *with* Orange Zest *and* Fresh Cranberry Sauce

SERVES 4

From Start to Finish:
45 minutes

Actual Working Time:
45 minutes

Make Ahead: Partially
(see steps 1 and 2)

Can Be Frozen: No

Best Seasons:
Fall and winter

A DEPARTURE from what we think of as all-American hamburgers, these sandwiches are just as delicious in their own right. The ground turkey patties are seasoned with orange and thyme, then grilled and topped with either white Cheddar or cream cheese. They are garnished with fresh cranberry sauce and served on warm buns.

Honeyed Cranberry Sauce (page 185)
1 pound ground turkey (*see Shopping Note*, page 326)
2 teaspoons grated orange zest
   (orange portion of rind)
2 tablespoons fresh orange juice
½ teaspoon dried thyme leaves
½ teaspoon salt
¼ teaspoon freshly ground black pepper
3-4 ounces thinly sliced medium-sharp
     white Cheddar or about 6 tablespoons
     (3 ounces) reduced-fat cream cheese
4 good-quality hamburger buns, split

1. Prepare Honeyed Cranberry Sauce. If not using immediately, cover and refrigerate. (*Sauce can be made 4 to 5 days ahead.*)

2. To prepare turkey burgers, place ground turkey, orange zest and juice, thyme, salt and pepper in a mixing bowl and mix well to blend. Shape into 4 patties. (*Burgers can be assembled 1 day ahead; cover and refrigerate.*)

3. Arrange a rack 5 inches from heat source and spray rack with non-stick cooking spray. Preheat grill. Cook burgers until they are completely cooked through, about 5 minutes per side. Watch carefully, because cooking time will vary, depending on intensity of heat and type of grill. Alternatively, the burgers can be sautéed: Spray a large, heavy skillet with nonstick spray and place over medium heat. Sauté, turning several times, until burgers are cooked through. During the last few minutes, top burgers with Cheddar or spread with cream cheese.

4. Place buns on grill or in skillet and toast lightly. To serve, place burgers in buns and pass cranberry sauce separately.

Menu Suggestion:
Prince Albert Pumpkin Brownies (page 382) served plain, with a dusting of confectioners' sugar, are a fitting dessert.

West Coast Club Sandwiches

SERVES 4

★

From Start to Finish:
30 minutes

Actual Working Time:
30 minutes

Make Ahead: Partially
(see steps 1 and 2)

Can Be Frozen: No

Best Seasons:
Summer and early fall

Shopping Note:

Leftover roast chicken or turkey can be put to good use in this delicious sandwich. Or you can buy roast chicken in the deli or meat department of most supermarkets. Buy a plain roast chicken without special seasonings for this recipe.

THESE CLUB SANDWICHES owe their success to the flavorful orange mayonnaise that embellishes them. It is quickly made with store-bought light mayonnaise, to which orange juice concentrate, orange zest and fresh herbs are added. Slices of roast chicken (bought already cooked), grilled red onions and juicy tomatoes all taste delectable combined with this special spread.

FOR MAYONNAISE

½ cup reduced-fat mayonnaise
   (*see Shopping Note,* page 248)

1 tablespoon orange juice concentrate, defrosted

1 teaspoon grated orange zest
   (orange portion of rind)

1½ tablespoons chopped fresh basil

1½ tablespoons chopped fresh cilantro

⅛ teaspoon crushed red pepper flakes

FOR SANDWICHES

1 tablespoon olive oil

2 medium-sized red onions (about 8 ounces each),
   peeled and cut into ¼-inch-thick slices
   Salt and freshly ground black pepper

8 slices best-quality whole wheat or white bread

8 ounces roast chicken, boned and skinned,
   preferably white meat (*see Shopping Note*)

6 slices turkey bacon, fried or microwaved
   until crisp (*see Shopping Note, page 335*)

1-2 medium tomatoes, thinly sliced

8 orange slices, cut ¼ inch thick, for garnish (*optional*)
   Good-quality black olives (such as Kalamata
   or Niçoise), *optional*

1. **To prepare mayonnaise**: Combine all ingredients in a small non-reactive bowl and stir well to blend. (*Mayonnaise can be made 1 day ahead; cover and refrigerate.*)

2. **To prepare sandwiches**: Heat oil in a medium skillet set over medium heat or brush it on a stovetop grill. When oil is hot, add onion slices and cook, turning several times, until onions are soft and lightly browned, 5 to 6 minutes. Onions may not retain their round shapes; this is okay. Remove from skillet or grill and season generously with salt and pepper. (*Onions can be prepared 2 to 3 hours ahead; leave loosely covered at room temperature.*)

3. To assemble sandwiches, toast bread. Spread 2 slices with about ½ tablespoon each mayonnaise. Arrange one-fourth of chicken on 1 slice and top with a generous portion of onions. Lay 1½ strips bacon and several tomato slices over onions and season well with salt and pepper. Top with remaining mayonnaise-coated toast slice. Slice sandwich in half on diagonal and skewer each half with a toothpick, if desired. Repeat to make 3 more sandwiches.

4. To serve, arrange sandwiches on individual plates and garnish each plate with several orange slices and a few black olives, if desired.

"Make-Your-Own" Smoked Turkey and Watercress Sandwiches

SERVES 8

★

From Start to Finish:
25 minutes

Actual Working Time:
25 minutes

Make Ahead: Partially
(see step 1)

Can Be Frozen: No

Best Seasons: All year

FOR THIS NEW CLUB SANDWICH, I let guests assemble their own creations. I put warm pita halves in a basket and arrange an array of fillings—sliced smoked turkey, sliced tomatoes, watercress and chopped walnuts—on a serving platter. A bowl of reduced-fat mayonnaise flavored with curry powder and apricot preserves makes a fine dressing for these sandwiches.

FOR CURRIED MAYONNAISE

1½ cups reduced-fat mayonnaise
    (*see Shopping Note,* page 248)
½   tablespoon curry powder
¼   cup plus ½ tablespoon apricot preserves
    or apricot spread

FOR SANDWICHES

8   pita breads (6-to-7-inch rounds)
1½ pounds sliced smoked turkey breast
8   ripe plum tomatoes, sliced lengthwise
2   bunches watercress, cleaned, tough ends
    cut off and discarded
1   cup coarsely chopped walnuts

1. **To prepare curried mayonnaise:** Combine mayonnaise, curry powder and preserves or spread in a mixing bowl and stir well. (*Mayonnaise can be made 1 to 2 days ahead; cover and refrigerate until needed.*)

2. When ready to assemble sandwiches, preheat oven to 350°F.

3. Place pitas on a baking sheet and place in oven just to warm, 5 to 8 minutes. Remove from oven and cut in half so you have 2 half-moon-shaped pockets.

4. To serve, place warm pita halves in a napkin-lined basket. Arrange turkey, tomatoes and watercress on a serving platter. Place mayonnaise in a bowl and walnuts in another bowl. Invite guests to assemble their own sandwiches.

Menu Suggestion:
A bowl of tart apples makes a nice dessert to follow the sandwiches.

Turkey, Curried Cheddar *and* Chutney *on* Whole Wheat

SERVES 6

★

From Start to Finish:
  25 minutes

Actual Working Time:
  25 minutes

Make Ahead: Partially
  (see step 1)

Can Be Frozen: No

Best Seasons: All year

Menu Suggestion:
  These sandwiches are
delicious with Butternut
Squash and Sausage Soup
(page 66) and a bowl of
apples, pears or grapes
for dessert.

MY HUSBAND AND SON, both picky eaters when it comes to sandwiches, love these multilayered creations. Lightly toasted whole wheat bread is spread with a mixture of cream cheese and grated Cheddar seasoned with curry powder. Sliced smoked turkey, a good dollop of mango chutney and thin slices of red onion are added. The result is a wonderful blending of flavors and textures. This recipe serves six, but it can easily be reduced to make fewer sandwiches.

    4   ounces reduced-fat cream cheese, softened
    4   ounces (1 cup packed) grated medium-sharp
          Cheddar cheese
    1   teaspoon curry powder
   12   slices whole wheat bread
  6-8   ounces thinly sliced smoked turkey, cut to fit bread
   ¾   cup mango chutney
    3   tablespoons chopped fresh flat-leaf parsley
    1   medium-sized red onion, peeled,
          halved lengthwise and thinly sliced

1. Combine cream cheese, Cheddar cheese and curry powder in a mixing bowl and mix well to blend thoroughly. (*Cheese mixture can be prepared 1 to 2 days ahead; cover and refrigerate. Bring to room temperature before using.*)

2. To assemble sandwiches, lightly toast bread. Spread a bread slice with 2 tablespoons cheese mixture, top with 3 to 4 slices turkey and 2 tablespoons chutney. Sprinkle 1½ teaspoons parsley over the chutney and place several onion slices on top. Cover with another slice of bread. Make 5 more sandwiches the same way. Cut sandwiches diagonally into quarters. Skewer quarters with toothpicks to secure, if desired. Arrange sandwiches on serving plates.

The Other BLT

I F I COULD HAVE ONLY ONE SANDWICH in the world, it would be a BLT. For this new version, I used roasted leeks in place of lettuce and reduced-fat mayonnaise scented with fresh basil. Turkey bacon replaces the traditional. (*See photograph, page 46.*)

4 leeks, about 1 inch in diameter
   Olive oil
   Salt and freshly ground black pepper
6 tablespoons reduced-fat mayonnaise
   (*see Shopping Notes*)
2 tablespoons chopped fresh basil,
   plus sprigs for garnish
8 slices sourdough bread (*see Shopping Notes,* **page 321**)
1 pound ripe tomatoes, cleaned and
   sliced ¼ inch thick
8 strips turkey bacon microwaved or fried
   until crisp (*see Shopping Notes*)

SERVES 4

★

From Start to Finish:
45 minutes
Actual Working Time:
45 minutes
Make Ahead: Partially
(see step 2)
Can Be Frozen: No
Best Seasons:
Summer and fall

Shopping Notes:
Hellman's makes a good
reduced-fat mayonnaise.
I like to use turkey bacon
because it contains only half
the fat of regular bacon,
and either microwave or
sauté it until crisp. Louis
Rich is a good brand.

1. Preheat oven to 475°F. Line a baking sheet with aluminum foil and spray with nonstick cooking spray.

2. Cut off and discard all but 1½ inches of green tops of leeks. Halve leeks lengthwise and rinse thoroughly under cold running water to remove all sand and grit. Pat completely dry. Arrange leeks, cut side up, on baking sheet and drizzle generously with oil. Season generously with salt and pepper, then bake until leeks are cooked through and just starting to brown around edges, about 10 minutes. Check after 5 minutes; watch carefully to avoid burning. Remove from oven and cool slightly. (*Leeks can be roasted several hours ahead; leave loosely covered with aluminum foil at room temperature.*)

3. When ready to assemble sandwiches, place mayonnaise in a bowl and stir in chopped basil. Lightly toast bread slices. Spread 2 toasted bread slices on 1 side with mayonnaise, then arrange roasted leeks on 1 slice and top with some sliced tomatoes and 2 slices bacon. Cover with other bread slice. Repeat to make 3 more sandwiches.

New-Wave Tuna Salad Sandwiches

SERVES 4

★

From Start to Finish:
20 minutes

Actual Working Time:
20 minutes

Make Ahead: Partially
(see step 1)

Can Be Frozen: No

Best Seasons: All year

Shopping Note:

Hummus, a Middle
Eastern sauce, is made
with chick-peas, which are
mashed and seasoned with
lemon juice, garlic and olive
or sesame oil. Typically, it is
used as a dip. *Hummus bi
tahini* is hummus to which
sesame paste has been
added. Either can be used
here. Hummus is available
in many supermarkets,
usually in a refrigerated
section with specialty foods.
It is also sold in Middle
Eastern food markets.

I DIDN'T THINK I would ever want to make tuna salad sandwiches without celery or pickle relish, but a good friend changed my mind. On a visit to the Adirondacks, my hosts packed a picnic lunch to eat on a canoeing trip. The tuna salad was like no other I had tasted before. My friend Tricia Winterer had combined some unexpected ingredients—hummus, sesame oil, cumin and cilantro—with tuna, green onions and reduced-fat mayonnaise. The results were superb. Back home, I re-created this tuna salad and packed it in pita pockets, along with sliced tomatoes and lettuce.

FOR TUNA SALAD

1 cup hummus (without extra seasonings
such as garlic and herbs; *see Shopping Note*)

1 12-to-13-ounce can white-meat tuna
packed in water, drained and flaked

¼ cup reduced-fat mayonnaise
(*see Shopping Notes,* page 335)

2 teaspoons dark Asian sesame oil

¼ cup chopped green onion, including
2 inches of green tops

¼ cup finely chopped fresh cilantro

1½ teaspoons ground cumin
Generous pinch cayenne pepper
Salt

FOR SANDWICHES

4 6-to-7-inch whole wheat pita breads,
cut in half to form pockets

4 plum tomatoes, cleaned and thinly sliced

8 leaves Boston or red leaf lettuce, cleaned
and patted dry

1. **To prepare tuna salad:** Combine all ingredients in a medium mixing bowl and stir well to mix. Taste and add salt and more cayenne, if desired. (*Salad can be prepared 1 day ahead; cover and refrigerate. Bring to room temperature 20 minutes before using.*)

2. **To assemble sandwiches:** Divide tuna salad equally and mound in pita pockets. Add several tomato slices and a lettuce leaf to each pocket. Arrange sandwiches in a basket or on a serving plate. Serve immediately.

Cajun Shrimp Po' Boy Sandwiches

SERVES 6

From Start to Finish:
45 minutes

Actual Working Time:
45 minutes

Make Ahead: Partially
(see steps 2 and 3)

Can Be Frozen: No

Best Seasons: All year

Shopping Note:
The size of shrimp is
determined by the count
of unshelled shrimp per
pound. This is a guideline:
Medium: 31-40 per pound
Large: 21-30 per pound
Extra Large: 16-20 per
pound
Jumbo: 10-15 per pound

MY FRIEND JIM BUDROS, cooking teacher extraordinaire from Columbus, Ohio, gave me the idea for these quickly assembled warm sandwiches. Long loaves of French bread are sliced lengthwise and filled with sautéed shrimp and red and yellow peppers. The shellfish and peppers are drizzled with a rich pan sauce, and the sandwiches are sliced and served hot. Since shrimp are expensive, you might like to reserve these for a special-occasion meal. (*See photograph, page 42.*)

4	tablespoons (½ stick) unsalted butter
½	cup red bell pepper strips (½ by 3 inch), about ½ pepper
½	cup yellow bell pepper strips (½ by 3 inch), about ½ pepper
¼	cup dry white wine
1	cup bottled clam juice
1	teaspoon salt
½	teaspoon cayenne pepper
¼	teaspoon white pepper
¼	teaspoon freshly ground black pepper
¼	cup Worcestershire sauce
2	pounds large (21-30 per pound) uncooked shrimp in shell, shelled and deveined, or 1½ pounds shelled, deveined, uncooked shrimp (*see Shopping Note*)
1	tablespoon fresh lemon juice
2	loaves French bread (about 20 inches long) cut in half lengthwise
½	cup chopped fresh flat-leaf parsley

1. Melt butter in a large, heavy nonreactive skillet over medium-high heat. When hot, add peppers and sauté until softened, about 3 minutes. Remove with a slotted spoon and set aside.

2. Add wine and clam juice to pan and cook until mixture has re-duced to ¾ cup, 3 to 4 minutes. Add salt, cayenne, white and black pepper and Worcestershire sauce and cook, stirring, for 1 minute. Add shrimp and cook until pink and curled, 3 to 4 minutes. Remove shrimp with a slotted spoon and set aside. (*Shrimp and peppers can be pre-pared 1 hour ahead. Cover with foil and refrigerate.*)

3. Reduce sauce in pan until it has thickened and is slightly syrupy, about 5 minutes. (*Sauce can be made in advance up to this point. Leave in skillet and reheat before continuing.*) Add lemon juice.

4. To finish, return shrimp and peppers to skillet with sauce and stir constantly until both are completely heated and sauce is hot, 1 to 2 minutes or more. Remove shrimp and peppers with a slotted spoon and mound on 2 bottom bread halves. Drizzle with sauce and sprin-kle with parsley. Top with remaining bread halves. Cut each sandwich into 3 equal portions. Serve warm.

Menu Suggestion:
Serve with Fresh Cole Slaw with Fennel Seed Dressing (page 248) and a plate of sliced tomatoes. Scoops of store-bought raspberry or strawberry sorbet garnished with mint sprigs can follow.

Shades of Reuben Sandwiches

SERVES 4

★

From Start to Finish:
40 minutes

Actual Working Time:
20 minutes

Make Ahead: Partially
(see step 1)

Can Be Frozen: No

Best Seasons: All year

THE REUBEN—piled high with corned beef, Swiss cheese and sauerkraut, slathered in creamy salad dressing and served either warm or cold on slices of rye bread—has long been one of America's most popular sandwiches. In this new version, more modest amounts of corned beef and cheese are used. Havarti cheese, which melts quickly, takes the place of Swiss; fresh shredded cabbage replaces the sauerkraut; and the dressing is a quickly assembled combination of light sour cream, grated apple, horseradish and caraway seeds. Once made, the sandwiches are wrapped in foil and heated in the oven until hot.

Horseradish Sauce with Grated Apple (page 193)
8 slices best-quality sandwich rye bread
8 ounces thinly sliced lean corned beef
6 ounces thinly sliced plain Havarti cheese
   (*see Shopping Note*, page 110)
½ cup thinly sliced cabbage

GARNISH SUGGESTIONS
Deli-style sour pickles
Small red and yellow cherry tomatoes
Green onions, trimmed of roots and all but
   2 inches of green tops

1. Prepare Horseradish Sauce with Grated Apple, and if not using immediately, cover and refrigerate. (*Sauce can be prepared 2 days ahead.*)

2. When ready to assemble sandwiches, arrange a rack at center position and preheat oven to 375°F.

3. Place 1 bread slice on a work surface and top with one-fourth of corned beef and one-fourth of cheese slices. Spread 1½ to 2 tablespoons sauce over cheese. Top with one-fourth of shredded cabbage. Top with another bread slice and wrap tightly in aluminum foil. Repeat to make 3 more sandwiches.

4. Bake until cheese melts and sandwiches are hot, about 20 minutes; check after 15 minutes. When done, remove sandwiches from oven with potholders. Carefully open foil wrappers and remove sandwiches. Slice sandwiches in half on diagonal and serve hot, with pickles, tomatoes and green onions, if desired.

Menu Suggestion:

These sandwiches are filling. Serve them with a green salad tossed in a light dressing and with a bowl of fruit for dessert.

Chili Steak Sandwiches
with Spicy Corn Relish

SERVES 8

From Start to Finish:
2 hours 35 minutes
(includes making relish and
1 hour for marinating)

Actual Working Time:
55 minutes

Make Ahead: Partially
(see steps 1, 2, 3 and 4)

Can Be Frozen: No

Best Seasons:
Summer and fall

TALL, COLORFUL AND STATELY, these sandwiches could easily be the main event of a special lunch or supper. Beef flank steaks are rubbed with chili powder and other spices and grilled, rather than fried. The steaks are thinly sliced, then mounded on sourdough bread and spread with corn relish and chopped watercress.

Spicy Corn Relish (page 186)
4 teaspoons ground cumin
1 tablespoon chili powder
2 teaspoons salt
2 teaspoons freshly ground black pepper
1 teaspoon ground coriander
½ teaspoon cayenne pepper
2 flank steaks (each about 1 pound),
   trimmed of all fat
2 round crusty sourdough or good-quality French
   bread rounds, about 8 inches in diameter
   (*see Variation*)
1 cup coarsely chopped watercress

1. Prepare Spicy Corn Relish, and if not using immediately, cover and refrigerate. (*Relish can be prepared 4 to 5 days ahead. Bring to room temperature about 30 minutes before using.*)

2. Combine cumin, chili powder, salt, pepper, coriander and cayenne in a small bowl and mix well. Rub both sides of flank steaks generously with mixture. Cover and chill for at least 1 hour or up to 8 hours. Bring to room temperature 30 minutes before grilling.

3. When ready to grill steaks, arrange a rack 5 inches from heat source and preheat grill. Cook meat for about 4 minutes per side for medium-rare. Cooking time will vary depending on type of grill and intensity of heat. Steaks can also be broiled 5 inches from heat for 4 to 5 minutes per side. Cool steaks for 5 minutes, then cut diagonally across grain into paper-thin slices. (*Steaks can be cooked and sliced 1 day ahead; cool, cover and refrigerate. Bring to room temperature 30 minutes before using.*)

4. To assemble sandwiches, cut 1 loaf in half horizontally and scoop out both halves, leaving hollowed-out shells. (Save scooped-out bread for bread crumbs.) Mound half of sliced meat in bottom half. Spread half of corn relish over meat and sprinkle half of watercress over relish. Place top of bread on sandwich. Repeat with second loaf. (*Sandwiches can be prepared 1 hour ahead; wrap in foil and chill.*) Cut each sandwich into quarters and serve.

Variation: I like to use large, round sourdough loaves, because they make a more unusual presentation, but 8 small individual sandwich rolls could be substituted.

Menu Suggestion:

Bowls of Orange and Basil Tomato Soup (page 58) are a delicious accompaniment. Fresh Fruit in Red Wine and Ginger Sauce (page 347) ends the menu.

Chapter 14

Blue-Ribbon Pies, Cakes, Brownies *and* Other Sweets

Warm Spiced Plums *with* Honey-Cream Sauce

T HIS DESSERT IS SIMPLICITY ITSELF. Sliced plums are sautéed with sugar to glaze them and are served with a quickly made honey-cream sauce.

FOR SAUCE

1   cup reduced-fat sour cream
2   tablespoons 1% milk
2   tablespoons honey

FOR PLUMS

3   pounds large, dark red or purple plums (*see Shopping Note*)
½   cup sugar, plus more if needed
    Scant ½ teaspoon ground cinnamon
8   fresh mint sprigs for garnish

1. **To prepare sauce:** Whisk together sour cream, milk and honey in a small mixing bowl until well blended. (*Sauce can be made 1 day ahead; cover and refrigerate. Bring to room temperature 30 minutes before using.*)

2. **To prepare plums:** Rinse and pat dry. Halve lengthwise, remove pits and cut halves into ¾-inch-thick wedges.

3. Place a large, heavy skillet, preferably cast-iron, over medium-high heat for a few seconds. Add plums and sprinkle with ½ cup sugar. Stir constantly until sugar dissolves and forms a glaze and plums are tender when pierced with a knife, 6 to 10 minutes, depending on ripeness of fruit. Do not overcook, or plums will become mushy.

4. Remove from heat and stir in cinnamon. Taste plums, and if too tart, add more sugar. (*Plums can be prepared 3 to 4 hours ahead and left at room temperature in skillet. Reheat, stirring, over medium heat before serving.*)

5. To serve, ladle hot plums into 8 dessert bowls and drizzle with honey-cream sauce. Garnish each with a mint sprig.

SERVES 8;
MAKES 1¼ CUPS
SAUCE

From Start to Finish:
30 minutes
Actual Working Time:
30 minutes
Make Ahead: Yes
(see steps 1 and 4)
Can Be Frozen: No
Best Season: Summer

Shopping Note:
This recipe is best made when plums are ripe and sweet, in late summer. The plums should be firm but give slightly to pressure when touched.

Ginger *and* Brown Sugar Grapefruit Compotes *with* Vanilla Ice Cream

SERVES 6

★

From Start to Finish:
2 hours 20 minutes
(includes 2 hours of
refrigerating)

Actual Working Time:
20 minutes

Make Ahead: Partially
(see step 2)

Can Be Frozen: Partially
(see step 2)

Best Seasons: All year

SOOTHING AND REFRESHING, this dessert is good in the heat of summer, when lighter foods are appreciated. Pink grapefruit halves are hollowed out and filled with scoops of vanilla ice cream. The grapefruit segments are mixed with brown sugar and chopped gingerroot and then returned to the shells and garnished with mint sprigs.

6   pink grapefruit
     Vanilla ice cream or frozen yogurt
⅓   cup firmly packed light brown sugar
4½   teaspoons finely chopped peeled gingerroot
     Fresh mint leaves

1. Cut grapefruit horizontally in half. Using a grapefruit knife or paring knife, cut all around grapefruit halves and between membranes to release segments. Place segments in a nonreactive bowl, discarding seeds. Cut out all membranes from 6 grapefruit halves; discard remaining 6 grapefruit halves.

2. Place a large scoop of ice cream or frozen yogurt in each grapefruit half. Cover and place in freezer to chill well, at least 1 hour. (*Grapefruit halves can be filled with ice cream or yogurt, covered with plastic wrap and frozen 1 day ahead.*) Add brown sugar and ginger to grapefruit sections in bowl and toss gently. Cover and refrigerate at least 2 hours or overnight.

3. To serve, spoon some grapefruit mixture over ice cream or frozen yogurt in each grapefruit half. Garnish with mint and pass remaining grapefruit mixture separately.

Fresh Fruit *in* Red Wine *and* Ginger Sauce

NOTHING COULD BE SIMPLER than this quickly assembled dessert. Fresh fruit is cut into bite-sized pieces and then marinated in a sugar syrup infused with red wine and fresh ginger. You can be creative in your selection of fruits: Include fresh berries in the spring and summer, apples and pears in the fall and oranges and grapes in winter.

8 cups bite-sized pieces assorted fruit
   (such as strawberries, melon, grapes,
   berries, apples)
1 tablespoon fresh lemon juice,
   plus more if needed
1½ cups water
¾ cup sugar
1 cup dry red wine
1 tablespoon finely chopped peeled gingerroot
   Fresh mint sprigs for garnish (*optional*)

SERVES 8

★

From Start to Finish:
   2 hours 35 minutes
   (includes 2 hours for
   chilling fruit)
Actual Working Time:
   35 minutes
Make Ahead: Yes
   (see step 3)
Can Be Frozen: No
Best Seasons: All year

1. Place fruit in a large nonreactive bowl. Add 1 tablespoon lemon juice and toss to blend.

2. Combine water and sugar in a medium, heavy saucepan over medium-high heat. Bring to a boil, stirring until sugar dissolves. Add wine and cook for 1 minute. Remove from heat and stir in ginger. Cool completely.

3. Pour cooled syrup over fruit. Cover and chill until cold, about 2 hours. Taste before serving, adding more lemon juice, if desired.

4. To serve, spoon into 8 dessert bowls or wine glasses and garnish with mint sprigs, if desired.

Glazed Winter Fruits *over* Pound Cake

SERVES 8

★

From Start to Finish:
35 minutes

Actual Working Time:
35 minutes

Make Ahead: Partially
(see step 2)

Can Be Frozen: No

Best Season: Winter

Shopping Note:

Sara Lee makes a delicious pound cake, available in traditional and lower-fat versions. Either works well in this recipe.

THIS IS A SIMPLE AND SATISFYING DESSERT I created for a cold winter evening. Just simmer dried fruits in a sugar syrup flavored with red wine, cinnamon and lemon zest. The dried fruits—apricots, apples, prunes and pears— look especially attractive served over slices of pound cake. Scoops of vanilla frozen yogurt or ice cream and cinnamon sticks are special garnishes. (*See photograph, page 39.*)

1¼ pounds mixed dried fruit
(such as apples, apricots, peaches,
pears and prunes)

2 cups water

1 cup sugar

1 cup dry red wine

1 teaspoon ground cinnamon

1½ teaspoons grated lemon zest
(yellow portion of rind)

1 16-ounce store-bought pound cake
(*see Shopping Note and Variation*)

1 quart vanilla frozen yogurt or vanilla
custard ice cream (*optional*)

8 cinnamon sticks (*optional*)

1. Chop dried fruit into large strips. If prunes are not pitted, pit them before chopping.

2. Place water, sugar, wine, cinnamon and lemon zest in a large, heavy nonreactive saucepan over medium heat. Stir constantly until sugar is dissolved. Add fruit and cook, stirring frequently, until fruit is tender and liquid has almost evaporated and become syrupy, about 10 minutes, depending on moistness of dried fruit. Remove from heat. If not using immediately, cool, cover and refrigerate. (*Fruit can be prepared 1 day ahead. Reheat fruit over low heat, stirring constantly. If mixture becomes too sticky, add a few tablespoons water.*)

3. To serve, cut eight ½-inch slices of pound cake and divide among 8 dessert plates. Top each generously with warm fruit mixture and, if desired, a scoop of frozen yogurt or ice cream and a cinnamon stick.

Variation: You might like to try this recipe without the pound cake. Simply divide warm fruit among 8 individual ramekins, soufflé dishes or custard cups. Garnish each serving with a scoop of frozen yogurt or ice cream and a cinnamon stick, if desired.

Apple Gratin *with* Cheddar Crust

SERVES 8 TO 10

★

From Start to Finish:
1 hour 35 minutes

Actual Working Time:
45 minutes

Make Ahead: Partially
(see step 3)

Can Be Frozen: No

Best Seasons:
Fall and winter

MY FRIEND TOM JOHNSON from Cleveland, Ohio, brought this warming dessert to the table one cold autumn night. Nothing could have been more inviting. The aroma of sliced apples baked with brandy-soaked prunes under a golden crust of walnuts, butter and brown sugar was irresistible. As a final flourish, the host sprinkled the baked apples with a grating of Cheddar cheese.

FOR FILLING

1   cup pitted prunes
1   cup sugar (*divided*)
½   cup brandy
½   cup water
6   large tart apples, such as Granny Smith
½   teaspoon ground cinnamon
¼   teaspoon ground cloves
1   tablespoon raspberry vinegar or
      red wine vinegar

FOR CRUST

¾   cup all-purpose flour
      Pinch salt
½   cup firmly packed light brown sugar
6   tablespoons (¾ stick) unsalted butter,
      chilled and cut into small pieces
1¼ cups coarsely chopped walnuts (*see Variation*)
1   cup (4 ounces) shredded mild Cheddar cheese

1. **To prepare filling:** Cut prunes into quarters and place in a mixing bowl. Combine ½ cup sugar with brandy and water in a saucepan and bring to a simmer. Pour mixture over prunes and let soak for 10 minutes. Drain and discard any remaining liquid from prunes and set prunes aside.

2. Peel, core and cut apples into 1-inch cubes. Place in a bowl and mix with remaining ½ cup sugar, cinnamon, cloves and vinegar. Add prunes and mix well.

3. Spray a 13-by-9-inch baking pan with nonstick cooking spray. Spread fruit mixture in baking pan and set aside. (*Gratin can be prepared 1 to 2 hours in advance to this point. Cover and refrigerate.*)

4. When ready to bake, arrange a rack at center position and preheat oven to 350°F.

5. **To prepare crust**: Place flour, salt and brown sugar in a bowl. Add butter and cut in, using a pastry blender or 2 table knives. Add walnuts and mix well; mixture will be crumbly. Sprinkle over fruit.

6. Bake until apple mixture is bubbling and crust is crisp, about 45 minutes. Remove from oven and sprinkle cheese over gratin; cheese will melt. Let cool for 5 minutes. Serve warm.

Variation: The walnuts used in this dish are known as English walnuts. If you can find black walnuts, which have a richer, more assertive flavor, substitute them for the English variety.

Honey *and* Ginger Roasted Pears

SERVES 8

★

From Start to Finish:

1 hour 15 minutes

Actual Working Time:

30 minutes

Make Ahead: Partially

(see step 4)

Can Be Frozen: No

Best Seasons:

Fall and winter

Shopping Note:

Häagen-Dazs makes a delicious almond-crunch frozen yogurt.

HONEY, LEMON, GINGER AND BROWN SUGAR are the simple ingredients that turn these pears into an elegant offering. Baked until tender, the pears are served warm with scoops of yogurt or ice cream and a garnish of mint and lemon zest.

8   ripe Bartlett pears

1   cup firmly packed light brown sugar

3   teaspoons ground ginger

6   tablespoons honey

3   tablespoons fresh lemon juice

2   teaspoons grated lemon zest
     (yellow portion of rind)

5   tablespoons unsalted butter (*divided*)

⅔   cup water

1   quart almond-crunch frozen yogurt
     (*see Shopping Note*) or premium vanilla ice cream

8   mint sprigs for garnish (*optional*)

8   ½-by-4-inch strips lemon zest for garnish

1. Arrange a rack at center position and preheat oven to 375°F. Spray nonstick cooking spray in 2 heavy 12-inch ovenproof skillets or flameproof baking dishes.

2. Peel, core and halve pears. Divide evenly among skillets, placing them cored sides down. Sprinkle with brown sugar and ginger.

3. Combine honey, lemon juice and lemon zest in a small bowl and stir well to mix. Drizzle over pears. Dot pears in each pan with 1½ tablespoons butter.

4. Bake until pears are tender when pierced with a knife, about 30 minutes. Turn pears over and bake for another 10 minutes. Remove from oven. (*Pears can be prepared 4 to 5 hours ahead. Cool, cover and refrigerate. Reheat, uncovered, in a preheated 375°F oven until hot.*)

5. To serve, remove pears from pan and place 2 halves on each of 8 dessert plates. Set aside.

6. Place skillets over burners on medium-high heat. Add ⅓ cup water to each skillet and whisk to incorporate syrupy mixture on bottom. Whisk 1 tablespoon butter into each and cook until sauce is slightly thickened, 1 to 2 minutes. Place a scoop of frozen yogurt or ice cream on each plate. Garnish each serving with a mint sprig, if desired, and a twist of lemon zest. Spoon warm sauce over pears.

Deep-Dish Apple *and* Cream Cheese Pie

SERVES 8

From Start to Finish:
2 hours 40 minutes
(includes 30 minutes for
chilling dough and 30
minutes for cooling pie)
Actual Working Time:
45 minutes
Make Ahead: Yes
(see step 7)
Can Be Frozen: No
Best Seasons:
All year, especially fall

THIS HAS BEEN MY FAVORITE APPLE PIE RECIPE for many years. It is baked in a springform pan and is taller than most versions. For the filling, sliced apples are baked over a delicious lemon-cream cheese layer and then topped with almonds, sugar and cinnamon.

FOR CRUST

1 cup all-purpose flour
3 tablespoons sugar
⅛ teaspoon salt
1 teaspoon grated lemon zest (yellow portion of rind)
5 tablespoons unsalted butter, well chilled
 and cut into small chunks
2-3 tablespoons ice water

FOR FILLING

4-5 Granny Smith apples, peeled, cored and
 cut into ¼-inch-thick slices (about 4 cups)
8 ounces reduced-fat cream cheese, softened
¼ cup sugar
1 large egg
½ teaspoon grated lemon zest
¼ teaspoon vanilla extract
⅛ teaspoon salt

FOR TOPPING

¼ cup sugar
½ teaspoon ground cinnamon
¼ cup sliced almonds

1. **To prepare crust** (*Food Processor Method*): Place flour, sugar, salt, lemon zest and butter in a food processor fitted with a metal blade. Process, turning on and off several times, until mixture resembles oatmeal flakes. With motor running, add water through feed tube

and process for several seconds more. Dough should adhere well when pinched firmly together.

(*Hand Method*): Combine flour, sugar, salt and lemon zest in a bowl. Cut in butter with a pastry blender or 2 table knives until mixture resembles oatmeal flakes. Gradually add water, mixing just until dough holds together. Transfer dough to a lightly floured surface. To ensure that flour and fat are well blended, smear ¼ cup of dough at a time across surface, using the heel of your hand to form a 6-inch strip; continue with remaining dough. Gather together and repeat once more.

2. Gather dough into a ball and flatten into a disk. Refrigerate, covered with plastic wrap, for 30 minutes, or until firm enough to roll out.

3. Place dough between 2 sheets of wax paper and roll into a circle 11 inches in diameter. Remove 1 sheet of wax paper and carefully mold dough, paper side up, into an 8½-inch springform pan. Remove remaining wax paper. Dough should cover bottom and come three-fourths of the way up side of pan. Refrigerate until needed.

4. **To prepare filling**: Arrange a rack at center position and preheat oven to 400°F. Place apple slices in a shallow baking pan and cover tightly with foil. Bake for 15 minutes just to soften apples slightly. Remove and set aside. Leave oven on.

5. Beat cream cheese in a medium bowl with an electric mixer on medium speed until creamy. Gradually beat in sugar. Beat in egg, lemon zest, vanilla extract and salt. Pour into prepared crust. Place baked apples over filling.

6. **To prepare topping**: Mix together sugar and cinnamon in a bowl and sprinkle over apples. Sprinkle almonds over top. Bake for 40 minutes, until crust is golden brown, checking after 20 minutes. If crust is browning too quickly, tent pie with foil.

7. Remove and cool to room temperature before serving. (*Pie can be prepared 3 to 4 hours ahead; cover loosely with foil and leave at cool room temperature.*)

8. To serve, remove sides from springform pan. Place pie, with bottom of pan still in place, on a serving plate. Cut into 8 pieces and serve.

Caramel Peach Pie

SERVES 8

★

From Start to Finish:
3 hours 15 minutes
(includes 1 hour to chill
dough and 45 minutes to
cool pie)

Actual Working Time:
30 minutes

Make Ahead: Yes
(see step 5)

Can Be Frozen: No

Best Season: Summer

Shopping Note:
Mrs. Richardson's
Caramel Sauce, which can
be found in most
supermarkets, is a terrific
product. The company
makes a traditional caramel
sauce as well as a light
version.

THIS PIE IS TRULY A SUMMER TREAT, one to make when peaches are in their prime. The golden crust—rich and flaky—is filled with sliced peaches seasoned with a hint of cinnamon. But what makes this pie extra special is the warm caramel sauce, which is drizzled over each slice when served.

FOR CRUST

1	cup all-purpose flour
2	tablespoons confectioners' sugar
⅛	teaspoon salt
4	tablespoons (½ stick) unsalted butter, chilled and cut into small pieces
2	tablespoons vegetable shortening, chilled and cut into small pieces
3½	tablespoons ice water, plus more if needed

FOR FILLING

5-5½	cups ¼-inch-thick slices peeled, pitted peaches (about 7 ripe peaches, 1¾ pounds)
1	cup sugar
¼	cup all-purpose flour
½	teaspoon ground cinnamon
¼	teaspoon salt
1	teaspoon fresh lemon juice

FOR TOPPING

⅓	cup pecans, toasted and coarsely chopped (*optional*), *see Cooking Technique*, page 278
½	cup warm caramel sauce, plus more if needed (*see Shopping Note*)

1. To prepare crust (*Food Processor Method*): Combine flour, confectioners' sugar and salt in a food processor fitted with a metal blade; add butter and shortening. Process until mixture resembles oatmeal flakes. With motor running, add 3½ tablespoons water through feed tube and process just until a ball of dough forms.

(*Hand Method*): Combine flour, confectioners' sugar and salt in a bowl. Cut in butter and shortening with a pastry blender or 2 table knives until mixture resembles oatmeal flakes. Gradually add 3½ tablespoons water, mixing just until dough holds together. Transfer dough to a lightly floured surface. To ensure that flour and fat are evenly blended, smear ¼ cup dough at a time across surface, using the heel of your hand, to form a 6-inch strip; continue until you have smeared all dough. Gather dough together and repeat one more time.

2. Gather dough into a ball and flatten into a disk. Wrap in plastic wrap, and refrigerate at least 1 hour or overnight.

3. When ready to bake, arrange a rack at center position and preheat oven to 450°F. Roll dough into an 11-inch circle and fit into a 9-inch pie plate. Fold in dough extending over edges and flute to form a border.

4. **To prepare filling**: In a large bowl, combine sliced peaches, sugar, flour, cinnamon, salt and lemon juice and mix well. Place in pie shell.

5. Bake for 15 minutes, then reduce oven temperature to 350°F and bake until peaches are tender and crust is golden, about 45 minutes more. Remove and cool for 45 minutes before slicing. (*Pie can be prepared 4 to 5 hours ahead; cover loosely with foil and leave at cool room temperature. Reheat in a 350°F oven until just warm, not hot, 10 to 15 minutes.*)

6. **To top and serve**: When ready to serve, sprinkle pecans over top, if desired. Cut pie into 8 slices and drizzle each piece with warm caramel sauce. Serve warm.

Blueberry Sour Cream Pie

SERVES 8

★

From Start to Finish:
3 hours 5 minutes
(includes 30 minutes for
chilling dough and 1 hour
for cooling pie)

Actual Working Time:
35 minutes

Make Ahead: Yes
(see steps 3 and 7)

Can Be Frozen: No

Best Season: Summer

THIS IS A PIE BEST MADE IN SUMMER. Plump fresh blueberries are combined with sour cream to make a filling for a golden crust. A streusel topping made with chopped pecans, butter and flour is a perfect finishing touch.

FOR PASTRY SHELL

1¼ cups all-purpose flour
2 tablespoons sugar
   Dash salt
8 tablespoons (1 stick) unsalted butter,
   well chilled and cut into small chunks
3-4 tablespoons ice water

FOR FILLING

1 cup reduced-fat sour cream
¾ cup sugar
2½ tablespoons all-purpose flour
¾ teaspoon almond extract
¼ teaspoon salt
1 large egg, lightly beaten
2½ cups (about 1 pint) cleaned,
   stemmed blueberries (*see Variation*)

FOR TOPPING

6 tablespoons all-purpose flour
4 tablespoons (½ stick) unsalted butter,
   well chilled and cut into small chunks
⅓ cup coarsely chopped pecans
2 tablespoons sugar

1. **To prepare pastry shell** (*Food Processor Method*): Place flour, sugar and salt in a food processor fitted with a metal blade; add butter. Process, pulsing on and off several times, until mixture resembles oatmeal flakes. With motor running, add 2 tablespoons water through feed tube and process just until a ball of dough forms. If mixture seems too dry or does not form a ball, add remaining 1 to 2 tablespoons water.

(*Hand Method*): Combine flour, sugar and salt in a bowl. Cut in butter with a pastry blender or 2 table knives until mixture resembles oatmeal flakes. Gradually add water, mixing just until dough holds together. Transfer dough to a lightly floured surface. To ensure that flour and fat are well blended, smear ¼ cup dough at a time across surface, using the heel of your hand, to form a 6-inch strip; continue until you have smeared all dough. Gather dough together and repeat one more time.

2. Gather dough into a ball and flatten into a disk. Wrap in plastic wrap and refrigerate for at least 30 minutes or longer, until firm.

3. Roll dough out on a floured surface into a circle 13 inches in diameter. Carefully ease dough into a 9-inch tart pan with a removable bottom or into a 9-inch glass pie plate. Fold over excess dough. If using a tart pan, press firmly to reinforce sides. If using a pie plate, crimp folded dough to make border. (*Pastry shell can be prepared ahead. Cover tightly with plastic wrap and refrigerate for 1 day.*)

4. To bake pastry shell, arrange a rack at center position and preheat oven to 400°F. Line shell with foil and then with dried beans or pie weights. Bake for 15 to 20 minutes, or until lightly browned. Remove from oven; leave oven on. Remove foil and beans or weights from shell.

5. **To prepare filling**: Combine sour cream, sugar, flour, almond extract, salt and egg in a large mixing bowl. Whisk until batter is smooth. Fold in blueberries. Spoon filling into pastry shell and smooth top with a spatula. Bake pie until just set, about 25 minutes. Remove from oven.

6. **To prepare topping**: Using fingertips, mix flour and butter in a medium bowl until small clumps form. Mix in pecans and sugar. Spoon topping over pie. Bake until topping browns lightly, about 12 minutes.

7. Cool to room temperature. Refrigerate, loosely covered, for at least 1 hour or up to 1 day.

8. To serve, cut into 8 portions.

Variation:

Some of my cooking students like to substitute raspberries for the blueberries. Be sure to make the pie using only fresh berries, not frozen ones, and gently fold them into the batter. Keep all the other ingredients the same.

Cream Cheese Pumpkin-Pecan Pie

SERVES 8

★

From Start to Finish:
3 hours 10 minutes
(includes 30 minutes for
chilling dough and 1 hour
for cooling pie)

Actual Working Time:
45 minutes

Make Ahead: Yes
(see steps 2 and 7)

Can Be Frozen: No

Best Season: Fall

Shopping Note:
Buy a 15-ounce can of
pumpkin puree, which
yields a little less than
2 cups. It is found with
the canned vegetables in
most supermarkets.

 RICH INDULGENCE, this is the ultimate pumpkin pie, the perfect end to a Thanksgiving celebration. The sinfully good crust includes chopped pecans and brown sugar, and the filling is made with pumpkin puree, spices, cream cheese and sour cream. A little cream cheese and sour cream are swirled into the filling just before baking so that the pie, when cooked, displays a beautiful marbled pattern.

FOR CRUST

¾ cup all-purpose flour
6 tablespoons firmly packed light brown sugar
¼ teaspoon salt
6 tablespoons (¾ stick) unsalted butter,
   well chilled and cut into small cubes
1 tablespoon cold water
¾ cup chopped pecans

FOR FILLING

8 ounces reduced-fat cream cheese, softened
6 tablespoons reduced-fat sour cream
½ cup sugar
2 large eggs
1 cup pumpkin puree (*see Shopping Note*)
¾ teaspoon ground cinnamon
¼ teaspoon ground ginger
⅛ teaspoon ground cloves

1. **To prepare crust** (*Food Processor Method*): Place flour, brown sugar and salt in a food processor fitted with a metal blade. Pulse several times to blend. Add butter and process until mixture resembles coarse meal, several seconds. With motor running, add water through feed tube, a little at a time, until dough is moist, not wet. Transfer to a mixing bowl and add pecans. Knead until a ball of dough forms and pecans are thoroughly incorporated.

(*Hand Method*): Combine flour, brown sugar and salt in a bowl. Cut in butter with a pastry blender or 2 table knives until mixture resembles oatmeal flakes. Gradually add water, mixing just until dough holds together. Transfer dough to a lightly floured surface. To ensure that flour and fat are evenly blended, smear ¼ cup dough at a time across surface, using the heel of your hand, to form a 6-inch strip; continue until you have smeared all dough. Gather dough together and repeat one more time. Add pecans and knead a few times to incorporate.

2. Gather dough into a ball and flatten into a disk. Press dough onto bottom and up sides of a 9½-inch tart pan with a removable bottom. Chill for at least 30 minutes. (*Dough can be prepared 1 day ahead; cover with plastic wrap and refrigerate.*)

3. When ready to bake crust, arrange a rack at center position and preheat oven to 375°F. Line crust with foil and fill with dried beans or pie weights. Bake until crust sides are firm, about 10 minutes. Remove foil and beans or weights and bake until crust begins to brown, about 10 minutes. Remove from oven and place on a cooling rack. Leave oven on while you prepare filling.

4. **To prepare filling:** Place cream cheese and sour cream in a large bowl and mix with an electric mixer on medium speed until smooth and creamy. Gradually add sugar and beat until well blended. Add eggs, one at a time, and mix well. Remove ⅓ cup filling and set aside.

5. Add pumpkin puree, cinnamon, ginger and cloves to cream-cheese mixture in large bowl and mix until well incorporated.

6. Pour pumpkin mixture into prebaked pie shell. Gently drop teaspoonfuls of reserved cream-cheese mixture onto pumpkin filling, then swirl very lightly with a knife to produce a marbled effect. (Be careful, or cream-cheese mixture will blend into pumpkin batter.)

7. Bake until firm, about 35 minutes. Remove from oven and cool on a rack for at least 1 hour. (*Pie can be prepared 1 day ahead; cover and refrigerate.*)

8. Serve cold or at room temperature. Cut into 8 portions.

Apple-Date Strudels *with* Honey Sauce

SERVES 10

From Start to Finish:
1 hour 30 minutes

Actual Working Time:
55 minutes

Make Ahead: Partially
(see steps 4 and 5)

Can Be Frozen: Yes,
unbaked (see step 4)

Best Seasons:
Fall and winter

Shopping Note:
Use unsweetened dates,
not the chopped ones that
are coated with sugar.

THESE STRUDELS ARE EASY TO ASSEMBLE, since they are made with store-bought phyllo dough. The phyllo sheets enclose a mouthwatering filling of diced apples, chopped dates and pecans. When baked, the dough becomes golden and flaky and the apples tender and juicy. A warm sauce made with apple juice or cider and honey is then poured over warm strudel slices.

FOR STRUDELS

1⅓ pounds Granny Smith apples, peeled, cored
 and cut into ¾-inch dice

½ cup dried pitted dates, coarsely chopped
 (*see Shopping Note*)

⅓ cup coarsely chopped pecans

⅓ cup sugar

½ teaspoon grated lemon zest
 (yellow portion of rind)

¾ teaspoon ground cinnamon
 Scant ¼ teaspoon freshly grated nutmeg

6 phyllo sheets (approximately 18 by 14 inches),
 defrosted according to package directions
 About 6 tablespoons (¾ stick) unsalted butter,
 melted

4 tablespoons unflavored dry bread crumbs
 Unsalted butter for baking pan
 Confectioners' sugar for topping

FOR SAUCE

1 cup apple juice or cider

½ cup sugar

1 strip (1 by 3 inches) lemon zest

3 tablespoons honey

1. **To prepare strudels**: Combine apples, dates and pecans in a large mixing bowl and toss to mix. Combine sugar, lemon zest, cinnamon and nutmeg in a small bowl and stir well. Sprinkle over apple mixture and toss well to incorporate. Set aside.

2. Place a phyllo sheet on a clean kitchen towel on a work surface, with a short end toward you. (Cover remaining phyllo sheets with a lightly dampened kitchen towel so they do not dry out.) Brush sheet generously with butter and sprinkle with 1 tablespoon bread crumbs. Repeat with a second sheet, then place a third sheet on top; butter it, but do not sprinkle with crumbs.

3. Place half of apple mixture on end of phyllo nearest you and spread filling horizontally to form a 4-inch-wide strip going almost to edges. Fold 2 long sides of dough over to enclose some of filling, then, starting at end with filling, roll dough into a log shape. Use a kitchen towel to help roll up strudel.

4. Butter a jellyroll pan or rimmed baking sheet. Use 2 spatulas to transfer strudel to pan. Brush strudel with melted butter. Repeat steps 2 and 3 to make another strudel, then transfer it to same baking sheet. (*Strudels may be made 1 day in advance. Keep covered with a lightly dampened kitchen towel and plastic wrap; refrigerate. Strudels can also be frozen; wrap tightly in plastic wrap, then in foil. When needed, do not defrost. Unwrap and put directly on a baking sheet in a preheated 375°F oven and bake as directed in step 6 but add an extra 10 to 15 minutes to cooking time.*)

5. **To prepare sauce**: Place apple juice or cider, sugar and lemon zest in a small nonreactive saucepan over medium-high heat. Bring to a boil, stirring, then reduce heat to low. Simmer for 5 minutes; remove from heat. Discard lemon zest. Stir in honey. If not using immediately, cool and refrigerate. (*Sauce can also be prepared 1 day ahead; cover, cool and refrigerate. Reheat when needed.*)

6. When ready to bake, arrange a rack at center position and preheat oven to 375°F. Bake strudels until golden, 20 to 25 minutes. Remove from oven and let cool for 5 to 10 minutes. Slice each strudel into 5 pieces, sprinkle with confectioners' sugar and serve with sauce. Serve warm.

Best-Ever Plum Upside-Down Cake

SERVES 8

From Start to Finish:
1 hour 10 minutes

Actual Working Time:
30 minutes

Make Ahead: Yes
(see step 8)

Can Be Frozen: No

Best Season: Summer

Shopping Note:

Santa Rosa plums work particularly well in this recipe. They are about 2½ to 3 inches in diameter and deep red with a golden flesh. They are available from June through October.

Cooking Technique:

It is important to use a skillet of the correct size. Too small a skillet will produce an undercooked cake; too large a skillet will yield a thinner, less attractive cake. To measure the skillet, turn it over and measure the bottom.

WHEN I WAS GROWING UP, pineapple upside-down cakes were a popular confection, but they were too sweet for my taste. A few years ago, during a visit to Chicago, I sampled a fabulous upside-down cake that was made with plums and seasoned with a hint of cardamom. It was less cloyingly sweet than traditional pineapple upside-down cakes. This is my version of that cake.

½	cup firmly packed dark brown sugar
5½	tablespoons unsalted butter, melted
1¼-1½	pounds large dark red or purple plums, washed and dried (*see Shopping Note*)
¾	teaspoon ground cardamom
1	cup all-purpose flour
½	teaspoon baking powder
	Pinch salt
3	large eggs
1¼	cups sugar
1	tablespoon fresh lemon juice
1	pint frozen vanilla yogurt or ice cream (*optional*)

1. Arrange a rack at center position and preheat oven to 350°F.

2. Select a heavy 9-inch skillet, preferably cast-iron (*see Cooking Technique*). Spray bottom of pan and sides generously with nonstick cooking spray. Place brown sugar in pan and pour in butter. Use a fork to blend butter and brown sugar well. Pat mixture with hands evenly over bottom.

3. Halve plums lengthwise, remove pits and slice into ½-inch-thick wedges. Starting around outside edge of pan, arrange plum slices in neat circular rows on top of sugar mixture. Sprinkle with cardamom.

4. Sift together flour, baking powder and salt; set aside. Beat eggs in a large bowl with an electric mixer on high speed for about 1 minute. Gradually add sugar in a thin stream. Continue to beat until mixture is thick and pale yellow, about 5 minutes.

5. On low speed, gradually add flour. If necessary, turn off machine and scrape down sides of bowl. Stir in lemon juice. Pour batter over plums.

6. Bake until top is golden brown, cake starts to pull away from sides of skillet and a tester inserted in center comes out clean, 35 to 40 minutes.

7. Remove from oven. Immediately run a knife around inside edge of skillet. Invert onto a large, round plate or serving tray. Let rest upside down for a minute so all fruit is released, then remove skillet.

8. Serve warm or at room temperature. It is best eaten the day it is made but can be covered and refrigerated 1 day ahead. Serve each slice with a scoop of yogurt or ice cream, if desired.

Country Chocolate Loaf Cake *with* Warm Chocolate-Coffee Sauce

MAKES 16
½-INCH-THICK
SLICES

From Start to Finish:
1 hour 55 minutes

Actual Working Time:
35 minutes

Make Ahead: Yes
(see steps 6 and 7)

Can Be Frozen: Yes
(see step 6)

Best Seasons: All year

THIS CAKE HAS AN UNUSUAL HISTORY. I discovered it in a little bakery in a hill town in eastern Provence. It bore no resemblance at all to classic French tortes but reminded me instead of American cakes. I pleaded with the bakery's proprietor for the recipe, but to no avail; she proudly guarded her bakery's secret. Over many months and after many trials, I was able to figure out that the cake was made with five simple ingredients: butter, sugar, flour, chocolate and eggs. I added a touch of cinnamon to the batter and also developed a warm chocolate coffee sauce to serve with it. The result was a cake that always reminds me of the narrow market street where I found my inspiration.

FOR CAKE

¼   cup plus 3 tablespoons all-purpose flour (*divided*)

8   tablespoons (1 stick) unsalted butter, well chilled and cut into small chunks

5   ounces semisweet chocolate, cut into small chunks

3   large eggs, separated

⅔   cup sugar

1   teaspoon ground cinnamon

FOR SAUCE

8   ounces semisweet chocolate, cut into small chunks

5½ tablespoons unsalted butter, well chilled and cut into small chunks

2   tablespoons powdered instant coffee, dissolved in ½ cup hot water

1. Arrange a rack at center position and preheat oven to 350°F.

2. Line an 8½-by-4½-by-2½-inch loaf pan with 2 layers of wax paper, cut so it extends 3 inches over both long sides of pan.

3. **To prepare cake:** Spray paper and pan generously with nonstick cooking spray. Sprinkle 1 tablespoon flour over paper and shake pan to coat generously. Shake out excess flour. Combine butter and chocolate in top of a double boiler set over simmering water and stir until melted and smooth. Remove from heat.

4. Beat egg yolks in a large bowl with an electric mixer on medium-high speed. Add sugar gradually in a thin stream and beat until mixture is quite thick and pale yellow, about 5 minutes. Reduce speed to low and pour in melted chocolate mixture. Add remaining ¼ cup plus 2 tablespoons flour and cinnamon and scrape down sides of bowl, if necessary.

5. Beat egg whites in a separate bowl until firm but not dry. Stir about ½ cup beaten whites into chocolate batter. Fold in remaining whites, a little at a time. Spoon batter into prepared pan.

6. Bake until a tester inserted in center comes out dry, 45 to 50 minutes. Remove from oven and let cool on a rack in pan for 30 minutes. Loosen edges with a knife and lift out, using wax paper as an aid. (*Cake will keep 4 to 5 days covered tightly in plastic wrap or foil in refrigerator. Bring to room temperature before serving. Cake can also be frozen; wrap in plastic and in foil. Defrost before using.*)

7. **To prepare sauce:** Place all ingredients in a small, heavy saucepan over medium heat. Stir until smooth, about 5 minutes. Remove from heat, and serve warm. (*Sauce can be made 1 week ahead. Cool, cover and refrigerate. Reheat, stirring, over low heat.*) Makes about 1⅓ cups.

8. To serve, cut cake into ½-inch-thick slices and drizzle with sauce.

Fruitcake Hater's Fruitcake

SERVES 12 TO 16

From Start to Finish:
3 hours 15 minutes
(includes 1 hour for cooling cake)

Actual Working Time:
50 minutes

Make Ahead: Yes
(see steps 3 and 4)

Can Be Frozen: Yes
(see step 3)

Best Seasons:
Fall and winter

WE ALL KNOW THE DESTINY of many holiday fruitcakes. They are fed to the birds, end up as doorstops or remain in the back of the refrigerator until June, when they are finally thrown away. This scrumptious fruitcake recipe is always devoured. I've replaced the usual cloyingly sweet red and green cherries with dried cranberries, dried apricots, currants and golden raisins. Orange juice and zest plus chopped walnuts add more character, and a delicious cream cheese icing coats the finished product.

FOR CAKE

3 large navel oranges
1 cup dried cranberries (*see Shopping Note*, page 183)
¾ cup golden raisins
½ cup dried currants
½ cup chopped dried apricots
2 cups sugar
½ pound (2 sticks) unsalted butter, softened
4 large eggs
1 teaspoon vanilla extract
3 cups all-purpose flour
1 teaspoon baking soda
½ teaspoon ground cinnamon
¼ teaspoon ground ginger
¼ teaspoon freshly grated nutmeg
1 cup buttermilk
1 cup chopped walnuts

FOR ICING

8 ounces reduced-fat cream cheese, softened
6 tablespoons confectioners' sugar
Dried fruit (cranberries, apricots, golden raisins and currants) for topping (*optional*)

1. Arrange a rack at center position and preheat oven to 325°F.

2. **To prepare cake**: Butter and flour a 10-inch tube pan (*see Variation*). Grate zest from oranges to make 3 tablespoons for cake and 2 teaspoons for icing; set aside. Squeeze oranges to yield ⅔ cup juice for cake and ¼ cup for icing; set aside. In a medium nonreactive saucepan, combine dried cranberries, raisins, currants, apricots and ⅔ cup orange juice. Bring to a boil, reduce heat to low and simmer for 5 minutes, or until fruit is plumped. Drain well and set aside.

3. In a large mixing bowl, cream sugar and butter with an electric mixer on medium speed until light and fluffy. Add eggs, one at a time, beating well after each addition. Add 3 tablespoons orange zest and vanilla extract; beat well. In another large bowl, combine flour, baking soda, cinnamon, ginger and nutmeg. Alternately add flour mixture and buttermilk to egg mixture, beginning and ending with flour mixture. Stir in walnuts and fruit. Pour into prepared pan. Bake until golden brown and a tester inserted in center comes out clean, about 1 hour 15 minutes. Cool in pan for 10 minutes. Transfer to a wire rack and cool completely, about 1 hour. (*If you want to freeze cake, do it before frosting. Wrap tightly in plastic wrap, then in foil, and freeze; defrost before continuing.*)

4. **To prepare icing**: Beat together cream cheese and confectioners' sugar until smooth. Add reserved ¼ cup orange juice and reserved 2 teaspoons orange zest; beat well. Spread on top of cake. Top with dried fruit, if desired. (*Cake can be made 5 days ahead; cover and refrigerate. Bring to room temperature 30 minutes before serving.*)

Variation: This recipe can be baked in mini-Bundt pans and will yield 12 smaller cakes. The mini-Bundt pans from the Williams-Sonoma catalog are the ones I like best; they are about 4 inches in diameter. Prepare the batter the same way and bake mini-cakes for about 30 minutes. Ice as directed and top with dried fruit. I wrap these cakes individually in clear cellophane, tie them with festive ribbons and give them as Christmas gifts—even to people who I know usually hate fruitcakes!

Dark Chocolate Walnut Layer Cake

SERVES 10 TO 12

★

From Start to Finish:
1 hour 35 minutes

Actual Working Time:
1 hour

Make Ahead: Yes
(see step 8)

Can Be Frozen: Yes
(see step 8)

Best Seasons: All year

NOTHING COULD BE MORE AMERICAN than chocolate layer cake, and this two-tier creation is a stately example. The cake has a fine texture, not too crumbly, and the dark chocolate icing is rich and smooth. Chopped walnuts, pressed against the sides of the cake, are a simple decoration.

FOR CAKE

3 ounces unsweetened chocolate, cut into chunks
8 tablespoons (1 stick) unsalted butter, softened
½ cup firmly packed light brown sugar
½ cup sugar
1 teaspoon vanilla extract
2 large eggs
1 cup all-purpose flour
½ teaspoon baking soda
½ cup buttermilk
¾ cup finely chopped walnuts

FOR ICING

4 ounces unsweetened chocolate, cut into chunks
8 tablespoons (1 stick) butter
3 cups confectioners' sugar
6 tablespoons milk, hot (*divided*)
¾-1 cup chopped walnuts

1. Arrange a rack at center position and preheat oven to 350°F.

2. **To prepare cake:** Butter and flour two 9-inch straight-sided cake pans. Line each with parchment or wax paper cut to fit pan, and butter and flour paper.

3. Melt chocolate in top of a double boiler set over simmering water. Stir until smooth and remove from heat. Set aside.

4. Cream butter in a large bowl with an electric mixer on medium speed. Gradually, in a thin stream, add sugars and beat until fluffy. Add vanilla, then eggs, one at a time, beating until incorporated. Lower speed and add chocolate.

5. Sift flour and baking soda together. On low speed, add flour mixture to egg mixture, alternating with buttermilk, beginning and ending with flour. With a wooden spoon, stir in walnuts. Divide batter evenly between pans and smooth with a spatula. Bake until a tester inserted in center comes out fairly clean, 25 to 30 minutes. Remove and cool in pans for 10 minutes. Run a knife around edges to loosen cake from sides of pan; invert and remove paper. Cool on racks.

6. **To prepare icing:** Melt chocolate in top of a double boiler set over simmering water. Stir until smooth and remove from heat.

7. Cream butter in a large bowl with an electric mixer on medium speed. Gradually, on low speed, add confectioners' sugar. When all sugar has been incorporated, beat in 2 tablespoons milk, then melted chocolate. Beat in remaining 4 tablespoons milk.

8. To ice cake, place a layer, flat side up, on wax paper. Ice top and sides generously. Place second layer, flat side up, over first layer and ice top and sides generously. Make a swirl pattern with a spatula or table knife on top of cake and press chopped walnuts around sides. (*Store for up to 1 day in an airtight container at room temperature. Cake can also be frozen; wrap tightly in plastic wrap and then in foil. Defrost in refrigerator before serving.*)

Golden Pumpkin Roll *with* Toffee Cream Filling *and* Warm Caramel Sauce

SERVES 12

From Start to Finish:
1 hour 25 minutes

Actual Working Time:
50 minutes

Make Ahead: Yes
(see step 8)

Can Be Frozen: No

Best Seasons:
Fall and winter

Shopping Note:
Hershey's Skor brand
"English Toffee Bits" and
Heath "Bits O'Brickle"
are two good products;
they are available in the
baking section of most
supermarkets.

THIS IS A WONDERFUL ALTERNATIVE to pumpkin pie for a Thanksgiving dinner. Pumpkin puree, along with ginger, cinnamon and allspice, flavors the cake roll. The whipped cream filling is enhanced with bits of English toffee and some rum. The chilled cake is served sliced and drizzled with warm caramel sauce.

FOR PUMPKIN ROLL

¾ cup cake flour
1½ teaspoons ground cinnamon
¾ teaspoon ground allspice
1¼ teaspoons ground ginger
⅛ teaspoon salt
6 large eggs, separated
⅓ cup sugar
⅓ cup firmly packed light brown sugar
⅔ cup pumpkin puree (*see Shopping Note*, page 360)
   Confectioners' sugar

FOR FILLING AND TOPPING

1 teaspoon powdered gelatin
2 tablespoons dark rum
1 cup whipping or heavy cream
3 tablespoons confectioners' sugar,
   plus extra for topping
10 tablespoons English toffee bits for baking
   (*divided*), *see Shopping Note*
1½ cups caramel sauce (*see Shopping Note*, page 356)

1. Arrange a rack at center position and preheat oven to 375°F.

2. **To prepare pumpkin roll**: Spray a standard 10½-by-15½-inch jelly-roll pan generously with nonstick cooking spray. Do not flour pan.

3. Sift together flour, cinnamon, allspice, ginger and salt; set aside.

4. Place egg yolks in a large bowl, and with an electric mixer on medium speed, gradually beat in sugars until mixture is pale yellow and thick, about 2 minutes. Mix in pumpkin puree. Gradually, on low speed, beat in dry ingredients.

5. In another mixing bowl, combine egg whites with a pinch of salt and beat on high speed until they are just stiff. Remove and mix one-quarter of whites into pumpkin mixture to lighten it. Fold remaining whites into batter in 3 equal additions. Spread batter evenly to edges of pan. Bake until cake springs back when lightly touched, 14 to 16 minutes.

6. When cake is done, remove it from oven. Lay a clean kitchen towel on a work surface and dust it generously with confectioners' sugar. Loosen cake around edges with a knife and invert immediately onto towel. (Tap back of pan with knife, if necessary.) When cake is un-molded, roll up cake and towel together, starting from a long side. Let cool completely, about 20 minutes.

7. **To prepare filling**: Place gelatin and rum in a small saucepan and place over low heat. Stir constantly to dissolve gelatin, about 1 minute; do not let rum get hot. Beat cream with an electric mixer until just firm. Beat in confectioners' sugar and rum mixture. With a rubber spatula, fold in 6 tablespoons toffee bits.

8. Unroll cake and sprinkle remaining 4 tablespoons toffee bits over it. Spread filling evenly over cake and roll it up again. (*Cake can be made and assembled 1 day ahead. Cover with plastic wrap and refrigerate.*)

9. To serve, transfer cake to a serving platter. Trim ends on a slight diagonal for a more attractive appearance, then dust with confection-ers' sugar. Heat caramel sauce and drizzle a little sauce over serving plate and cake. Serve extra sauce separately. (I often collect fall maple and oak leaves in varying hues of orange, yellow and red, arrange them on serving plate and place cake on top.)

Vanilla *and* Chocolate Layered Cheesecake

SERVES 10

★

From Start to Finish:
9 hours 20 minutes
(includes 1 hour for cooling
and 6 hours for chilling
cheesecake)

Actual Working Time:
30 minutes

Make Ahead: Yes
(see step 8)

Can Be Frozen: No

Best Seasons: All year

Shopping Note:
Chocolate graham
crackers are available in the
cookie section of most
supermarkets. Make crumbs
by placing crackers in a
food processor fitted with a
metal blade; process until
crumbly. Or place crackers
in a plastic bag and crush
with a rolling pin.

CHEESECAKE IS AMERICA'S FAVORITE DESSERT, and this one features two flavors—chocolate and vanilla—in separate layers. The crust is made of crushed chocolate graham crackers and chopped pecans, followed by a dense dark chocolate tier, topped with a vanilla layer. (*See photograph, page 48.*)

FOR CRUST

½ cup very finely chopped pecans
½ cup finely ground chocolate graham cracker crumbs
   (*see Shopping Note*)
2 tablespoons firmly packed light brown sugar
3 tablespoons unsalted butter, melted

FOR FILLING

4 ounces semisweet chocolate, cut into small chunks
2 ounces unsweetened chocolate, cut into
   small chunks
1 pound reduced-fat cream cheese, softened
1 cup sugar (*divided*)
1 tablespoon cornstarch
4 large eggs
½ cup reduced fat sour cream
1 teaspoon vanilla extract

FOR GARNISH

1 ounce semisweet chocolate or 2 tablespoons
   coarsely ground chocolate graham cracker crumbs

1. Arrange a rack at center position and preheat oven to 350°F. Spray an 8½-inch springform pan generously with nonstick cooking spray.

2. **To prepare crust:** Toss pecans, graham cracker crumbs and brown sugar together in springform pan and pour in butter. Mix well with a

fork until pecan mixture is thoroughly moistened. Pat evenly over bottom of pan. Set aside.

3. **To prepare filling**: Melt semisweet and unsweetened chocolate together in top of a double boiler set over simmering water. Stir until smooth and shiny. Remove and set aside.

4. Beat cream cheese in a large bowl with an electric mixer on medium speed. Add ½ cup sugar and beat until mixture is smooth, about 3 minutes. Add cornstarch and mix for a few seconds more. Add eggs, one at a time, beating just until blended. Add sour cream and vanilla and beat just to blend.

5. Remove 1½ cups batter and place in another bowl; add melted chocolate to this bowl. Stir well to mix, then stir in remaining ½ cup sugar. Pour chocolate batter into pan. Spread evenly with a spatula. Gently pour remaining plain batter on top. Spread evenly and gently with a spatula, taking care to maintain separate layers.

6. Wrap outside of pan with a double thickness of aluminum foil. Set in a larger pan and surround with 1 inch of very hot water.

7. Bake until set and a knife inserted in center comes out almost clean, about 50 minutes. Turn off oven and let cake cool in oven for 1 hour. Remove and let cool to room temperature, about 1 hour.

8. Cover with plastic wrap and refrigerate for 6 hours or overnight. (*Cake can be made 2 days ahead; keep covered and refrigerated.*) When ready to serve, remove sides of springform pan and transfer cake to a serving platter.

9. **To garnish**: Using a vegetable peeler or a sharp paring knife, shave chocolate onto top of cake, or sprinkle 2 tablespoons graham cracker crumbs over cake.

Lemon Cheesecake *with* Cranberry Topping

SERVES 12

From Start to Finish:
 9 hours (includes 6 hours
for chilling cheesecake)

Actual Working Time:
 45 minutes

Make Ahead: Yes
 (see steps 5 and 6)

Can Be Frozen: No

Best Seasons:
 Fall and winter with
cranberry topping, summer
with fresh berries as
topping

M Y FRIEND CAROLYN CLAYCOMB, a chef from Columbus, Ohio, thought of combining the tastes of lemon and ginger in this dessert. The crust is made with gingersnap crumbs, and the lemon filling includes fresh gingerroot. I added a glistening deep red cranberry topping. With the cranberries, the cake makes a beautiful dessert for the holidays, but it is equally good adorned with fresh strawberries, raspberries or blueberries at other times of the year.

FOR CRUST

1	cup gingersnap crumbs
3	tablespoons unsalted butter, melted
2	tablespoons sugar

FOR FILLING

1¼	cups sugar
2	pounds reduced-fat cream cheese, softened
2	large eggs plus 2 egg whites
1½	tablespoons finely chopped peeled gingerroot
1½	tablespoons grated lemon zest (yellow portion of rind)
¼	cup fresh lemon juice

FOR TOPPING

¾	cup water
1	cup sugar
	Dash ground cinnamon
2	cups fresh cranberries, washed and picked over (*divided*)
1	teaspoon cornstarch, dissolved in 1 teaspoon cold water

1. Arrange a rack at center position and preheat oven to 325°F.

2. **To prepare crust:** Combine gingersnap crumbs, butter and sugar in a 9½-inch springform pan. Using 2 forks, blend well and press mixture into bottom and partially up sides of pan. Set aside.

3. **To prepare filling:** In a large bowl with an electric mixer on medium speed, beat sugar and cream cheese until well blended, 3 to 4 minutes, or beat well by hand with a wooden spoon. Add eggs and egg whites, one at a time, beating well after each addition. Beat in gingerroot, lemon zest and lemon juice.

4. Pour filling into prepared pan. Bake until a knife inserted in center comes out clean, 65 to 75 minutes. If cake starts to get too dark on top, cover loosely with aluminum foil.

5. Turn off oven. Let cheesecake remain in oven with door closed, 1 hour. Cover with plastic wrap and refrigerate cake for 6 hours or overnight. (*Cake can be made 2 days ahead, cover and refrigerate.*)

6. **To prepare topping:** Combine water, sugar and cinnamon in a medium, heavy saucepan and set over medium-high heat. Cook, stirring, to dissolve sugar. When mixture comes to a boil, add half of cranberries and stir until they start to pop, 2 to 3 minutes. Stir in remaining cranberries and cornstarch mixture. Cook until thickened, 2 to 3 minutes more. Remove and cool. (*Cover and refrigerate for up to 2 days.*) Makes about 2 cups sauce.

7. To serve, remove sides from springform pan and transfer cake to a serving platter. Use a slotted spoon to arrange cranberry topping on top of cake. Save any extra liquid from cranberries and drizzle over slices.

Margarita Cheesecake

SERVES 10

★

From Start to Finish:
8 hours 5 minutes
(includes 6 hours for
chilling cheesecake)

Actual Working Time:
30 minutes

Make Ahead: Yes
(see step 6)

Can Be Frozen: No

Best Seasons: All year

Cooking Technique:
Although the thin strips
of lime zest lend visual
appeal to this cheesecake,
they also add an extra shot
of lime flavor to each
serving. Do not omit this
garnish.

THIS LIGHT, AIRY CHEESECAKE is as cool, refreshing and irresistible as the famous drink from which it takes its name. It can be made ahead and is perfect to serve after spicy grilled foods.

FOR CRUST

1 cup graham cracker crumbs

3 tablespoons unsalted butter, melted

FOR FILLING

1½ pounds reduced-fat cream cheese, softened

1¼ cups reduced-fat sour cream

½ cup plus 2 tablespoons sugar

2½ tablespoons Triple Sec (orange-flavored liqueur)

2½ tablespoons tequila

2½ tablespoons fresh lime juice

4 large eggs (*see Healthful Variation*)

FOR TOPPING

½ cup plus 2 tablespoons reduced-fat sour cream

2½ teaspoons fresh lime juice

2½ teaspoons sugar

1 tablespoon very thin strips of lime zest
(green portion of rind), *see Cooking Technique*

2-3 teaspoons graham cracker crumbs

1. Arrange a rack at center position and preheat oven to 350°F. Spray an 8½-to-9-inch springform pan with nonstick cooking spray.

2. **To prepare crust:** Place graham cracker crumbs and butter in pan. Mix well with a fork until all crumbs are moistened. Use your fingers to pat crumbs evenly on bottom and about 1 inch up sides of pan.

3. **To prepare filling**: Place cream cheese and sour cream in a large bowl and beat with an electric mixer on medium speed until softened, 2 to 3 minutes. Add sugar gradually in a thin stream. Reduce speed to low and add Triple Sec, tequila and lime juice. Beat until incorporated. Add eggs and beat just to blend.

4. Pour filling into prepared pan. Bake until set and a knife inserted in center comes out almost clean, 45 to 50 minutes. Turn oven off, and remove cheesecake from oven.

5. **To prepare topping**: Whisk together sour cream, lime juice and sugar and spread over cake.

6. Return cheesecake to oven, shut door, and let sit for 45 minutes more. Remove; cool completely, cover with plastic wrap and refrigerate for 6 hours. (*Cheesecake can be made 1 day ahead; keep covered and refrigerated.*)

7. To serve, remove sides of pan and transfer cheesecake to a platter. Garnish by making a border with lime zest on top of cake and sprinkle graham cracker crumbs in center.

Healthful Variation: You can use egg substitute in place of eggs.

White Chocolate- *and* Pecan-Studded Brownies

MAKES 32
BROWNIES

★

From Start to Finish:
1 hour

Actual Working Time:
35 minutes

Make Ahead: Yes
(see step 5)

Can Be Frozen: Yes
(see step 5)

Best Seasons: All year

T HESE DARK, ALMOST FUDGELIKE BROWNIES owe their special appeal to the little chunks of white chocolate and the chopped pecans that stud them. The brownies will keep four to five days, but my students tell me that they never last that long at their houses.

3 ounces unsweetened chocolate,
cut into small pieces

12 tablespoons (1½ sticks) unsalted butter,
softened slightly

½ cup sugar

½ cup firmly packed light brown sugar

3 large eggs

¾ cup all-purpose flour

¼ teaspoon salt

6 ounces white chocolate, cut into ¾-inch chunks

1 cup coarsely chopped pecans
Confectioners' sugar

1. Arrange a rack at center position and preheat oven to 350°F. Spray bottom and sides of a 13-by-9-inch baking pan with nonstick cooking spray. Sprinkle bottom and sides with flour; shake out excess. Cut a sheet of aluminum foil to fit bottom of pan; spray and flour foil and shake out excess.

2. In top of a double boiler set over simmering water, melt unsweetened chocolate, stirring until it is smooth and shiny. Remove from heat and set aside.

3. In a large bowl, cream butter with an electric mixer on medium speed. Gradually add sugars. On low speed, pour in melted chocolate. Add eggs, one at a time, and mix only until incorporated. Beat in flour and salt. With a spatula or wooden spoon, stir in white chocolate and pecans.

4. Pour batter into prepared pan and spread evenly with a spatula. Bake until a tester inserted in middle comes out almost clean (there might be a few specks of chocolate on it), 20 to 25 minutes. Remove and cool to room temperature.

5. When cool, invert brownies onto a work surface and peel off foil. Cut brownies into 32 pieces. Invert again and sprinkle lightly with confectioners' sugar. Store in an airtight container for up to 4 to 5 days. (*Brownies can also be frozen; wrap in plastic wrap, then in foil. Defrost when needed.*)

Prince Albert Pumpkin Brownies

SERVES 9

★

From Start to Finish:
1 hour

Actual Working Time:
25 minutes

Make Ahead: Yes
(see step 6)

Can Be Frozen: Yes
(see step 6)

Best Seasons:
Fall and winter

PUMPKIN REPLACES CHOCOLATE in these spiced, moist, dense confections. Although the brownies are delicious offered unadorned, they are elevated to new heights when served warm with scoops of vanilla ice cream and a drizzle of hot caramel sauce. I created them for Prince Albert of Monaco, who was the guest of honor at a special fall dinner at our home one crisp, cool October evening.

8	tablespoons (1 stick) unsalted butter, softened
1	cup firmly packed light brown sugar
1	large egg
1½	teaspoons vanilla extract (*divided*)
1	cup all-purpose flour
1	teaspoon baking powder
¼	teaspoon salt
¾	teaspoon ground cinnamon
¼	teaspoon ground ginger
	Generous ⅛ teaspoon ground cloves
¾	cup pumpkin puree or canned pumpkin, without seasoning (*see Shopping Note*, page 360)
½	cup coarsely chopped pecans
¼	cup reduced-fat cream cheese, softened
1	egg yolk
2	tablespoons sugar
	Fall maple leaves in different colors for decorating (*optional*)
1	quart vanilla ice cream or frozen yogurt
	Caramel sauce (*see Shopping Note*, page 356)

1. Arrange a rack at center position and preheat oven to 350°F.

2. Butter an 8-inch square baking pan and coat it with flour.

3. Place butter in a large bowl and beat with an electric mixer on medium-high for several seconds. Gradually add brown sugar and beat until completely incorporated, about 2 minutes.

4. Add egg and 1 teaspoon vanilla extract and beat just to blend. Reduce speed to low and beat in flour, baking powder, salt, cinnamon, ginger and cloves. Beat in pumpkin puree or canned pumpkin and fold in pecans. Spread batter evenly in prepared pan.

5. Combine cream cheese, egg yolk, sugar and remaining ½ teaspoon vanilla extract in a small mixing bowl and whisk until smooth. Drop heaping teaspoons of mixture over batter in pan. Gently swirl cream cheese mixture into batter with a table knife to give marbled appearance.

6. Bake brownies until a tester inserted in center comes out clean and top of batter is firm, about 35 minutes. (*If not using immediately, cool completely and store in an airtight container for 2 to 3 days. Reheat brownies, covered, in a preheated 375°F oven for 15 minutes before serving. Brownies can also be frozen; wrap in plastic, then in foil. Defrost before using.*)

7. To serve, cut brownies into 9 squares. Arrange squares on individual dessert plates lined with maple leaves, if desired. Place a scoop of ice cream or yogurt beside each brownie. Heat caramel sauce and drizzle over brownies and ice cream.

Variation: These brownies are good served at room temperature simply sprinkled with confectioners' sugar.

Cranberry Ginger Squares

MAKES 16 SQUARES

★

From Start to Finish:
2 hours 10 minutes
(includes 45 minutes for
chilling filling and 20
minutes for chilling
topping)

Actual Working Time:
40 minutes

Make Ahead: Yes
(see step 5)

Can Be Frozen: No

Best Seasons:
Fall and winter

Shopping Note:
Crystallized ginger has
been cooked in a sugar
syrup and coated with
coarse sugar; it is available
in specialty-food stores and
many supermarkets. If you
can't get it, substitute an
equal amount of peeled,
chopped gingerroot.

THESE DELECTABLE MORSELS ARE ADDICTIVE—an indulgence worth every bite. Composed of a walnut butter crust, a lemon-and-ginger cream cheese layer and a glistening cranberry topping, they are perfect for the holidays, when fresh cranberries are available.

FOR CRUST

1 cup all-purpose flour
¼ cup confectioners' sugar
8 tablespoons (1 stick) unsalted butter,
   chilled and cut into small chunks
½ cup coarsely chopped walnuts

FOR CREAM CHEESE LAYER

8 ounces reduced-fat cream cheese, softened
6 tablespoons sugar
1 teaspoon grated lemon zest
   (yellow portion of rind)
4 teaspoons fresh lemon juice
1 tablespoon very finely chopped
   crystallized ginger (*see Shopping Note*)

FOR CRANBERRY TOPPING

12 ounces fresh cranberries, washed and picked over
1½ cups sugar
5-6 tablespoons water

1. Arrange a rack at center position and preheat oven to 350°F. Line an 8-inch square baking pan with aluminum foil.

2. **To prepare crust** (*Food Processor Method*): Place flour, confectioners' sugar and butter in a food processor fitted with a metal blade. Process for about 30 seconds or more, pulsing off and on, until mixture resembles coarse meal. Add walnuts and pulse 4 or 5 times more to incorporate. Remove dough and press into pan to form an even layer.

(*Hand Method*): Place all crust ingredients except walnuts in a mixing bowl and cut butter into flour with a pastry blender or 2 table knives until mixture resembles coarse meal. Finely chop nuts and stir in. Press into pan to form an even layer.

3. Bake until crust is light golden, 20 to 25 minutes. Remove and cool to room temperature in pan.

4. **To prepare cream cheese layer**: Place cream cheese in a medium bowl and combine with sugar, lemon zest, lemon juice and ginger. Stir well to mix. Spread over cooled crust in pan. Refrigerate, covered with plastic wrap, until firm, about 45 minutes.

5. **To prepare topping**: Place cranberries, sugar and water in a medium, heavy saucepan over medium heat. Stir until sugar is dissolved. Continue to cook, stirring constantly, until berries pop and are soft and mixture is quite thick, about 10 minutes. Transfer to a bowl and refrigerate until cool, about 20 minutes. Spread topping over cream cheese layer. (*Squares can be prepared 1 day in advance; cover and refrigerate until needed.*)

6. To serve, cut into 16 squares.

English Toffee Cookies

MAKES 18 TO 20
(3-INCH) COOKIES

From Start to Finish:
1 hour 35 minutes

Actual Working Time:
35 minutes

Make Ahead: Yes
(see step 8)

Can Be Frozen: Yes
(see step 8)

Best Seasons:
All year, but especially
good at Christmas

T HESE BUTTER-RICH SHORTBREAD COOKIES have an un-expected crunch because they are studded with little toffee bits. Baked to a light golden brown, the cookies are cooled and then drizzled with a chocolate glaze.

FOR COOKIES

1⅓	cups all-purpose flour
¼	cup sugar
⅛	teaspoon salt
8	tablespoons (1 stick) unsalted butter, well chilled and cut into small pieces
½	teaspoon vanilla extract
½	cup English toffee bits for baking (*see Shopping Note,* page 372)

FOR CHOCOLATE GLAZE

2	ounces semisweet chocolate, broken into small chunks
¼	cup heavy cream

1. Lightly butter a cookie sheet.

2. **To prepare cookies** (*Food Processor Method*): Place flour, sugar and salt in a food processor fitted with a metal blade. Distribute butter evenly over flour and sprinkle with vanilla extract. Process, turning on and off for several seconds, until mixture is crumbly and butter is well incorporated. Add toffee bits and process for a few seconds more. (*Hand Method*): Place dry ingredients in a mixing bowl, add butter and vanilla extract and use a pastry blender or 2 table knives to cut butter into flour. Stir in toffee bits with a wooden spoon.

3. Transfer dough to a work surface and knead for 2 to 3 minutes. Gather dough into a ball and flatten into a disk. Cover with plastic wrap and refrigerate for 1 hour. (*Dough can be made 1 day ahead and re-frigerated. Let soften slightly at room temperature before rolling out.*)

4. When ready to roll out dough, arrange a rack at center position and preheat oven to 350°F.

5. Place dough on a lightly floured sheet of wax paper. Sprinkle with a little flour and cover with another sheet of wax paper. Roll out to a thickness of ¼ inch. Cut out cookies with a 3-inch star, round, heart-shaped or other cookie cutter. Use a spatula to transfer cookies to baking sheet, spacing them about 1 inch apart.

6. Bake until lightly golden, 12 to 15 minutes. Remove and cool for 1 minute on baking sheet, then transfer to a rack and cool completely. If necessary, trim cooled cookies with a knife to remove any uneven edges.

7. **To prepare glaze**: Place chocolate and cream in top of a double boiler or a saucepan set over simmering water. Stir gently until chocolate has melted and is smooth and creamy.

8. Let cool for a few minutes. Place warm glaze in a zipper sandwich bag. Seal bag, taking care to remove any excess air. Snip a tiny end off one corner and drizzle glaze over cookies. Cool until glaze is set, 30 to 60 minutes. Store carefully in an airtight container. (*Cookies can also be frozen. Double bag in self-seal food-storage bags.*)

9. Serve cookies mounded in a basket or on a serving platter.

Gingerbread Ice Cream Sandwiches

SERVES 8

From Start to Finish:
3 hours 25 minutes
(includes 2 hours of
freezing time)
Actual Working Time:
45 minutes
Make Ahead: Yes
(see step 6)
Can Be Frozen: Yes
(see step 6)
Best Seasons:
All year, especially
summer

Shopping Note:
Molasses can be either
sulfured or unsulfured. The
unsulfured variety is lighter
and has a clearer sugarcane
flavor.

THESE SPECIAL ICE CREAM SANDWICHES are made with freshly baked gingerbread, topped with warm caramel sauce and topped with sliced peaches and mint. I discovered them at Baang, a restaurant in Greenwich, Connecticut. Krista Kern, the pastry chef, willingly shared the recipe with me.

⅓	cup boiling water
¾	cup dark molasses, preferably unsulfured (*see Shopping Note*)
¾	teaspoon baking soda
2	cups all-purpose flour
2	teaspoons baking powder
2	teaspoons ground ginger
½	teaspoon ground cinnamon
¼	teaspoon ground cloves
	Scant ¼ teaspoon salt
6	tablespoons (¾ stick) unsalted butter, softened
¾	cup firmly packed dark brown sugar
1	large egg
1½-2	pints best-quality vanilla or peach ice cream, softened slightly
1	1-pound jar caramel sauce, heated until warm (*see Shopping Note*, page 356)
4	large ripe peaches or 6 ripe apricots, peeled and sliced (*optional*)
	Fresh mint sprigs for garnish (*optional*)

1. Arrange a rack at center position and preheat oven to 350°F. Coat a 15½-by-10½-inch jellyroll pan with nonstick cooking spray and line with parchment paper. Coat paper with nonstick spray.

2. Combine water, molasses and baking soda in a mixing bowl and mix well. Set aside.

3. Sift together flour, baking powder, ginger, cinnamon, cloves and salt in a bowl and set aside.

4. Cream butter in a large bowl with an electric mixer on medium speed until fluffy. Gradually add brown sugar and beat until incorporated. Beat in egg. Reduce mixer speed to low and alternately add dry and liquid ingredients, beginning and ending with dry ingredients. Pour into pan and bake until a tester comes out clean and cake springs back when touched, 20 to 25 minutes. Remove and cool for 15 minutes. Remove from pan, removing paper; set aside.

5. When pan is cool, clean it and line it again with parchment paper. Spread softened ice cream in an even layer on half of pan (an area about 7 by 10 inches) and fold paper over top. Freeze until firm, about 1 hour.

6. When gingerbread is completely cool and ice cream is firm, cut gingerbread into 2 equal halves (each about 7 by 10 inches). Place 1 layer on a baking sheet. Remove paper from ice cream and place on top of cake layer. Freeze for 30 minutes to firm slightly. Top with remaining cake layer and freeze until firm, about 30 minutes. (*"Sandwich" can be made 2 days ahead. Cover well with plastic wrap and keep frozen.*)

7. When ready to serve, trim edges of cake so they are even. Cut into 4 squares and cut each square diagonally into 2 triangles for a total of 8 triangular slices. Arrange each sandwich on a serving plate and drizzle each with warm caramel sauce. Garnish with fruit slices and a mint sprig, if desired.

Index